DREAMING IN CHINESE
WILLIAM TSUNG

MEMOIRS FROM A TAIWANESE PRISON

PROSPEROUS CAT

PUBLISHING

Dreaming in Chinese by William Tsung

Published by Prosperous Cat Publishing LLC
3640 Concord Pike #1152
Wilmington, DE 19803

Cover by Nathan Alexander Rico.
IG: ricoartistico

Edited by Jesse Winter and Alex Kempsell from Duo Storytelling.

Library of Congress Control Number: 2022923217
ISBN: 979-8-9874527-0-7

Printed in the United States of America

First Edition

PROSPEROUS CAT
PUBLISHING

You ain't gotta like me, you just mad 'cause I tell it how it is, and you tell it how it might be.

—Sean Combs

To my mom, dad, and family in Taiwan, especially my grandma. I'm sorry for all the trouble I caused and for making everybody worry.

CONTENTS

INTRODUCTION

Home is the place where, when you have to
go there, they have to take you in.

—Robert Frost

I thought Taiwan was a great place at first.
I ran red lights on my moped and parked wherever I wanted. My friends owned bars and nightclubs. The food was fantastic, and the women were beautiful. It was a nonstop party. But what the fuck did I know? I lived in a bubble. Taiwan is not the bastion of human rights that she claims to be.

The Taiwanese government has been conducting a "war on drugs" since the early nineties, but like the American war on drugs, it's really a war on people. What I've seen and experienced is the human cost. This war's dark legacy is ever-rising drug use and overcrowded prisons. But drug laws in Taiwan and China, in particular, have always been strict. The harshness is a holdover from the Opium Wars; narcotics are perceived as a deadly poison smuggled in by foreigners to destroy society from the inside. There is a social stigma attached to drug use. The media often presents addicts as mentally ill and a danger not only to themselves, but to their families and society. Many people think that I, or individuals in similar positions, deserve to be in prison. Prison in Taiwan isn't a prison. It's more like a zoo—cruel and unusual.

I hope to start a nuanced, layered conversation about prison and criminal justice reform in Taiwan. I want to bring attention to the treatment and conditions inside Taiwanese prisons. Not all crime is the same, and not all criminals should be treated equally. If this book can inspire people to fight for better living conditions in Taiwanese prisons and a reform of the judicial system, that would be unicorns and rainbows. In my dreams, I see the international community shaming Taiwan for its human rights violations, and Taiwan trying to change and make amends. But that's just the idealist in me talking.

Growing up, I never learned to care about mental health—especially for men. It was a weakness I just needed to get over because it was shameful to family, and everything had to appear perfect to save face. As a result, it's hard for me to deal with my emotions, let alone talk about them. I just don't have the vocabulary for it. I'm scary good at compartmentalizing. I put my feelings in a box and tried to bury them as deep as I could. My time inside didn't help. I just got better at it. When I got out, people asked what happened. They wanted a play-by-play. Nobody asked how I felt.

Walking around and trying to act tough all the time while being unable to talk about how I feel is exhausting. It's mentally draining, and some people crack. It's why I use drugs; I'm self-medicating. I don't want to feel or think about anything. That's not a healthy way to deal with trauma because when the feelings come, they erupt like a volcano. Who do I talk to when I want to vent? I now try to talk about my feelings freely, acknowledging that some might think I sound like a bitch. Talking about it helps.

When I was inside, I had nobody to talk to. So I wrote. I kept a journal. If I couldn't cry, at least my pen could. It was cathartic. They confiscated the journals I kept during my trial because nobody told me I couldn't bring them out when I made bail. I snuck out the rest of my journals when I left. After all, I am a convicted smuggler—if I can get something in, I can get something out. But smuggling written records of the things I experienced—it felt different, like I was a spy. Code name: 626 (the area code of the neighborhood I'm from).

This book's first few drafts were in journal form and kept my emotions out of it. I'd never written anything that long before, and it was easier for me to organize the book based on "facts," not feelings. But what are feelings but internalized facts? Writing this was a strange experience, and it changed the way I viewed masculinity. When I was young, I used to get beaten all the time. Sometimes I would cry because it hurt. I was a kid.

Whenever I cried, I would get beaten again. "Boys don't cry." It took so long to get to a point where I could freely talk about my feelings.

Before prison, if you told me the world could be a mean and cruel place, I'd reply with, "It's a cold world. That's why they make sweaters."

During, I learned how to accept and control my emotions, especially sadness, anger, and disappointment. And if I felt these things, I'm sure other people did too. When it was all about survival, to get through it, I had to put all my feelings, thoughts, and emotions into that box again.

These days, if you told me the world could be a mean and cruel place, I'd reply with, "Yeah, but that doesn't mean I have to be."

As I wrote this book after my release, I realized what was so difficult about it: to open that box was to relive prison all over again. There were times when I didn't know if I would finish. I felt sorry for myself and suffered in silence, forever toiling in my own obscurity. Or, when life gives me lemons, I could make lemonade and slang it.

I hope you enjoy my lemonade.

CHAPTER 1

ARREST

It is said that no one truly knows a nation until one has been inside its jails. A nation should not be judged by how it treats its highest citizens, but its lowest ones.

—Nelson Mandela

January 21, 2016

I knew something was wrong when I landed. I used my Taiwanese passport instead of American to enter Taiwan because the line was shorter. After the passport check, I accidentally walked in the wrong direction, toward a dead end. Out of the corner of my eye, I noticed a security guard shadowing me. Why was I being followed? This had never happened before . . .

While I waited for my stuff, I noticed police officers with two gray K9 units nearby for "random drug checks." Felt too coincidental to be random.

After what seemed like an eternity, my bags glided down the chute. Both dogs sniffed my luggage and left. I picked up my things and made my way to customs. A pair of officers stood in my path with another dog. He sniffed at my stuff and made no gestures. I stood at the end of the line. When I got to the front, they selected me for a "random check." At first, it was one customs officer, but once they opened my luggage, eight Ministry of Justice Investigation Bureau (MJIB) agents ambushed me.

I'd brought few clothes because my wardrobe was in Taiwan. In the bag were edibles, snacks, vitamins, and gifts for the family. They ran spot tests on everything. Initial tests came back negative. No drugs? They were befuddled. Why were they so sure they were going to find something? My stomach felt funny. The man in charge told them to run it again. This time, a cop said the edibles tested positive for ketamine.

There wasn't any ketamine in those edibles. The positive test was never explained to me, so I can only assume it was a lie.

People craned their necks to get a glance as they walked around the three-ring circus happening at customs. The officials never took me to the back. I was at a customs table, trying my best to look relaxed while surrounded by police. It felt like they were causing a scene on purpose.

The short middle-aged cop almost smiled when he said, "You smuggled drugs over."

I shook my head. "It's not drugs, it's my medicine. I want to speak to a lawyer."

"You don't have that right here," he said sternly.

I fidgeted. "I want to call my family—"

"Shut up!"

I slumped in my chair.

"Stand up." He grabbed my arm and stood me up. "We're taking you to the airport police station to be questioned by MJIB detectives and customs officials."

The police recorded the whole situation and took a picture of me with the phony positive test result. I frowned. Dammit, I was a long way from home.

* * *

People stared as they paraded me to the airport's station. There were murmurs and whispers as they cleared a path, judging me with their eyes.

There was peace and privacy at the station. For them, at least, I still felt like a trophy buck. They searched my stuff, bent me over, and searched my cavities.

"We'll confiscate your computer, iPad, clothes, sneakers, and luggage," a cop said.

I scrunched my face. "Am I getting anything back?"

"You lose anything used in the commission of a crime."

I chuckled darkly.

Somewhere, some cop's kid is looking fresh right now.

* * *

They escorted me to the MJIB headquarters to spend the night. I was taken into custody on January 22, 2016, at 3:00 a.m. on suspicion of drug smuggling and trafficking. The interrogation would continue the next day. By the time I got to a cell, it was 3:30 a.m. It had no bed, blanket, or pillow. They kept the lights on, so I wouldn't be able to sleep. I lay on the cold, concrete floor and thought, *What an idiot I am. I should have left my medicine at home.*

An officer handed me breakfast at 6:30 a.m. I sat in the cell until 11:30 a.m., when I had my mug shot and fingerprints taken. Interrogated at 4:00 p.m.—eight hours without sleep, including the flight.

During the interrogation, I denied any wrongdoing and repeatedly asked for a lawyer or translator. They refused both. I asked to speak to my family, but the officer told me to shut up. I kept asking and asking, and the police got frustrated. But what else was there to say? I don't speak Pig Latin.

Born and raised in America, English is my native language. My Chinese reading and writing, at the time, were at an elementary school level. I could hold a conversation in Chinese, but if my freedom hung on every word, I was definitely not fluent enough to go through an interrogation or court without a translator. A lot of the vocabulary was over my head.

Two officers smoked outside during a break in the interrogation. I stared at the room's wall. The patio was outside the interrogation room, and they had left both doors open.

I overheard one officer ask the other, "How did we even know? I've seen nothing like this."

"We got a tip from a guy who claimed to be his client. He said it was heroin, not weed."

"What's the guy's name?"

"Lǐjīngzhé (李京哲)."

That was a familiar name. I'd met him once. My friend, Panasonic—half-Brazilian, half-Taiwanese, married, tall, with long legs—had an upscale bar on a marina with an ocean view. Lǐjīngzhé used to be a bartender there. Panasonic and I had been drinking and chatting when he came up to us and asked, "Can I buy some edibles off you?"

My head snapped back. "I don't know what you're talking about?"

"Ah, c'mon, man. I heard you have some exotic stuff."

"I dunno what you heard, but it's not true." I didn't know why somebody I'd just met would ask a question like that out of the blue.

"I'm hooking you up, putting money in your pocket."

No, you're not. I don't trust anybody that says that. "Now, this is getting annoying. I don't know why you think I need money or that you're doing me a favor, but you're not. You can go fuck right off."

He squared up. He wasn't a threat. I didn't even bother physically reacting.

"Calm down, William," Panasonic said. "He's our bartender. We're all friends here."

I had shrugged and gone back to my beer.

Lǐjīngzhé gave my name to the authorities after. He also stole money—about 50K NTD—from Panasonic's bar, then quit. I went back to LA for three months, and when I came back, they caught me at the airport. That was the only time I'd ever met him. *I can't believe this dude snitched me out. What the hell did I ever do to do him?* He was a spoiled, punk-ass rich kid. I wished he were a gangster. We could've settled it on the street, like gentlemen.

A lieutenant walked in toward the end of the interrogation, looked over my responses on the computer, and said, "Oh no, this won't do." He typed something on the computer and printed it out. "Sign it."

"Can I have a translation of this?"

"No. Sign it, or else."

Three officers crowded around. A bead of sweat fell from my brow. I signed.

The police finally allowed me to call Small Auntie because they wanted her to come pick up the rest of my luggage. They didn't want it brought to the prison. I had seventy-six edibles: twenty-two Rice Krispies Treats, twenty-five pretzel sticks, and twenty-nine caramel popcorn packs.

It may seem like a lot, but I have terrible anxiety. I go through a bag a day. Weed was illegal in Taiwan, but edibles were a gray area. And with my license, I thought the penalty wouldn't be as harsh. In hindsight, I was a fucking idiot.

They kept the Rice Krispies Treats and planned to hand Auntie the other fifty-four snacks. When I realized she would be taking the rest home, I confessed that all seventy-six bags contained weed. Didn't want her to get in trouble.

At first, the police didn't believe me. They said they'd send them to a lab for analysis.

"It's a small world. I went to elementary school with your auntie," said an officer after she left.

"You should call him Uncle," joked another.

After that farce of an interrogation, they escorted me to the prosecutor's office and placed me in a holding cell in the court basement. The proceedings were in Mandarin. The prosecutor said the evidence was enough to press charges. There was a judge, a court clerk, and finally, a translator. He was an older, husky man with a buzz cut and a frumpy face.

"Speak English?" I asked in English tepidly.

"English, okay," he replied with a heavy Chinese accent.

I exhaled. "What is this?"

"Courthouse." He gestured around the room.

I sucked my teeth. "I didn't say, 'Where is this?' I asked, 'What this is?' Trial, arraignment, what?"

He looked confused.

I raised my voice. "How come you don't know?"

"Quiet, so we can begin," said the judge in Mandarin.

Frumpy-Face stuttered translating for the judge in English. "We accuse you of smuggling a ph-phase 2 contraband, no-narcotic, for r-rush hour."

"Rush hour?" I scrunched my face. "You mean *traffic*? Trafficking?"

"Yes, trafficking." He looked grateful I knew English. "How do you reply?"

As if it was even a question. "Not guilty."

"What are you doing in Taiwan?" he asked softly in Mandarin.

"Judge didn't ask that." I rolled my eyes. "What are your qualifications as a translator?"

5

Either he didn't understand or he ignored my question. "Do you know anybody here?"

"Judge didn't ask that either. You just nosy or what?" I stared at him and gestured around the room. "How come we're speaking Chinese if you're a translator?" I lifted my chin, pointed at him, and said in Mandarin, "Your honor, this dude's English sucks. Is there anybody else who can translate?"

"No, there isn't," said Frumpy-Face. "You can't understand me because I have an English accent." He straightened his back. "I speak the Queen's English." He replied with an accent so heavy I would've laughed if it weren't such a serious situation.

Chinatown bargain basement version of a translator.

"The Queen's English, huh?" I cackled. "Whatchu trying to say? Americans can't understand British people? You don't have an English accent and definitely don't speak the Queen's English." I would've been more animated if it weren't for the cuffs.

"You don't understand me because you can't understand English. Don't pretend like you do," he sneered.

His attitude made my blood boil. He was masquerading as an aristocrat when he probably couldn't even read *The Cat in the Hat*. "Oh, I understand English. What you're speaking isn't it. If it's like this, I'd rather take my chances in Chinese." I asked the judge in Mandarin, "Can I fire him?" I looked at Frumpy-Face and bared my teeth.

He glared.

"Everybody calm down," said the judge sternly. "Mr. Tsung, you're charged with smuggling and trafficking, sales, possession, and personal use. Altogether, they carry a minimum sentence of twelve years to life."

I shuddered and sweated. Twelve years to life? For some snacks? She must've been out of her mind. "Is there bail?"

She looked at my file. "You're a flight risk and denied bail."

"How am I a flight risk?" My eyes darted around the room, looking for an exit.

"You hold two passports, and although one is Taiwanese, you don't have a national identification card and are therefore not a full citizen. Nor do you have a job here."

I hung my head and slouched.

"Since it's your first offense in Taiwan, I'll lower the minimum to seven years."

Seven was better than twelve, but this felt like a sentencing. I'd hoped for a trial, but I wasn't sure what this was. It wasn't an arraignment—that came later. This court appearance ensured they had enough to detain me. The prosecutor had two months to charge or release me.

* * *

After some time in the holding cell, three policemen with assault rifles and bulletproof vests escorted me to Kaohsiung's second prison. Being sandwiched by policemen in full body armor felt surreal. Did they think somebody was going to hit the transport and break me free like El Chapo?

They took mugshots and fingerprints upon arrival. I took off my shirt for the cavity search.

"Whoa, you're fat," the officer said.

I took my pants off. "I don't think so."

He patted my torso, then grabbed my stomach flab and jiggled it. "Oh, no? What's this?"

"Prosperity." I pulled away.

"Bend over, smartass."

I bent over and winced as he did his thing.

"You'll lose some weight during your time here, chubby," he said as I put my clothes back on.

Must've been the highlight of his day.

There didn't seem to be any method to the maddening way they sorted detainees. Violent offenders were placed with petty thieves, short-timers with lifers. People frequently cycled in and out because of sentence-related prison changes or requests to go to the factory. Some made bail.

They placed me in a cell with two men, who I immediately sized up. Both were skinny, and one was taller than the other but shorter than me. I was relieved to be bigger than them.

"I'm Santino," the taller guy said. He nodded at the shorter guy, who was missing teeth. "He's Michael." At first, they stood on opposite sides of the cell. They seemed guarded and kept their distance.

I pointed at myself. "William."

Santino gave a knowing look. "You're not from around here, are you? You have an accent."

I smiled. "I'm from Monterey Park. It's in Los Angeles." I pointed in the direction I thought LA was.

He smiled back and looked longingly out the window. "Did you come straight from the airport?"

They didn't seem as defensive. I nodded.

"That sucks." His smile disappeared. "This your first time in Taiwan?"

"Nah, I lived with my grandma in Kaohsiung for three years. Went back to America for two weddings and got a job offer. I came back to grab my things and tie up loose ends." I chuckled awkwardly. "Funny how things work out."

"Do you have anybody that can visit?" Michael asked as he stared out the window.

"Yeah." I slumped a bit. "But I don't know if they know where I am."

The walls looked like they were once white, but now they were stained yellow. I spread out my arms and could almost touch both walls—which is saying something since I'm five foot ten.

"Whatchu doing?" Santino asked.

"Can't believe how small this cell is," I groaned.

He chuckled. "Prison in America is like a hotel, huh?"

I'd been in the weed industry since before it was legal. I'd been inside of a few cells. "Compared to this? Yeah." I jumped and tried to touch the ceiling.

"It's high to prevent suicide. Each cell is only meant for two people." He gestured around the cell. "But because of overcrowding, they cram in three."

This tiny cell wasn't big enough for one grown person, let alone three. I thought I'd see a bed and a toilet, but nope—nothing. It was an empty room with a hole in a corner on the floor, which was separated from the rest of the room by a pony wall. I wasn't sure what I'd been expecting, but it was definitely more than this. A small fan attached to a wall, a floor-level toilet, and no shower.

I stood and stared at the toilet for a moment.

"You don't know how to use it, do you?" asked Santino.

"Nope." I sighed. "Never used one. I've seen them around, mostly here. I prefer Western-style toilets. This is just a hole in the floor."

"They're nicknamed *squatters* because you squat instead of sit." He bent his legs to demonstrate. "Squat refers to your posture, not if the toilet flushes. Some are dry."

"I don't know which direction to face." I grunted and spun around in a circle. "Do I take my pants off or what?"

He stood up and indicated the proper direction. "Take them off and face the wall, away from us."

I had to pee, so I undressed. "Do I pee standing?"

Both looked away. "No!" Santino said. "Squat, but pee the other way, facing us. And no running water."

I squinted. "What do you mean, 'no running water'?"

"We get water for ten minutes to wash dishes after every meal and for thirty minutes at two to shower."

The water was potable. Each cell had a faucet like the kind on the side of a house.

"How do we flush?" I asked.

"Fill those with water"—he pointed at some buckets—"and pour it down."

"No trash can?" I looked around. "Or toilet paper?"

"Wipe with your hand, then wash afterward. They allow us to buy napkins but not toilet paper. Nobody uses toilet paper to wipe their ass anyway. Can't throw stuff down the toilet because it'll get clogged." He pointed at the squatter, then gestured around the cell. "Can't put them in the trash because it'll smell. The cell is small, and space is at a premium. Dump the buckets on your head to shower. Shower, piss, wash dishes, do laundry, and brush your teeth over the toilet. It's the only drain we have."

My heart raced. I ran my fingers through my hair, then needed to sit down. I sat silently against a wall for a while, then spent the rest of the day with my face in my hands or staring into space.

I thought they'd let us out for dinner, but they fed us through the hole in the wall. It was like we were in solitary. We slept on tatami mats on the floor. When there were two people per cell, there was space between mats. With three, they overlapped, and our pillows touched. Santino slept next to a wall, and I slept on the other, with Michael between.

Santino looked at me while he prepared for bed. "You have nothing, huh?"

"Until I have a visitor . . ." I sighed. "No."

Santino gave me his extra pillow and a towel. I hadn't expected him to hook me up. I felt like Blanche DuBois from *A Streetcar Named Desire*: "I've always depended on the kindness of strangers."

The first night was rough. It was so cold I borrowed a blanket from a trustee. A trustee is an inmate who assists in the prison's operation. They're given a little trust, hence the name. They wear shirts that are numbered one through nine. Number one was the head, but the other numbers denoted job responsibilities, not hierarchy.

"How come when you talk to a guard, you pretend you don't speak Chinese, but then you ask the trustee for a blanket in Chinese?" Santino asked after the trustee left.

I chuckled. "You noticed, huh?"

"Because it's pretty good, considering you're not from here."

The compliment made me smile. "Thanks, man. I speak Chinese at home and learned English in school. I figured it would be easiest on me if they just assumed I don't speak Chinese. Fewer interactions means fewer opportunities for conflict."

"Pretty slick."

While I shivered myself to sleep, an inmate bawled in the distance, and a corrections officer (CO) shouted at him to shut up.

*   *   *

It was tough to sleep. Michael asked me to face the wall because I snored so loud. When Michael got up to pee, he woke me, too. I'd landed on a Thursday night, and it was already Saturday when I woke up. Every fucking day, even on weekends, a gong sounded at 6:30 a.m. to wake inmates. I hated the gong. It would soon become as synonymous with the prison routine as a rooster crowing is with farm life.

"What happens on weekends?" I wondered aloud.

"On weekends and holidays, it's twenty-four-hour lockdown. Only the guards walk around," Santino replied.

"It's eerily quiet."

He nods. "You get used to it."

"What do people do?"

"Read, watch TV, listen to the radio, write letters, or sleep. There's not much else to do. They let us watch TV or read until eleven instead of ten since it's the weekend. Trash and everything else wait until Monday. Mondays are busy."

Santino watched a small personal TV he'd bought from the commissary. Michael wrote letters home. What the hell was I supposed to do for forty-eight hours straight? I stared at a wall. This barely qualified as a cell—no bed, no tables, no chairs, no restroom. It was a tiny room with a hole.

Most countries differentiate between prison and jail. Jails are usually for short sentences. Prisons are for longer, more serious crimes because they incarcerate the more serious offenders. Prisons are stricter than jails. Taiwan doesn't—it's all prison. However, she has a penal camp. It's a minimum-security institution for first-time nondrug-related, nonviolent offenders. Inmates work outside on farms and get to go home for a weekend. I've met only three people who transferred to camp, and they were all white-collar criminals. Maybe prison camp is Taiwan's version of Club Fed.

*　*　*

On the fifth day, Small Auntie visited for the first time.

I have four aunts in Taiwan. In Chinese, we differentiate by age. The oldest auntie is Big Auntie; Small Auntie is the baby.

Personal time and quiet time were the same: rot in my cell. We were rarely let out—only for doctors' appointments, visitation, and mail. Each cell door was as tall as my chest. Had to crouch to get in and out. The door had two deadbolts on the top and bottom, a chain, and a key lock. When the guards felt lazy (which was often), they didn't even unchain the door and just unlocked it. We slithered in and out.

The visiting room had rows of what looked like three-fourths of a telephone booth. Each inmate sat on a stump in a booth, separated from visitors by glass. There were dividers on each side so we couldn't interact with each other. There was one phone receiver—a landline with no buttons—on my side, two on the other. We were allowed up to two visitors at a time.

Small Auntie was already there when I sat down. I avoided eye contact because I felt so guilty. The dirty glass helped hide my shame.

"Thanks for coming," I said. "How'd you know where to find me?"

She took a deep breath. "It was two days before they told us you'd been arrested, then another two before they said where you were. There's no transparency. I kept getting the runaround."

Family has a way of finding each other. I hated to ask, but I was in a tough spot. "I need you to buy commissary."

"What's that?" She pushed her glasses further up her nose. "You're the first person in this family to be incarcerated."

Commissary is a penitentiary store from which inmates can purchase products such as hygiene items, snacks, writing instruments, and the like. We weren't allowed to have cash. Instead, we could make purchases through an account with funds earned as wages or provided by friends and family members. After I submitted the forms, commissary took a week to arrive. They were filled out in triplicate and included a fingerprint. We had to buy the ink pads. If a visitor ordered commissary on my behalf, it'd come the next day. There was a maximum of 2,000 NTD per visit, but I could only purchase some items. It's prohibited for inmates to trade commissary, but certain items were used as currency—cigarettes, batteries, tea, stamps. We were allowed to buy one pack of cigarettes a week (60 NTD), which were rationed. Four per day, Monday through Friday. My cigarettes were purchased on Wednesday and arrived the following Friday (ten days). Everybody smoked the same kind, and people usually took out the filter. They often took commissary away for infractions. I explained all this to her, and she nodded.

She rummaged through her purse for a pen. "What do you need?"

"Toothbrush, toothpaste, a tatami mat, blanket, towel, snacks," I blurted. "Everything!"

"Okay, what el—"

The line disconnected.

She pointed at the receiver and mouthed, "What happened?"

I hung up mine and nodded at the CO, who strolled toward me. Another came to her side and said something to her. Slowly, she got up and left, but she kept her eyes on me until I was out of sight. I sniffled as I watched her leave.

They tacked on up to 30 New Taiwan dollars (30 NTD = $1) to everything, but they up-charged clothes the most. Those were marked up 30 NTD to 50 NTD. They made inmates buy everything—bowls, chopsticks, toothbrushes, toothpaste, detergent, dishwashing liquid, soap, clothes, and so on. I had a bamboo mat with padding, two pillows, and a blanket.

When inmates were processed, they received one set of clothes: long pants (or shorts, depending on the season), a dress shirt, and a jacket. They let me keep the boxers I'd been wearing. Some of the poorer inmates didn't change clothes for a few days because they couldn't afford it.

When I got back to my cell, I sat down next to Santino.

"Who visited you?"

"Small Auntie." I couldn't hide my smile.

He looked out the window. "What's she do?"

"She used to own a Beijing-style duck restaurant. It was good," I lamented. "But she's retired now."

"Visitors make a difference, huh?" Michael added. "My wife comes. Sometimes she brings my kid." His voice got higher when he mentioned his family. "Are you married? Do you have any kids?"

"I'm single, no kids," I said proudly.

Santino looked at me. "Same. My mom visits."

"Whatchu in for?"

He looked me up and down. "Dealing heroin, sixteen years."

I turned to Michael. "You too?"

"Yeah, dealing. Not heroin—meth. Only got ten."

I couldn't believe he'd said "only."

Michael looked malnourished and was always restless. Santino had acne and seemed annoyed at him all the time.

Michael turned to Santino. "How come you're nicer to William than you are to me?"

I looked at Michael. "What are you talking about?"

"Santino let you borrow a pillow. He didn't loan me one. Anytime I ask for something, he's snarky. He's nicer to you."

Maybe because I'm bigger than him. Didn't know what to say. It was true, but the comment caught me off guard. "It's all in your head."

"I want to work for Santino when I get out."

I felt like I'd walked into a buddy sitcom. "Why? Aren't you already dealing meth?"

"There's more money in heroin," he replied smartly.

"You ever tried heroin?" Santino asked.

"Smoked it once, then fell asleep." I chuckled. "Didn't like it."

"Ever tried meth?" Michael asked enthusiastically. Tweakers always get so excited when they talk about meth.

"Nah, I know some people who went crazy." I paused for a few moments. Had to choose the right tone and words because I didn't want to piss him off. "Personally, I hate it and have never touched the stuff. Think it's poison."

"Heroin is just as bad," Santino replied. "When I use, I don't even feel good. I just don't feel bad anymore. I had two girlfriends, and we used to get so high that sometimes my dick wouldn't get hard." He chuckled, then hung his head.

I felt bad for him.

"Smoke break!" A CO shouted.

The cell was overcrowded, but we were three dope-dealing peas in a pod. I'd never been locked up abroad. They could've put me with serial killers for all I knew, but these guys gave me hope this nightmare might turn out okay. They were like me: guys in their early thirties who didn't like to wake up early. We were pretty lax with the schedule and wake-up times. If wake-up was 6:30 a.m., we'd wake up for roll, then go back to sleep.

*   *   *

Commissary arrived the following day. Six days in, and I finally got to brush my teeth! I felt human again.

"Hey, it's you!" Santino blurted while reading the paper.

He read the article out loud. Apparently, I was the first person to bring edibles into Taiwan, and it was a big deal. The article didn't mention the snitch. It said the police had had their eye on me since December and caught me due to fine police work. I couldn't help but laugh. Santino cut it out and gave it to me as a memento. But a guard confiscated it during a random search.

Infamy. Don't know how I felt about that. I was on every news channel and most newspapers in Taiwan and a few in Hong Kong and

Macau. Later, my friends and family would tell me they'd repeated that mediocre-at-best propaganda for days. They wanted the police to look competent. If you look at the dates of the articles and clips online, the story changes depending on the date. Fucking keystone cops. They swore they caught the Azn Nino Brown.

After I made the news, everybody knew who I was. People sent food and came and introduced themselves. The Taiwanese media unknowingly gave me instant street cred inside. They were all drug traffickers and were curious whether I was open to working together upon release. I said sure, figuring it was all a miscommunication, and hoped it'd be sorted out soon. But if not, and I was going to be there a while, my safety was paramount. The best way to stay safe was to have friends. All they wanted was knowledge about what I brought over anyway. If knowledge was power, I considered myself an information broker. Trading harmless info for my safety was a great deal.

An unfortunate consequence of time in any prison is that people make connections in the underground world that the authorities want them to leave behind.

* * *

"Pack your things," the head CO said on the seventh day. "You're moving cells."

I walked closer to the front. He looked about retirement age—tall, with a hunchback. "What'd I do wrong?"

"Nothing."

"Then, I don't want to move." I crossed my arms. "It's been a week. I want to stay here."

"It's not up to you."

"Fuck me," I grumbled, then slowly packed. Michael helped. "I didn't know what to expect, but thanks for making this as smooth as possible for me. Don't know what I would've done without you guys." I shook Michael's and Santino's hands, and we embraced.

Santino wrote down his information and handed it to me. "You'll be all right. Look me up when you get out."

I trudged to my next cell.

My next celly was Sun, and I sized him up. "Whatchu in for?"

"Murder." He took off his glasses and wiped them down. "I got into a fight with a guy and accidentally killed him."

Damn, that escalated quickly. My first week in, and they put me with a murderer.

I put my hands on my hips. "Whatchu looking at?"

"Twenty-five to life. I'm appealing." He sighed. "Used to be an LED technician."

Defenses were on DEFCON 1. I'd never been so close to a killer before. He didn't look like the type. Then again, not all murderers look the same.

"Do you know why you moved?" he asked.

I shook my head.

"In Taiwan, the people who've been locked up longer get the privilege of choosing their cellmates. I've been here for one and a half years. I learn English in my spare time and wanted you to teach me."

I said as little as possible. Like I'd be his education or entertainment. I wanted to do my time in peace and bounce as quickly as I could.

* * *

"Wake up," Sun said the next morning, shaking me.

"Huh?" I rubbed my eyes. "Why?"

"Morning roll call," he said matter-of-factly. "Get up and make your bed."

I thought everybody sat in their beds for roll like Santino and Michael. "Why? Can't I sit and sound off from my mat?"

"Get up and do it. In this cell, that's how it is."

"This is pointless." I woke up and made my bed, slowly. "Brownnoser," I said in English. "It's not like if we follow the rules, they treat us better, bitch." I doubted he understood me, but I hoped he did.

I was angry at him for the rest of the day. That night, after lights out, I rolled over to see him watching me.

"You shouldn't sleep like that," Sun said as we lay on our mats.

I inhaled sharply. "Like what?"

"With two pillows."

I used one for my head and another as a body pillow. I sat up, "Why not?"

"It might bother other people."

I raised an eyebrow. "Does it bother you?"

He took off his glasses and put them away. "No."

"Then shut the fuck up," I growled.

He turned away from me.

I lay back down and slept with both pillows.

* * *

He tried to tell me when to use the restroom, insisted my towel hung a certain way, and yelled when it wasn't. He soon got on my last nerve. Didn't know why he thought he could tell me what to do or why I'd listen. I hate being told what to do. Nobody tells me anything. Maybe he thought it was because he was a murderer and I was only a smuggler—like he was trying to pull rank. Pudgy bastard had a bald, bespectacled head that I could see the top of. I was taller, bigger, younger, and meaner. I wasn't worried if things escalated, but I slept with one eye open.

People had always called me an asshole, and it was true. But I'd never realized what it was like to deal with a real asshole until I was trapped in a cell with a bigger asshole than me.

It's strange how Taiwan mixes people on death row with people who recently arrived. In less than a week, I'd shared a cell with a man looking at twenty-five to life. He wasn't the only one either. The wing had a few on death row. Sometimes he cried when he watched TV and folded origami. He peppered me with questions about America. It got old fast. I felt like an organ-grinder monkey, dancing for his amusement.

After five days, I'd had enough. One morning, I didn't put my towel back to his preference.

"How many times do I have to tell you?" he seethed. "Put it like this. How stupid are you?" He pointed a finger at me.

"Shut the fuck up." I squared up and made eye contact. "I'm happy they're executing you. If they'd let me, I'd pull the trigger myself. It saddens me they won't let me watch. Fuck you for real." I swaggered toward him.

He raised his voice. "You can't talk to me like that," he said, then backpedaled.

17

Suddenly, a guard called my name for visitation. Small Auntie had come to see me. What would've happened if she hadn't come when she did?

On the way back from seeing her, the head CO took me aside. "There's an Englishman in for arson. His Mandarin isn't good. I want you to help translate for him."

The Brit was in the cell with Sun when I returned.

"What do you want to do?" The head CO looked at Sun. "You could share with two foreigners. Both can teach you English. Isn't this what you wanted?"

"I don't want William here anymore." Sun looked at me, then at the guard. "He threatened me before leaving for visitation."

The CO took his hat off, scratched his head, and looked at me. "Is this true?"

"I don't think so." I shrugged. "He always trying to tell me what to do. He's the bully. Self-defense." I crossed my arms. "He's the one who wanted me here. I was happy where I was."

He nodded and moved us to a cell behind his desk. I suspected he wanted to monitor me after Sun's complaint.

* * *

The Englishman, Nigel, was my fourth celly. He was around my age but looked older. Balding and sporting a beer belly, he had yellow teeth so crooked they looked like they were running away from each other. Had more wrinkles than me too. White people's skin ages like cheap leather left out in the sun. Nigel had left Britain at eighteen, lived in Taiwan for ten years, and had an eleven-year-old son in England he never saw. He taught English for years but hated it, quit, and opened a night market booth that sold pork gyros.

Nigel had been charged with arson and intimidation. After work one night, he'd gone to Family Mart and bought a hamburger. They didn't have any ketchup, so he returned it even though it was prepared. A week later, he returned to the Family Mart after a night of drinking and tried to buy a burger, but the employee refused to sell to him. Nigel got angry and yelled. They still refused and told him to leave. Nigel got on his moped, rode to a nearby gas station, filled an empty liquor bottle with gasoline, and drove back. He dipped a rag in gas, stuffed it in the bottle, lit it, threw it onto the sidewalk in front of the Family Mart, and drove off. As he rode off, an employee came out to put out the fire with an extinguisher. From his moped, Nigel looked at the employee and slid his finger across his throat.

Cameras are everywhere in Taiwan, and they'd recorded everything.

The next day, the police raided his apartment in Sizihwan and found him sunbathing on the roof. "Ten policemen stormed the apartment building, searched my apartment, and interviewed my neighbors," he lamented. "I messed up because I still had the receipt for the liquor and gasoline in my pocket."

He was all over the news. Everything was news in Taiwan, especially foreigners. The headline is usually some variation of, "Look at these foreigners causing trouble."

The judge allowed bail. Nigel hopped on a plane the next day and fled to England with no intention to return. They put a hold on his passport, but it took a few days. He left before it took effect and spent three months in England.

"I hated it," he told me.

He'd checked online for arson penalties, saw it was only a year or less, and faced the consequences. They arrested him at Taoyuan Airport.

I liked Nigel at first. It was nice to have somebody who spoke English. It provided a sense of normalcy among all the chaos and confusion. But that was about it for his good traits. He couldn't read or write Chinese but claimed he spoke it. Didn't do laundry or brush daily. Slept all day, then complained he couldn't sleep at night.

There are rich people, there are poor people, and then there are white people. The guards allowed Nigel cigarettes every three days instead of the usual ten. To pay them back, Nigel ordered twice the amount. Must be nice to be white. Asians in America get bullied and picked on. Apparently they didn't get the memo.

His mother in England repeatedly called the British consulate because she wanted to speak to him. Officially, inmates had to wait three months before receiving their first call, but apparently, if you're white, it's within two weeks.

As they scheduled his call, I asked the head CO, "Where's my phone call?"

"Nobody is calling for you." The other guards laughed.

I clenched my fists at the sound of their laughter. I felt like a caged tiger in a zoo, teased by some kids who only dared because of the bars between us.

"After sleeping on it," the head CO said the next day, "I've decided since Nigel gets a call, I'll give you one too."

I walked closer to the front and smiled. "Thank you. May I ask why?"

"It's only fair."

I didn't know or particularly care why he suddenly changed his mind, but I was happy he did. We bought prepaid phone cards for the calls. They took over a week to arrive.

"They delayed your cards," the head CO said. "If I order them, they'll come by three today. I'll order for you. When yours comes, give it to me."

He allowed me a call after all. I felt great, then noticed my tooth was aching. Fuck.

CHAPTER 2

YELLOW IS THE
NEW BLACK

**Do not pray for an easy life, pray for the
strength to endure a difficult one.**

—Bruce Lee

February 8, 2016

Chinese New Year, or CNY. It's the most celebrated and observed holiday in Chinese culture. It's like Thanksgiving and Christmas rolled into one. I love CNY!

Three years before I got arrested, during my first year in Kaohsiung, I discovered fireworks sold at the local stores. Fireworks were illegal in California—bottle rockets, Roman candles, mortars, and so on. I bought 3K NTD, about $100, of fireworks and shot them off every night for a week. There was a big box left over. I kept them on the balcony for a few days, then Grandma made me get rid of them because she didn't want explosives in her house.

CNY was the worst holiday to experience locked up in the intake cells. Way worse than Christmas, and it wasn't particularly close. Christmas was only a day, and there were no decorations. It felt like just another day.

CNY was, like, a week. My cell door didn't open for seven fucking days. Felt like they put me in a box and threw away the box. You at least let your dog out to pee once or twice a day.

I finally saw the dentist. He was only available on Tuesdays. My tooth had ached for eight days—since CNY Eve. He tapped my tooth, told me I needed a root canal, then pulled it out.

Gingerly, I touched my cheek. "Can I get a crown?"

"We don't do that here," the dentist told me. I heard my tooth drop in the metal tray with a thud. "Nothing cosmetic. I make it so it doesn't hurt."

I was given a temporary crown. He didn't sand it down, so it felt big in my mouth. The next day, I received antibiotics.

Nigel constantly complained that the other prisoners and guards never addressed him. They talked to me, and I translated. The issue wasn't that they didn't understand him—they did. But he didn't understand them. It wasn't like he made much of an effort either. He'd ask me to speak to a guard whenever he needed something, then complained they wouldn't talk to him. Eventually, I grew sick of his whining and refused to translate. Would've felt sorry for him if he weren't such a dick. The place was terrible enough as it was, but it would've been so much worse if I couldn't speak Chinese.

My cell got tossed for the first time. I hid my battery but didn't know I had to hide my sparks too. They confiscated those. Batteries themselves weren't contraband as long as I didn't have too many. No matches or lighters were allowed. To light our cigarettes, we got creative and used batteries and the foil from cigarette boxes, which we folded and cut with nail clippers. Strips had to be cut thin; too fat, and they wouldn't combust, just burn out.

The guys in the cell next to mine showed me how to make and use makeshift lighters. They were glued together from a used cardboard box, molded in the shape of two batteries, and even had positive and negative signs. Inside were the nail-clipped foil strips. Insert two batteries, and it created a circuit. When I touched a foil strip to the top—boom! Azn MacGyver. A napkin or tissue caught the flame, which burned long enough to light a cigarette. A pair of batteries lasted about a month. When it didn't ignite and burned out, the battery was about dead.

* * *

On the thirtieth day, they moved me for the fourth time. Each move annoyed me. They couldn't even let me rot in peace.

While we settled into our new cell, Nigel got into an argument with a guard over nothing. He was salty that nobody talked to him and threw a hissy fit. His voice got louder and louder. He shouted in English, "I don't want to be ignored anymore! I don't want William translating!"

"Okay, no problem," the guard replied in Mandarin.

Nigel's voice softened, and he said in heavily accented Chinese, "What do you mean?"

The guard turned to me. "He didn't understand what I said, did he?"

"Nope." I snickered.

He hid a smile. "Let me get this straight . . ." He took off his hat, scratched his head, and sighed. "He doesn't understand, but doesn't want you to translate for him either?"

"Correct," I jabbed. "He's crazy."

The guard laughed and walked away.

The situation made Nigel angrier. He was a petulant child who needed to be babysat whether he liked it or not. He screamed something about being ignored and wanting the guard to come back. Nigel was incoherent when the guard returned.

The guard waved me to the front. "William, translate this verbatim." He looked at me, then at Nigel. "You're not at home and can't do whatever you want. You better adjust to your new surroundings. If you don't want William translating for you, too bad. He's the only English speaker we have. He's your translator, and he's here to help. I'm an officer. You don't talk to me like this." He shook a disapproving finger. "Do it again, and I'll send you to solitary confinement.'"

Nigel stewed in a corner after he left.

"What do you call people who speak three languages?" I asked.

"Trilingual," he responded.

"What do you call people who speak two languages?"

"Bilingual."

"What do you call people who speak one language?"

"I don't know. What?"

23

"British." I cackled.

He wasn't amused, just looking for somebody to blame for his shitty life. "You need to stop knocking people about their shitty Chinese. What about the people who live in America for ten years and can't speak English?"

"What about the people who lived in America for five years and can?" I scoffed. "Why do you compare yourself to the worst?"

"You sound like my wife. I've tried learning Mandarin. It's bloody hard, okay?" he snapped. "It's easier to speak English."

Ahh, I see. Everybody should learn English to converse with him, yet there I was, translating everything for this entitled, ignorant, privileged, walking advertisement for contraception.

✳   ✳   ✳

Nigel and I met on February 7. His first court appearance was on the twenty-fourth and before mine.

"I'm surprised they denied bail," he said when he returned.

"How come?" I sat, leaned against the wall, and tilted my head. "They let you bail out the first time, and you fled. Why would they let you bail again?"

"Well . . ." His voice broke. "I came back."

I shook my head. I didn't know why he felt so entitled, but I wanted to know the juicy details. "What did the judge say?"

"She asked, 'At your original bail hearing, you said Taiwan is your home. Why'd you run?' I think I'm bipolar. I went back to England to see a doctor. 'Bail is 50K NTD,' she said, but then she pivoted. 'You don't have a job in Taiwan, your apartment lease expired, you don't even have any furniture, and you're divorced. Bail denied.'"

Nigel hated to socialize with other expats and foreigners. He preferred places with locals because he was special there. In big cities like Taipei, he was just another foreigner. There were plenty of them. He thought he was different, but we see them all the same.

"I've been here for ten years," he said smugly. "The foreigners staying for one or two years are glorified tourists."

"Who are you to judge other foreigners?" I clicked my tongue. "You're what Taiwanese think foreigners are: troublemakers and outside agitators.

Your rap sheet is pages long, full of DUIs and drunk and disorderly conduct."

"I'm more Taiwanese than you are." His face turned red. I couldn't see if his neck matched.

"To us," I smirked, "you're another dumbass foreigner."

The next day, his ex-wife visited.

"This will probably be the last time I visit you," she told him. "I looked it up online. Foreigners, if convicted of a crime, are banned from Taiwan for ten years. I don't want to leave, and if you can't come back for a decade, I don't know how it'd work."

It is frustratingly annoying, translating for entitled people. What grinded my gears was that Nigel claimed he could speak Chinese, but it was obvious he couldn't. It's okay if you can't, but you don't have to pretend like you can. When you're a guy, if you look like you're trying or pretend to not know how to do something, it'll often get done for you. In other words: women do it. I often reminded him who was doing who a favor. He made my life more difficult. I didn't have to translate, and I didn't appreciate being treated like a servant.

* * *

February 29. Of course my dumb ass would get arrested right before a leap year. I hoped this didn't affect my sentence. Two years is 730 days, but Taiwan was so vindictive, it wouldn't surprise me if they tried to give me 731 days.

"Any updates?" Small Auntie asked when she visited the next day.

"I have an arraignment at some point." I shrugged. "A two-part trial, then sentencing."

She nodded. "Do you know when?"

"Nah." I looked down and away. "They don't tell me until the day before."

"That sucks. I'll see if they'll tell me."

Without getting visitors often, a prisoner's got no way to live comfortably. The 300 NTD was only enough for essentials. Fortunately, Small Auntie had the time for weekly visits. I stocked up on snacks and necessities. Inmates could purchase stackable boxes, often used as tables.

Friends and family could send me books, up to three per visit, which Small Auntie brought in. They wrote my name and inmate number on the cover. Newspapers, pornography, and books with scribbled notes weren't allowed. They screened everything overnight. Anything that came in on Friday I wouldn't get until Monday.

* * *

"Put that over there," I told Nigel as I sorted through Auntie's commissary.

"I'm not scared of you!" he bellowed. "Stop telling me what to do. I'm not your bitch."

I didn't know what triggered him, but fuck it. "Whatchu gonna do about it?"

"I'm not your bitch." He balled his fists and paced. "You're not my dad. Stop telling me what to do. I'm not your bitch." He shouted for a guard, who sprinted over with a trustee.

"William is a bully, and he makes me do chores," he whined.

The CO looked at me, and I shook my head. "He doesn't have a problem eating my food. He's a racist and doesn't want me translating."

The CO put Nigel on the other side of the wing.

My fifth celly was John. He was on parole for fraud, then caught a gun charge. While he was out on bail, they caught him dealing meth. With my first three cellies, I was definitely not in charge. But when I met John, I let him know the deal.

"In this cell, I call the shots."

He did everything: washed the dishes, mopped the floor, washed and hung our clothes, got food, put food away, and did other odd jobs. When I finished showering, he stood by with a towel ready. I gave him food and cigarettes. John had little money, and nobody ever visited. The only person who'd visit was his sister, and they got locked up together on the same charge. I couldn't help but feel bad for him. I donated him an extra toothbrush and boxers. By this point, I'd made a lot of friends inside. People often sent food, so I made sure he had enough to eat.

John was the loudest snorer I'd ever met. Louder than me. Suddenly I understood what people go through when we sleep in the same room. Somehow he gargled while he slept, while also talking. And when I say talking, I mean he had full conversations. Sometimes he woke himself up with his own voice. It was so weird. Because of the meth, he had muscle spasms and twitched throughout the detox. I put a box between us so I wouldn't get kicked.

Whenever John talked about his case, he seemed certain they would take it easy on him. I pressed him because I wondered why he was so sure.

"I snitched out a dude for a lighter sentence." He slouched and hung his head.

I couldn't even look at him. "Someone snitched me out," I hissed. "Fuck snitches."

He retreated and opened his arms. "I didn't snitch out my friend, just somebody I didn't like. If they catch him, I cut my sentence in half. Nobody gets hurt."

"None of that is true. Even if it was, the game and universe police themselves. Karma is real." I'd become agitated. Never heard anybody admit they're a snitch. "I'm superstitious, and snitching is bad juju. Why do you think they have witness protection? It's a dangerous world. Who knows what'll happen? Might fall down some stairs, get hit by a car, be struck by lightning. Karma is only a bitch if you are."

For a snitch, John cried a lot—once off and on for four days straight. The longest cry was an hour.

"I'm thinking about home," he said between sniffles.

"Everybody's thinking about home," I replied with disdain.

His voice broke. "They'd've had locked me up all over Taiwan."

Did you cry at every stop?

It was weird to be waited on when I woke up. Felt like Eddie Murphy in *Coming to America*. John asked my permission for everything. "I'm going to masturbate tonight. Is that okay with you?"

"Sure, go nuts. Don't get any jizz on me."

I quickly got annoyed with John. He kicked things when bored, marched in place for no reason, and sang out loud whenever I loaned him my radio. Thankfully, he requested a factory transfer on the seventeenth day. After he left, I realized he'd never used the toothbrush I gave him. Not once in sixteen days!

But thanks to John, I realized how lucky I was and how good I had it. Visitors at least once a week, sometimes twice. I slept on a bamboo mat with padding, two pillows, and a blanket. I'd made friends; people looked out for me. I had a bunch of snacks and drinks, a TV, books to read, and a radio. All things considered, I was blessed. On visitation days, my visitors would bring fried chicken, pizza, or some delicious food. I'd eat my meal, watch TV, and smoke a cigarette. What cage?

John had slept on the floor with no mat or blanket, and used borrowed prison library books for pillows. Nobody ever wrote. He had nobody. It was hard not to feel empathy and compassion for him and others like him. It's rough.

There's a difference between being a bully and enforcing my law. I was only reminding him of his place, I thought. When he left, I noticed two people inside me. William, a.k.a. Dr. Jekyll, and Mr. Hyde, f.k.a. Wizzo. I was as savage as ever. I needed to be to survive and keep sane. What do I mean by savage? I could talk until my face turned blue, but a mofo only knows what a mofo knows. Some people understand logic and reason, but everybody understands an ass-kicking. I felt like an easy target. Alone, a foreigner in a foreign place, and because I was American, people thought I had money. I didn't. I was ready and able to defend myself over any slight, real or perceived. William was the guy giving away toiletries and food to my cellies who were less fortunate. Wizzo wanted to stomp anybody dumb enough to step to him with malicious intent or just looked at him wrong. He'd stomp them until they're comatose and would feel like a punkass bitch if he didn't.

It was hard not to feel for some of these men. This system is beyond fucked up. The conditions and treatment were inhumane. We didn't even get the necessities. Seemed like Taiwan shifted the responsibility of the incarcerated from the government to the inmates. A person's experience depended on who they were, how much money they had, and the frequency of their visitors.

*　*　*

Small Auntie visited and told me Pops had had a heart attack. He smoked and didn't exercise, yet I felt guilty. Was I responsible for this? It wouldn't surprise me if seeing me on the news had given him the heart attack. I slept with one eye open and was constantly aware of my surroundings.

Being locked in a cage with murderers, sexual predators, and addicts was stressful. If it was stressful for me, it must've taken a toll on my parents. They must've been worried all the time. I didn't want to give anybody another heart attack.

CHAPTER 3

KANGAROO COURT

People have to go through trials and tribulations to get where they are. Do your thing—continue to rock it.

—Kendrick Lamar

March 19, 2016

The government had two months to charge or free me, and my first court appearance was two days before that deadline expired. Inmates didn't know their court date until the day of. Weekday mornings, a trustee used the mic and notified those who had court. Guards lined us single file at the wing's far end so we could be searched, then herded to intake.

At intake, I exchanged my slippers for old, smelly sneakers. It disgusted me to wear secondhand sneakers, especially without socks. I signed and fingerprinted the master list next to my name, then sat. When I was called, I stood and stated my name, birthday, and inmate number. After, they cuffed us in fours and pointed to the bus.

A guard handed me lunch on the way to the bus: two hard-boiled eggs and a *mantou* (bread). They separated the bus into three sections, which had two benches on each side that sat up to twelve per bench. The driver and most of the guards sat in the first section, inmates sat in the second, and the third was for those in solitary. Everybody in the third section was shackled and chained. Figured they must've done something bad to deserve that. Felt sorry for them, but happy they didn't shackle me.

It was a nice spring day. I wanted to feel a breeze, but the windows didn't open. It'd been over two months since I'd seen the outside. I'd forgotten how frenetic it is.

People talked about their cases, and I thought about mine. Maybe I was naive, but I hoped I could resolve it shortly with a hefty fine—worst case, maybe a few months.

It was just a bunch of cops jerking each other off. They got their names and faces in the news, probably parlayed this into a promotion. Their altar of propaganda needed a human sacrifice.

I never thought I'd committed a crime—it was only weed—but the conditions and treatment were unacceptable. Didn't know Taiwan treated people that way, especially her own people. If China did this to Taiwanese citizens, there'd be mass protests. Yet nobody cares that Taiwan claims to be a bastion of human rights while running gulags.

The courthouse was by Kaohsiung's Love River. We walked through a gauntlet of policemen en route to the basement holding cells. Must've been every cop in the area. They brought us in sets to be searched, then placed in holding. I stuck my hands through the bars to be uncuffed. The cell had rows of benches but only one toilet for forty people, which was in the corner separated by a little wall. There was graffiti on the walls, usually a person's name and date. Guards placed a kettle of water with paper cups outside the bars, within arm's reach.

Moments after I got there, a bunch of guys crowded around the front of the cell.

One dude whistled.

"Aye, aye, aye!" yelled another.

A few hung on the bars like monkeys.

What're they doing?

"Heyyy!" cooed a female voice.

Oh, a woman! No wonder it was so loud. Some of these guys hadn't seen a woman in months, years.

"Shut up," barked the CO as he walked over.

Those to be questioned and posted bail were in separate cells. All the cells were the same. We were called individually for court, which was upstairs on the second and third floors. Two police officers sandwiched me on the way up. In the courtroom, I was uncuffed and placed in the defendant's seat.

The courtroom resembled an American courtroom, except the prosecutor and defendant faced each other instead of the judge. Both attorneys wore robes. My lawyer's were black with silver trim, and the female prosecutor's were pink, also with silver trim. The judge sat on an elevated bench behind two recorders. Frumpy-Face was there as well. When I saw him, I shook my head. *Fuck me.*

I complained in Mandarin before proceedings began. "You guys can't understand him, but his English is terrible. Is there anybody else?"

"No," the judge replied.

I looked around the courtroom for other options, as if one would magically appear. "If he's my translator, your honor, then I don't want one."

She looked at like me like I was a waiter who'd gotten her order wrong. "You asked for a translator. We provided one."

"You don't understand me because you can't understand English," sneered Frumpy-Face with an accent so heavy white people don't even sound like that when they're mocking Asians speaking English.

"Saying you can speak English," I growled, "doesn't mean you can."

A policeman leaned in and whispered in Mandarin, "Can't speak English, can't speak Chinese. You're screwed."

I glared at him

He side-eyed me. "Pay attention to the court."

"Quiet!" the judge announced.

They officially charged me with smuggling and trafficking a schedule 2 narcotic for distribution and sales. Minimum sentence was seven years, the maximum—life.

For a thirty-minute court appearance, I was gone from 8:00 a.m. to 5:00 p.m. because we waited for everybody to finish. I was strip-searched twice and cavity searched once.

"You missed dinner," the CO said when I got back. He handed me a small cardboard bento box and my daily cigarettes.

Court days were the worst.

* * *

My sixth celly was Brad. Broke and divorced, he didn't shower, wash, or change clothes daily. He flossed his teeth with a rubber band. I gave him a toothbrush when he arrived. Didn't use it until four days in.

Small Auntie and Pops visited. Surprised he made it. He should've been home recovering. Instead, he was there, looking disappointed and sad.

"Tell them you're American," he said. "You have a license. They can't do this." Pops was a bespectacled man with a medium build, a hunchback, and great salt-and-pepper hair.

I took a deep breath. "I tried, but I don't think either of us understands Taiwanese laws. Weed is a lot more serious here than LA. I'm pleading guilty and throwing myself at the court's mercy. I don't see another way."

"Are you sure you want to do this?" he asked solemnly.

I wasn't, but a long drawn-out trial wasn't in my best interest either. I prayed the judges would go easier on me if I made it easier for them.

The first session of the two-part trial was on March 29. I got a different translator, a thirty-something man. I think he was an American-born Chinese—an ABC. His English was fluent, but his Chinese was uneven. Anybody was an improvement over Frumpy-Face, though. I saw the evidence the state had against me, which wasn't much. The state had a log showing my travel history to and from Taiwan. They displayed my luggage, edibles, doctored confession, and pictures of edibles. They didn't have a witness. In Taiwan, there's no witness protection. The prosecutor lowered the minimum to three and a half years with a two-part trial because I confessed. My lawyer requested bail, and the judge said she'd get back to me.

A week later, I got a letter that my bail had been denied. I wasn't too sad about bail. The faster I did my time, the faster I could go home. The judges decided I was a flight risk, and they weren't wrong. I played hopscotch with borders. Flight risk and proud of it!

* * *

I dreamed that Eminem and I were signing autographs at a mall. A fan asked me for a picture. I told him, "Not now, I'm busy."

Em pulled me aside and said, "You should be nicer to your fans, William."

"Damn, Marshall. You gone Hollywood."

He slugged me. I hit him back, and we needed to be separated by security. I like how, in my dreams, Eminem and I are on a first-name basis.

They added a third person to my cell because of overcrowding. The reasoning seemed odd until I realized words don't mean the same thing in Taiwan. By *overcrowded*, they meant that every single penitentiary was past full capacity, so what was a duo became a trio.

Bob was a tweaker and a thief with forty-one counts of burglary. He'd gotten into an argument with my third celly, Sun, and moved. I hadn't shared a cell with two people since my first days, and it took some getting used to. I slept against the wall with the fan and window, Bob was in the middle, and Brad was farthest from me.

One night while I slept, I felt something on my chest. I thought it was a mosquito and slapped it out of instinct. When I realized it was a person's hand, I sat up and looked. It was the thief. Bob had been running his fingers across my chest. I hit him in the face.

"It was an accident! I was dreaming!" he insisted.

Fucking lying tweaker. Pretty calm response for someone who was supposedly dreaming.

I pointed at him. "Don't do that to me, especially when I'm sleeping. Tomorrow, you're going to submit a factory request. I don't want you in the same cell anymore."

Bob left the next day. He'd lasted almost a week.

After two weeks, an inmate could submit a written request to go to the factory. For drug offenders, it was four weeks. People submitted requests by Wednesday and moved on Thursday. Every week, a CO would ask if anybody wanted to go. He described all the benefits and how to apply "You earn points toward your early release and get more cigarettes—ten daily instead of four."

Extra cigarettes and early release weren't enough incentive for me to work. I'd have rather rotted in a cell.

Penitentiaries are a big business in Taiwan. Each one is a gulag, a forced-labor camp. They sold products to the public via the government's Corrections Agency Handmade Goods Marketplace website. Most inmates produce goods under Taiwan's "one prison, one specialty" policy, Monday through Friday. Usually, it's six or seven hours of work, but eight isn't uncommon.

Clearly, they are under financial pressure to increase revenues. Slave labor allows them to sell high-quality handcrafted commodities at bargain prices, without the need to adhere to minimum-wage requirements. But does indentured servitude help achieve prisons' overarching purpose of helping criminals turn over a new leaf and reenter society? Well . . . perhaps that's not Taiwan's goal.

* * *

Mrs. Juice and Houston visited. They were the first friends who came to visit me. Mrs. Juice and I go way back from college. She moved home after graduation and lived in Taipei as a wife, mother, and model. I met most of my Taipei friends through her, Houston included. He was a big-bellied, bespectacled, finance bro from Houston. He liked to race cars, and we went go-karting whenever I was in town. He'd surprised me the first time he beat me in a go-kart race. It wasn't like I was good or anything, but this bro outweighed me by fifty pounds. In a go-kart, he looked like Bowser from *Mario Kart*, and Bowser smoked me.

"Are you okay?" Mrs. Juice asked. "We're worried about you." She sounded concerned and maintained eye contact.

"I'm fine." I smiled. "Thanks for visiting."

"We got you, homie," Houston replied. "We're here to make sure you're okay." His eyes darted around the room. "You get into any fights yet?"

"No, not yet. I'm not trying to either. Some are cooler than others, but most seem like okay dudes." I saw them look around and take in the environment. Must've been jarring. They looked so uneasy.

A CO walked by, stopped, and hovered. They did this a lot when I had visitors. Not so much when I spoke Chinese, but all the time in English. I'm sure they didn't expect to hear Taiwanese people converse in English in a prison visiting room.

Houston side-eyed the guard and nodded. "I put 8K NTD in your account—"

"And I bought you KFC," Mrs. Juice blurted.

"Thanks." I blushed. "How'd you know where I was?"

"We called the Ministry of Justice to find out which prison, then called to confirm." Houston sighed. "It wasn't easy."

* * *

Jerry, the guy in the next cell, sent a kite (a note passed between inmates) that said he wasn't happy in his cell and asked if he could move into mine. Because of high suicide rates, inmates weren't allowed to be alone in a cell. If a celly was gone for whatever reason, the guards shuffled people. I'd met Jerry when his celly had court last week.

"Sure," I replied, "but it's full. As soon as somebody leaves, you can come."

The nighttime hand-on-chest incident with Bob the thief happened shortly after that, and Jerry took Bob's place. He moved in three days after I received the kite.

They'd caught Jerry with twenty kilos of ketamine and five kilos of heroin. He was married at twenty-two, but his pregnant wife was only seventeen. He hoped to bail in time for the birth of his child. His presence transformed the cell. He made paper speakers for my radio, which amplified the sound. It played in the background throughout the day. The cell felt homier because he crafted a few shelves and taught Brad how to properly clean the restroom. The squatter sparkled.

"Brad is in for rape," Jerry said as we smoked a cigarette on his second day.

I looked around. "How do you know?"

"Outside of the cell, there are ID cards with our names, ages, dates of arrest, and charges." He took a puff and passed the cigarette to me. "Mine and yours say drugs. Brad's says rape."

"Can't read or write that well." I took a few puffs. "When people tell me their crime, I have no reason to think they're lying." I passed the cigarette back. "I never checked."

I acted cool, but I was heated. All I could do was stew until I got the chance to complain.

The following morning, when I picked up my mail at his desk, I asked the head CO, "Why'd you put me in a cell with a rapist?"

"It wasn't to punish you. I don't know if you know, but in Taiwan, thieves and rapists are the lowest of the low here. I put him with you because I hoped you wouldn't find out. If I put him in another cell, he might get bullied."

"Can you move him to another cell?" I pleaded.

"I can't move him unless he wants to, and he doesn't. He's worried he'll get bullied if he moves."

I was so pissed. The entire way back to my cell, my fists clenched and unclenched. When I got there, I confronted Brad.

"How come it doesn't say drunk driving on your name card?"

"Because I'm in for rape," he calmly replied.

"What the— Why'd you tell me and everybody else you're in for drunk driving when you're in for rape?"

"Well, I was out on bail, then I got caught for rape."

Fuck him. Jerry and I taxed his cigarettes and split them between us. We each had six, and he had none. Everything made sense. Whenever they allowed us to smoke or exercise, he never wanted to be out of the cell for long and had no other friends except for another rapist. Birds of a feather.

* * *

April 19 was my last court appearance. While I dressed, I told Brad, "You woke me up four times last night. I told you before to be quieter when you wake up. This isn't working. When I get back, you'll move your ass to another cell."

In court, they gave me the best translator. An older woman. Her English was accented but fluent. There were three judges instead of one: an older presiding judge and two younger judges. The presiding judge asked if I had any last words before they sentenced me.

This was my chance to get everything off my chest. I took a deep breath.

"I want to say I'm not a bad person. I made a mistake. To be clear, I confessed to smuggling. I did it and I'm sorry, but I didn't confess to anything else. The police coerced the rest. I was under duress. Matter of fact, if you check the tape, you'll see a gap because when I asked for a lawyer or remained silent, they stopped the tape, took me outside, and threatened me. You can see portions where a supervisor comes in, looks at my responses, and changes my answer." I exhaled.

"What do you mean, *coerced*?" asked the judge.

"Exactly what I said. I wasn't treated fairly or justly." I straightened my posture and began gesturing. "Look at when I got arrested. It was a fifteen-hour plane ride. I didn't sleep on the plane. I was arrested at 2:30 a.m., and by the time I got to a cell, it was three, maybe 3:30 a.m. There was no bed. I lay on the floor, no pillow or blanket, and they kept the lights on the whole time. They didn't let me sleep, and they didn't interrogate me until 1:30 p.m. the next day. For no reason, I was kept up the whole day." I counted on my fingers. "Over twenty-four hours with no sleep before they interrogated me. While interrogated, they denied me a lawyer and translator."

Papers rustled.

"We're going to go over your confession, and you tell us what you said and what they changed," the judge said. "Why didn't you bring this up earlier?"

"I tried!" I shouted, then lowered my voice. "But I had terrible translators, and nobody listened or cared. It seemed like all everybody cared about was their face on the news."

We went over the confession line by line and got to a part where I confessed to smuggling for distribution. The lieutenant had written a full false statement in which I confessed to intending to smuggle drugs for profit.

"That's not what I said," I declared. "I confess to smuggling. I'm not trying to get out of it. I did it and will accept the consequences. It's twelve kilos, but it's not all weed. Most of it's packaging and food. If I'd known it was this serious, I would've never brought 'em over. I thought I'd face a fine or the state confiscating them." I was animated. "I didn't understand the laws. I thought my medical license would protect me. It's all a miscommunication."

"You're stupid." The presiding judge laughed. "Is this your first time in Taiwan, Mr. Tsung?"

I shook my head. "No, but it's not legal in every state in America, yet the airlines still let me fly with it. I have a license—it's my medicine. If I flew into a state where it wasn't not legal, they'd confiscate it or fine me." I pointed at the evidence. "It's not time, and it's certainly not years. I crossed two customs with it, Los Angeles and Hong Kong. They all knew. I wasn't hiding it. How can I hide seventy-six bags? It was in plain sight. If you want to blame somebody, blame the state of California. I paid taxes on this."

"Well, what would you like your sentence to be?"

I cleared my throat. "A fine." I don't come from money, but fines aren't punishments. A fine is how much it costs for me to break the law.

"We can't do that. You have to do time."

I threw my cuffed hands into the air. "Why?" They landed on the table with a clang.

"Because this is the first time we've encountered marijuana snacks in Taiwan. I don't want other people to do what you did and think they can get off scot-free."

"Then . . .," I sighed wearily, "charge me with smuggling a prescription drug for personal use, because that's what it is. I'd like the minimum, please."

The judges huddled. It was quiet for a few moments.

"I-I also request to do my time in the south, in the same place, because it's closest to my family," I mumbled. "I heard all foreigners are supposed to go to Taoyuan Prison, which is four hours away and inconvenient if anything happened."

"That's not our decision. It's the prison's," replied a judge.

My lawyer chimed in. "What about bail so he can spend some time with Grandma before sentencing?"

"How do you feel about bail?" the presiding judge asked. "What do you want to do?"

"If you let me out"—I sighed deeply and stared at the floor—"I prom-ise I won't run."

"If you don't post bail, do you wish to come to your sentencing?"

"I don't want to come. My lawyer can tell me."

"We set bail at 50,000 NTD." That was equivalent to $1,544. "Do you have it?"

"Yes."

"Bail granted."

I wanted to jet-pack out the door and never look back. I bounced up and down in my seat.

"For bail, you're not required to check in. You may travel within Taiwan, but you're not allowed to leave the country. We'll mail you your sentence, along with where and when to surrender."

I couldn't believe what had happened. They'd mailed me a letter that denied bail, but now I was free? The court flip-flopped like that? Maybe it wasn't that serious after all. Laws are bullshit until they're not.

After they granted bail, the police walked me downstairs and uncuffed me. I felt free, as if woken from a bad dream. Reality slapped me in the face when I heard the cell door clang shut. They'd placed me in the cell for those who bailed. I thought about Jerry. I felt bad, leaving him alone to deal with the rapist. Pops and Uncle were there but didn't have cash on them because they didn't know I'd get bail. It took them a few hours to hit the bank and come back.

"How come you're not out yet?" taunted a guard. "Maybe you won't post bail after all, and we'll just take you back to prison."

There was no flowery time lapse. I did what I did every day: sat and stared at a wall until somebody got me.

The sun was so bright. I hadn't experienced the sun or fresh air in three months. Not even when I had court because the bus parked in the basement. We went upstairs, not outside. I saw Pops and Uncle when I stepped out. I'd never been happier to see them. Pops is taller than my uncle, but shorter than me. Pops's big brother somehow looked younger, maybe because he didn't have as a much white hair and better posture.

Uncle handed me a cigarette. "Must be nice to breathe fresh air again, huh?"

I lit it and took a puff. "Got that right."

"If you want to smuggle yourself out of the country, your mother and I'd understand. We won't be mad," Pops said on the way to the apartment.

The comment caught me off guard and I paused. "Let me ask Mom."

Because of the time difference, she was asleep, but I left a message. She called back when she woke up.

Pops and Uncle didn't tell Grandma what happened. They had denied bail so often we assumed they'd do it again. When she saw me, she was ecstatic.

Grandma was a little old lady. Her hair was short, white and curled like Betty White's. She couldn't have been over four foot ten, and she dressed in flowery silk blouses all the time. I get my style from her. Her feet were tiny because they were bound when she was younger. Small feet were in vogue for women back then.

She came over, felt my face, and gave me a big, long hug. "If I was younger, I'd beat you. I was so worried."

I smiled. "I'm happy you're old, Grandma."

"How much weight did you lose?" She grabbed a handful of my stomach.

"Little under four keys."

"Four kilos!" She exclaimed. "I could eat for over two weeks."

I chuckled and pulled away.

She turned to Pops and asked, "So it's over?"

"Not quite," Pops sighed. "He's out on bail. We're awaiting sentencing, and at some point, he's going back in."

"At least he's out."

I told my people I was out. Houston said he was celebrating his birthday the next night in Taipei with dinner and drinks. I could come up, eat, drink, and stay at his house. It'd be great to see everybody. I hung out with Grandma, Uncle, and Pops until they fell asleep.

CHAPTER 4
FLIGHT RISK

Out on bail, fresh out of jail, California dreaming!

—Tupac

April 20, 2016

took the high-speed rail to Taipei. Houston's apartment was in Xinyi, in the most expensive complex in the city. It was full service—like living in a hotel—and was spotless. From his living room was a view of Taipei 101. I nicknamed him Houston because he was my first friend from Texas. I didn't know Houston had such a big Taiwanese community until we became friends. Southern hospitality, barbecues, guns, cars, football—he was like a cowboy in a Taiwanese dude's body. All he was missing was a cowboy hat and spurs.

For his birthday, Houston rented out a barbecue restaurant, complete with an open bar. My first drinks in months, and I overindulged. After dinner, we bar-hopped. Between bars, somebody handed me a joint and said, "Happy four-twenty." A friend with weed is a friend indeed.

The next day I woke up with the meanest hangover—good thing I had plenty of weed to take the edge off. When Houston got off work, we had dinner, then he dropped me off at the high-speed rail.

"Stay out of trouble," he pleaded as I hopped out of his Benz.

* * *

Three days out, my legs finally stopped feeling sore. My muscles had atrophied while I was inside. Life outside was tiring. So much walking around.

"What do you do all day?" Grandma asked.

"Well, today, I got a full physical, updated my booster shots, saw a dentist, and got a gym membership." I flexed. "I'm eating five meals a day. It might be awhile before I eat well."

* * *

I didn't know how long I'd be out or how long my sentence would be. The uncertainty was the worst part of the system. It was like there was a guillotine hanging over my head, and I couldn't tell when it'd fall. To keep my mind off the impending doom, I hung with Jason. Born in Taiwan, raised in Vancouver, Jason was the first Kaohsiung friend I made. We met at a bar on Christmas.

We smoked a J and hit the JD. What's a JD? In Mandarin JD (酒店 Jiǔdiàn) means hotel, but it has another meaning in Taiwan. The most apt comparison would be a hostess bar or a strip club. There are different JDs, but they're all more or less the same: liquor, karaoke, and women. Clients rent rooms, buy liquor by the bottle, and pay women to keep them company. The mama-san could pick, or they pick themselves, à la Heaven on Earth from *Rush Hour 2*. Depending on the JD, women entered individually or in groups. First come, first serve. The earlier people go, the more options they have.

Prostitution should be legal, regulated, and taxed. Pimping is exploitative and illegal for that reason. If two grown adults come to a decision, who are we to tell them what they can and can't do, especially if they're not hurting anyone? The laws are all twisted here. How can a rapist get less time than a drug dealer? People ask for drugs; nobody asks to get raped. I never thought selling or smoking weed was wrong. People treat marijuana like it'll cause the downfall of society. How could it? If it could, maybe that society wasn't that sturdy to begin with.

* * *

My sentencing was May 10. I didn't attend, and my lawyer didn't either. Had I known he wouldn't go, I would've gone. I think Small Auntie hired him because they were friends, not because of his legal prowess. Drugs weren't even his area of expertise, the fraud.

They convicted me of smuggling a prescription drug for personal use. I wanted my grandma's opinion.

"You got off light," she said. "I think I'll still be alive when you get out." She was ninety years old.

I had ten days to appeal but decided not to. I could do two years. Those walls wouldn't change me. Besides, what I went through wasn't a fair or even an actual trial. What made me think I'd get a fair appeal?

I smoked a joint and went to the movies. How easy it'd be to smuggle myself out of the country. I even got quotes, between 100K ($3,183) and 500K ($15,917) NTD. I'd get on a boat to Fùjǐn, and the captain would stamp my passport. From there, I'd make my way to a major city and hop on a plane to the States. But I could never come back. Never is a long time, and I have family here.

* * *

On July 10, I was on my moped, riding home after a late-night snack at the night market, when I saw Lǐjǐngzhé's (the snitch) car parked outside a neighborhood bar. It was the first time I'd seen any trace of him since he'd snitched me out. Heated and unsure what to do, I pulled over and checked my cell phone to confirm it was his. There was a picture of his car on my phone. Just because he was unharmed didn't mean I didn't have an eye on him. I stalked this rat like a tiger in the tall grass.

I lit a cigarette and considered my options: (1) Do nothing. Going home was the smartest move. I didn't need any more problems right now. (2) Run up into the bar, turn his face into a hamburger patty. He wakes up in the hospital; I go to prison again. Unlikely, but I refused to let him slide. I needed to send a message. (3) I pick up the biggest rock I can find and pretend I'm Ryu in the bonus stage in *Street Fighter*.

I went with door number three. I smashed every car window and keyed it on both sides from hood to trunk.

A week later, a policeman showed up at my door. "Were you driving a white moped with this license plate?"

I popped my head out and looked around. He was by himself. "Yes, I was."

"A car has been vandalized, and you need to come to the precinct for questioning."

"I don't want to," I growled and tried to close the door on him.

He stuck his foot in the crack. "You must."

I relented and let him in. "What if I don't?"

"Then," he put his hands on his hips, "we'll come back and arrest you."

I exhaled. "How about the precinct tomorrow?"

"Tomorrow is fine."

I asked Small Auntie to come with. "We'll be there at 8:00 p.m."

* * *

"What do you know about a Porsche that's been vandalized?" The cop asked when I sat down at the precinct.

I'm going to die with the lie. "Nothing."

He sighed and played surveillance footage from a street camera. There was no doubt it was me. The tattoo on my calf was clear. *Dammit.*

I took a deep breath. "All right, I did it."

"Why'd you do it?" He filled out paperwork.

I couldn't tell the truth of what I'd done, which was what Batman does to criminals: intimidate through terror. "I was in a bad mood. I shouldn't have done it. I won't do it again."

"Were you drunk?"

Seemed to work. "No. Drunk driving is dangerous and illegal."

He shook his head.

"Will bail get revoked?" I asked meekly.

"No. It's a nonviolent, nondrug-related crime. It'll probably be settled out of court."

"Great," I smiled and stood up. "We done here?"

"Yes. Don't do it again."

The justice system appeared nonsensical, but fuck it. I was free. I considered that a win.

* * *

"I'm sick of your shit," Mom screamed when she called the next day. "You smashed somebody's car? What the heck were you thinking?"

I sat on the couch, looked out the window, and braced for a long lecture. "How'd you find out?"

"Small Auntie called. What the heck were you thinking?"

"It's the snitch! Every breath he takes is mercy."

"Shut up. We don't talk like that in this family."

"Doesn't make it a lie," I snarled. "The cop said it's petty vandalism, nonviolent, and nondrug-related. The max is only three months."

"Only three months!" she roared. "Another three months?"

"Under six months, I can pay 1K NTD per day instead of time." I counted on my fingers. "That's 92K, give or take, to make it go away."

"You think you're so smart, huh? This better work out the way you hope it does. I just want you home, okay? Whatever it takes to get you home as soon as possible. You don't need any more trouble."

"I know. My bad. I should've left, but at least I didn't run into the bar and turn his face into a hamburger patty."

"Behave yourself. I'm sick of your shit." She hung up.

At least it was quick. I put down the receiver. Landlines were still common in Taiwan.

My grandma pulled me aside. "This is what I was worried about. Kaohsiung is a small city."

"He's not in Kaohsiung anymore. He moved to Taichung shortly after I Ryu'd his car."

Her neck snapped back. "How do you know this?"

"I'm Batman," I grunted.

"Shut your mouth. You think this is funny?"

I hung my head.

"It kind of is." She chuckled. "You're not even from here. Imagine if some Taiwanese dude went to Monterey Park, punked you, and you left."

I cackled.

"I'm calling your lawyer now to ask how soon we can throw you in jail to keep you from any more trouble."

* * *

A few days later, a cop called Small Auntie and asked if I wanted to settle out of court. I never asked why they contacted Small Auntie instead of me or my parents, but I suspected a few reasons: (1) She was with me at the police station during questioning. (2) I didn't have a cell phone, so the only way to reach me would be on my grandma's landline. (3) I was released under her for bail.

On the twenty-second, I received a Ministry letter that said I'd get my iPad and laptop back. I went to retrieve them that day. I was worried that if I lagged, the government would keep them.

I received a prosecutor's letter on the twenty-seventh, which said the government wouldn't press charges because I was stoned when I landed. I got faded in LA, where it's legal. As if it were even an option, Taiwan wished it had that kind of jurisdiction.

* * *

My surrender date arrived via letter, but the wording was convoluted. It had two dates on it: August 13 and 16. I asked Small Auntie for clarity.

"I received a letter that says August twenty-third."

We asked the lawyer. "My letter says July seventeenth."

Neither of us had received that letter. August 13 was my second warning. The latest I could surrender was August 23. Why'd they have three surrender dates? August 13 was a Saturday—and no one can surrender on a weekend. August 16 was two weeks from that day and a week before the twenty-third. That was my day, I decided.

* * *

August 15, my last day out. Jason and I smoked a J, ate Japanese barbecue, and hit a JD.

From my understanding, I'd be deported upon release. Most people got kicked out of bars or nightclubs. My trouble-making ass gets kicked out of countries. It was hard going from the airport to prison. Now I had time to prepare, both mentally and physically. It was easier. I'd spent the past months bulking up. I weighed 187 pounds when I'd gotten out; now I was 210 pounds. Hopefully some of it was muscle. Friends, family and loved ones would know where I was this time. That was a relief.

"Don't worry, Grandma. I'll be fine. I won't let anybody punk me."

"I believe that. Thing is, you can't bully anybody. Don't cause trouble. Keep your big fat mouth shut and your head down. You're not in America. You can't solve all your problems by fighting and smashing things."

Grandma was the real mobster in the family. I'd miss her the most over the next two years.

While everybody slept, I stood in front of a mirror, took off my shirt, and postured to hide how frightened and anxious I was.

How do I come back from this? This is the end of my life.

Staying positive didn't mean I didn't have negative thoughts. It meant I didn't let negative thoughts consume me. A season of isolation and loneliness is when a butterfly gets his wings. You know what I would be? *A motherfucking butterfly.*

CHAPTER 5
FRESHMAN DORMS

You only do two days; the day you go in and the day you come out.

—Avon Barksdale, The Wire

August 16, 2016

I didn't want to get out of bed. If I didn't get out of bed, the day couldn't start. If the day couldn't start, I wouldn't have to go to jail.

"You got your favorite for breakfast." My grandma watched me stuff a *xiao long bao* in my mouth.

"Mm-hmm."

"When do you turn yourself in?"

"Two o'clock, and Small Auntie is taking me." I played with my food. "Beijing duck for lunch."

"All your favorites, huh?" She chuckled softly. "What, do you think you're going to die?"

"No, though people have been staring like I will." I popped another bao into my mouth. "It just might be a while before I eat these again."

Freedom felt like it was on fast-forward.

It was sprinkling outside the courthouse, but I didn't care. I stood in the rain, smoked a cigarette, and savored my last precious moments of freedom.

They placed me in the same cells for court. The smell of urine and sweat made me gag. I had forgotten how bad it was. After a couple of hours, they pulled me out and brought me to a brightly lit room. Two officials were seated at a table stacked with dossiers.

"Do you know what you're convicted of?"

"Smuggling."

"Do you know what your sentence is?"

"Two years."

"Do you have questions?"

"I wanna stay in Kaohsiung."

"Do you have other pending charges?"

"No."

They looked at each other.

Fuck, I thought. *They're going to dick me.*

"You'll stay around the Kaohsiung area because you were caught at the Kaohsiung airport," one of them said, finally. "Therefore, in our jurisdiction."

I exhaled and strutted back to the cell.

After everybody finished, guards cuffed us in fours and herded us to the bus. It didn't have enough seats. My group and the one next to us sat on the floor. I could've surrendered at Yan Chao; it would've saved a lot of time and trouble.

At intake, a guard searched me, bent me over, and did his thing, then took my clothes. The prison uniform was a light-gray dickeys-type button-up with dark blue dickeys-type shorts. I had trouble finding clothes that fit. I settled for 3XL. All I was allowed to bring in with me was an extra pair of boxers, yet some people had toothbrushes, towels, and undershirts. Must've been repeat offenders. There's no other way they knew the system so well. I wished somebody had told me. An official counted my cash and took my passport and ID cards. A few trustees entered to handle the paperwork. I knew a couple from my earlier stay.

When one of them saw me, he exclaimed, "Hey, everybody, William's back!"

"You got fatter," said another.

"Ate too good on the outside," I crowed.

"No talking!" the CO shouted. "Everybody shut up!"

My inmate number was 4020. Four thousand and twenty. Hard not to see the humor. Guards took our shoes and made us walk barefoot to our cells in Ling Wing. The floor was wet from the rain.

The cell was a little bigger than before but had the same layout. They placed my six-person group in a ten-person cell that already had two inmates. Newcomers slept on one side, incumbents on the other. I slept second from the top, next to the guy who had the wall spot. A rolled-up towel was my pillow. It was cramped, and the mofo next to me kept rolling onto me.

* * *

The gong brought everything back. It was as if I had never left. Guards rounded up the newcomers after breakfast and herded us to intake for cell assignments and mugshots.

"You're assigned to Ming wing, cell 15. Sit on the floor outside the hallway, and fill out paperwork—electric razor requests, health forms, emergency contacts, et cetera—before entering. When you're done, we'll shave your head."

Cell 15 was the same as yesterday and had nine people, including me. Realistically, four could probably sleep comfortably on the floor, and *that* would've been a stretch. I'd assumed all the cells would be the same, that I'd be in a two- or three-person one. I didn't know there were different-sized cells, let alone why. System kept throwing me curveballs. The two-person cells were for those awaiting trial.

The CO made me sleep in front of the camera to monitor me. It felt Orwellian. Every cell had cameras and speakers. Whenever the speaker came on, we stopped what we were doing and listened.

"Anybody know how long I have to be here?" I wondered aloud.

"Everyone has to spend at least one month in the dorms," one guy replied. "They're for incoming inmates."

I nodded at him. "Thanks, man. I'm William."

He nodded back. "Jessie." He was short, chubby, and balding with a widow's peak.

"How many of these are there?" I looked around and sized up the other cellies.

"Two of these wings, minimum two weeks each." He pointed across the wing. "Freshmen and sophomore dorms are across from each other."

Guards didn't tell me shit. I heard everything from my cellies, though I didn't know how reliable any of this information was.

"They constantly cycle people out of freshmen dorms into sophomore, but once a person leaves, there's always another—"

"How long do we get out of our cells?"

"Ten minutes."

I shook my head. Don't know why I expected better treatment.

"Unless there's a doctor's appointment or something."

"They only turn the water on for showers and for ten minutes after every meal to wash our dishes," said the guy next to Jessie.

I looked at the water. It didn't look clear. "Is it drinkable?"

"No!" Jessie and the other guy said together.

"We always buy bottled from commissary," the other guy explained. "Some days they don't turn it on to save money."

"What happens then?"

"On those days we use bottled to flush, do dishes. We skip showers."

The cell had a water cooler that held five liters and the two five-gallon jugs we used to refill it. Every day, we put the five-gallon jugs outside, through the hole in the wall, to get refilled. Penitentiary water looked and tasted funny, but bottled water always ran out by the weekend. For the shower, we had a trash-can-sized bucket and two rain-pail-sized buckets filled with water.

I looked at the buckets, then at all of us. "How do we all shower?"

"Two at a time, one next to another," Jessie replied. "We only get thirty minutes of running water a day," replied Jessie.

"For ten people?" I did the math quickly. "That's only three minutes each."

"Less, including laundry," he lamented.

* * *

"Start meditation!" the trustee shouted at 8:00 a.m. the next morning.

Meditation sounded nice, but people sat in their roll call spots with their legs crossed and faced the wall. I noticed the two small ceiling fans turn off when "meditation" began.

"Hey." I nudged Jessie. "They turned them off by accident."

"It's not an accident," he replied. "They turn them off during meditation, from eight to eleven and one-thirty to four."

Why would they do that?

It was the hottest part of the day. It was stuffy and felt like a sauna. How was I supposed to meditate like that?

Throughout the weekday "meditations," we wore shorts, undershirts, and our light-gray dickeys-type button-ups. Weekends were more relaxed—shorts and undershirts. Only guards walked around.

On the third day, Small Auntie visited. I tried to walk out but was stopped by the CO.

"Whenever you leave the cell," he explained, "you exit ass-first and enter face-first." The door was only about four feet high; everybody crouched coming and going.

They sent everything through the hole in the wall: commissary, food, nail clippers, razors, documents that needed to be signed or given, books—everything. They placed food outside the hole in metal bowls, family style. We ate, washed the bowls, then put them back outside. I bet it looked creepy at dinnertime, all those arms coming out of holes.

At the end of a long day, I tried to sleep, but they kept the lights on.

* * *

Auntie's commissary came. She'd bought everything I needed: pillows, a blanket, a mat, padding, a toothbrush, toothpaste, extra undershirts, and a few books. She could bring up to three books per visit. I gave her about thirty books I bought while on bail to bring in, a few pictures, and a book of sixty stamps to mail me. I kept both in the envelope they came in.

The day of the commissary delivery was the first time I'd brushed my teeth since I surrendered. I held my towel to my face. I'd never been so thankful for a towel. Until then I'd been air-drying—standing around buck naked until the water evaporated. No more using a rolled-up towel as a pillow. I also bought two mats. I didn't want the mat I slept on to touch the floor.

I applied for my National Health Care insurance card and had a check-up, but it was a check-up in name only.

"Do you feel okay?" the doctor asked.

"I feel fine."

"Okay, you may go."

A pointless meeting, but it felt refreshing to get out of a cell, if only for a little while.

As he escorted me back, the CO said, "Show me your hands."

I held out my hands. Every day, he'd check that my nails were trimmed and that I'd shaved. He looked at my hands, then my face, and nodded.

"Tuck in your shirt," he scolded my celly as he dropped me off. "And you! Button yours!" he huffed at another as he locked the door.

I groaned. "Fucking guy thinks he's a drill sergeant."

"Yeah. Towels have to be hung a certain length too," Jessie replied, pointing to the towels, which all hung two bricks down from the rack.

"Lot of the guards are army guys," said the guy next to me. "For Taiwan, it's considered a good job."

"A good job? Their job fucking sucks. Nobody dreams of being a prison guard when they grow up." I sucked my teeth. "We have to be here. They come willingly."

He nodded. "It's a stable, reliable government job. But you're right. There's a shortage of guards."

"Not surprised."

"It's gotten so bad the government resorted to assigning army draftees."

"Oh!" I snickered. "That's why some of them look like teenyboppers."

*　*　*

It was pretty nice how we shared. Whenever anybody in the cell had a visitor, they bought the max 2K NTD–worth of commissary and stocked the cell. With so many people, we had visitors almost daily who supplied us with plenty of outside food. Food and drinks went fast, but that wasn't a problem. Our cell was small; we didn't have space for surplus. I had the easiest job: I dried the dishes. Even though the CO still made me sleep in the middle, I was getting used to the sleeping arrangements. Eight people wasn't so bad.

It rained for four days straight. Rain—those were God's tears. He was sad I was there.

I know I was.

* * *

During meditation, I sat with my arms around my knees instead of cross-legged. I didn't know I had to sit a specific way.

"What's wrong with your legs?" a guard asked sarcastically.

"Nothing."

"First warning."

I got a warning for that? My head snapped back.

"Two more, and you get sent to the black room"

Taiwan's version of solitary. It was supposed to be shittier than the regular cells. *What could be shittier than this?*

* * *

Small Auntie brought fried chicken.

"My celly gave me a Taiwanese name. They call me Masa," I said proudly.

She sighed and ran her fingers through her short salt-and-pepper hair. "What's wrong with William?"

"Nothing." I straightened up and smiled. "Masa sounds cool, and it's easy to remember."

"There's an old Taiwanese show, and Masa is the name of a gangster on it."

Whoopsie-doodle. I couldn't have known.

On the way back to my cell, I checked in at the CO's desk. He looked me up and down, then asked, "Who came to see you?"

I nodded toward the visitation area. "My auntie."

"What'd you guys talk about?"

"Family business," I mumbled. "How I'm doing. Stuff like that."

"How *are* you doing?" He picked lint off his shirt. It looked freshly pressed.

"I'm all right." I shrugged slightly. "It is what it is."

"You need to check your attitude." He jabbed a finger at me. "You're not in America, so take this seriously."

I bugged out. "I am taking this seriously."

"Well." He gave me a dirty look. "What have you learned?"

"*Learned?*" I raised my voice. "Staring at a wall all day? Nothing. Not a damn thing."

"It's your fault," he replied smugly.

"You think your job is important, but it's not." I smirked. "You're a glorified babysitter." Sometimes I felt like "Battle Hymn of the Republic" should play in the background as I spoke.

"Second warning. One left."

Fuck. I should've kept my big fat mouth shut.

* * *

Midmorning, a guy sat in the hallway and shouted, "I will not socialize when I walk around!"

Another dude shouted, "I will not lie down if it isn't nap time!"

Punishment for minor infractions was to sit in the hallway and shout, usually twenty times per infraction. Not sure what the point was, if there even was one. Felt like kindergarten.

One of my cellies had been going through heroin withdrawal. He coughed blood and was having a tough time. We called a guard over, who took his blood pressure and temperature.

"It's up to you to see a doctor and take care of yourself, not me," he scolded.

It made little sense—dangerously so. Taiwan made people go to rehab after they detoxed.

* * *

I had a doctor's appointment because my gout flared up. Ten people were in line for it, which was common in Taiwan. Inside, our diet was tofu and bean based because it was cheap. Coupled with a lack of exercise, this didn't bode well for my health.

After my appointment, the CO put me in another line instead of taking me back.

"What's this?" I stood and refused to move. "I finished. I'm done."

58

He pushed me toward the line. "She's in charge of rehab."

"I don't need rehab. The judge said so." I folded my arms and stood my ground.

"All drug cases, with few exceptions, need rehab."

"I'm one of those exceptions!" I exclaimed.

He pointed at a chair. "Sit. Let's see what the doctor says. You're already here anyway. If you're telling the truth, it shouldn't be a big deal."

I sat and waited.

"Hello," I said to the doctor when I stepped into her messy office. "This is a mix-up. I shouldn't be here. I'm a foreigner. I'm not—"

"Name and date of birth?" She didn't even look up.

"William Tsung. September 27, 1984. But ma'am, I don't have to go to rehab. Judge said so. I even got—"

"National ID number?"

"Don't have one."

"How can you not have one?" she screamed at me like I'd killed her dog. "They issue all citizens a national ID number upon birth. You're supposed to have it memorized by now! All you addicts are the same. So high when you come in . . ."

I fidgeted, unsure what I'd done wrong.

"Wait," she said, looking me over. "Are you a Taiwanese citizen?"

"No."

"Then you don't need to go."

I sucked my teeth. I'd been trying to tell her that for the past three minutes!

* * *

In the morning, they crammed another dude into our cell. If ten was crowded, eleven was packed. When we tried to take our midday naps, we slept on our sides with our legs on the wall, and the new guy slept in the space between our heads. Luckily, two guys cycled out in the afternoon, and I finally slept somewhat comfortably. It was the first time I'd used my mat and padding. We only had space for them if the cell had fewer than eight people; otherwise, everybody slept on the floor with a pillow because they wouldn't fit. Sure, we were always on the floor, but there was a big difference between sleeping on the floor with a pillow and sleeping on a padded tatami mat. It's the simple things in life, really.

Took a urine test, the first of two. Everybody with drug charges needed to take drug tests because use is a crime. It had already been two weeks; I didn't know why they'd waited so long.

Guards took the inmates who needed to take a test out of their cells and made us pee in a cup in the hall. All thirty of us. It was smelly and messy. We poured the piss into a small container, labeled it, sealed it, and put it in a garbage bag. There was so little oversight it would have been so easy to switch labels.

They denied my application for National Health Care because my Alien Resident Card expired. I'd have to pay full price in cash for medical treatments. Taiwan has arguably the best National Health Care system in the world, yet it didn't apply to foreign inmates.

By definition, incarceration means I was the state's responsibility, right?

Small Auntie mailed a letter with her household registration and the medicine my outside doctor prescribed me. I brought the note to the doctor and had him prescribe the same. The stuff they'd given me earlier was ineffective.

* * *

I washed my light-gray button-ups for the first time—eighteen days after I'd received them. We wore them Monday through Friday for meditation. Took at least a day or two to dry. We hadn't gotten water the weekend before, so this was my first chance.

Transients wore cleaner clothes than we did.

* * *

One night, as we got ready for bed, I was leaning against a wall. A tweaker came up to me, touched my penis, and asked, "You ready for bed?"

I shoved him, hard. He flew and landed on the floor with a loud thud. I took a few steps toward him, fortunately (for him) some cellies got between us.

"He was joking," Jessie said.

"It ain't funny!" I roared.

"He was just playing," the tweaker's friend insisted.

"It was a joke." The tweaker nodded.

Fucking tweakers. I walked to the corner farthest from him to cool off. Jessie lit a cigarette as they talked me down.

* * *

Small Auntie visited again on September 5. I was so happy to see her but felt guilty she wasted her time visiting me in this godforsaken place.

My second urine test was only three days after my first. It felt sudden. What a waste of time and money. I suspected these prison tests were fake. I mean, we took them, but I don't think they're sent to a lab. Tests aren't free. I heard they cost 500 NTD ($18) each, and there's no way the government paid for all that. Never heard of anybody being caught by a test they took inside. I suspected they made us do them so they'd look like they were doing a good job, but I'd smoked a handful of joints two weeks prior and apparently tested clean, twice. I was glad I didn't catch another charge, but if they were legit, I should've.

* * *

No running water for the second day in a row. The cell smelled. Lately there'd been a lot of visitors. We had so many snacks, which we traded some for smokes. At least the cigarettes covered the stench.

Ten in a cell made it tough to sleep. I slept on my side because of my broad chest. We slept with our heads in the middle, so the camera could see our faces. Sometimes when people yawned or thrust their hands in their sleep, they'd wake up whoever was sleeping across from them. Arguments and fights happened at least once a week. I stopped keeping track of all the fights because I rarely saw what happened. I heard commotion, voices raised, and maybe saw people escorted out.

A trustee hooked us up with a bowl of ice, and we enjoyed some iced coffee and soda. Cokes are better with ice.

I went to Diao Cha, Taiwan prison's version of Hogwarts's sorting hat, with three of my cellies and forty-two others from my wing. Diao Cha was where we submitted the paperwork for work assignments. Guards herded us into a room that looked like a temple that'd been converted into a meeting room. It had long rows of tables and chairs.

At the top of all my paperwork, I wrote, "I can't read Chinese." I told a trustee, and he told the dude next to me to translate. Out of defiance, I told him not to worry about it and sat there. A little later, a trustee pulled me out of my seat and brought me to a CO at a table in the back of the room. He asked me questions in Chinese and filled out my paperwork.

A projector played an eight-minute video about bullying and rape on a loop in the room's front. The story was about a young man's first time being incarcerated. After he was processed and put into a cell, some older dudes told him, "This place is different. You're with the big boys now." A tattooed, thuggish looking older man gave him a chicken leg for dinner. At night, while everybody slept, the older guy woke up the young'un and forced him to give him a hand job. Three new guys entered the cell the next day. When everybody slept, the older guy woke up, lay down next to the young'un, and tried to rape him. One of the new guys tried to stop the guy, and they tussled. Finally, the new guy pushed the cell's panic button, and guards came. The older guy tried to cover it up, but the new guy ratted him out. A CO questioned everybody separately. He told the young'un that he should've spoken up sooner—that they were there to protect him. The new guy got an award for snitching. They put the older guy in solitary and shackled him to the floor.

The moral of the story? Don't take a chicken leg from anybody. We nicknamed rapists Chicken Leg Big Brother as an inside joke.

I think the whole point of Diao Cha was to sort us into the jobs we were most qualified for, but it was a waste of time. Everybody ended up in a factory anyway. Somebody had written answers in my book. Other people copied off each other. I just filled out everything myself. No way was I going to copy off a dude with an elementary school education.

Guards took us out of our cell at 1:00 p.m., and we didn't get back until 4:00 p.m. We'd missed cigarettes, showers, and laundry. We took one-minute showers over the toilet, with no soap or shampoo; it was against the rules to shower when it wasn't time—same with laundry.

After the shower, Jessie produced a cigarette. "Saved you guys one."

"For real? That's cool of you." We fist-bumped.

"Well, there's three of you, and we thought you'd share."

After dinner the three of us washed our clothes on the low. It was worth the risk. I'd worn the same clothes for three days. They turned on the water for ten minutes after meals. We usually had a guy who washed and another who dried. This time we had a guy do dishes while the other did laundry and used his body as a shield from prying eyes. The rest of us huddled around to obstruct as much of the view as possible.

* * *

Jessie and I cycled out after nap time. My new cell was the same as the ones in the freshmen dorms, but this wing had fewer inmates, which meant fewer people per cell. It felt so much bigger.

The move took all afternoon, and we missed shower time. The trustees let us shower in groups of ten. No soap or shampoo. What was the point of a shower without soap or shampoo? It wasn't even a shower; I just dumped water on my head.

I was assigned to cell 2 with Jessie and six others. It was unoccupied. The CO had designated it for people with serious medical conditions; one guy had a broken leg, another guy had asthma, and another had a bad back.

The cell had an actual toilet, not a squatter, but it had no seat. We sat or squatted on the rim and dumped water down to flush it.

I finally stopped sleeping in the middle. Now I had the best spot: under the window. I wouldn't wake up with sun in my face anymore. My cellies, however, still did.

* * *

Trustee #5 always asked me to spell English words whenever he passed by to distribute food. I saw him four or five times a day, for maybe a minute or two each time. One time, he wanted to know which was *desert* and which was *dessert*. Another time, he had me explain the difference between *there*, *their*, and *they're*.

Whenever a CO questioned me, I lied about my Chinese proficiency. They took it at face value. Trustees, usually present during questioning, saw through my game because of the inconsistency. How can I claim my Chinese isn't good yet hold conversations? They assumed my English was good because I sounded like a white guy speaking not-particularly-good Chinese.

* * *

"Brother, do you smoke?" Trustee #5 asked during his lunch rounds.

I'd just finished eating, and a cigarette would be nice. "Yeah, I do."

"I'll be right back."

He came back and handed me two cigarettes. I looked around for a CO before accepting. "Thanks. I appreciate it."

"Don't worry about it. You won't be here much longer."

I lit one of the cigarettes and took a puff. "What do you mean?"

"All foreigners get transferred to Taipei." He walked away.

I slouched and hoped he didn't know what he was talking about.

"Who knew William had juice here?" Jessie said.

I cracked a smile and raised my chin ever so slightly. Inside, English was my ticket to a more comfortable life.

* * *

I kept my things organized. I had to; I never knew where I was going to lay my head at night. I was always ready to pack and go at a moment's notice. Everything was in my bag, in the same place. At all times, I knew where it was and if anything was missing.

While I brushed my teeth in the morning, I noticed my pictures were out of their envelope. I kept stamps with them—one form of prison currency. Upon further inspection, thirty-three stamps were missing.

During breakfast I announced, "Last night, before I went to bed, I had forty-eight stamps. Now, I only have fifteen. I don't want to accuse anyone of being a thief, so I'm gonna say I misplaced it. Whoever 'found' them can give them back, and we won't have a problem." I made eye contact with each person.

"William, that's a serious accusation," warned Jessie.

I didn't listen to him. "I'll give it until after breakfast, then I'm going to sort this out."

I wasn't sure why someone would have stolen from me. If any of my cellies had asked, I would've given them some. Karma is real. Please don't steal.

"I think I saw them on your bed," said the celly with the broken leg.

I unfolded my mat and looked. They weren't there. I hadn't expected them to be.

"If you misplaced it, you owe us an apology," Jessie chided.

"True, but if I didn't, we're going to have a problem." I looked at each of my cellies. "If the stamps don't appear, I'm going to tell a trustee I want to see last night's video. Tape don't lie."

"It's a serious offense," said Jessie. "They're going to toss the cell, take our cigarettes, and send us all to the black room." He pointed his finger at me. "You too."

I ignored him and looked around. "Just give me back my shit, and we're good."

"Keep looking."

"I'll check my box." I straightened my posture. "But if they're not there, I wanna see the tape."

I knew they weren't in my box, but I wanted to give the thief time. Midway through, Broken Leg stopped me.

"Don't look anymore. I found them. They're in my book."

"Why were they there?" I asked. In my head, I'd already held court in the street, and he'd been convicted and sentenced.

"I found them last night and didn't know who they belonged to. I put them in my book and forgot." He opened his book, showed me, and handed them back.

Lying sack of shit. He'd written his inmate number on the back of each one. Had he put my pictures back in the envelope, I wouldn't have noticed until later. If he'd taken less, I probably wouldn't have noticed at all. He'd even taken them out and folded them differently to look like they were his. I bet he thought that I wouldn't notice or that if I did, I wouldn't make a big deal of it because I was a foreigner. He was a thieving piece of shit.

He apologized twice.

I kicked his broken leg. "We're good."

Generally speaking, kicking someone's broken leg is wrong. But prison had its own ethics and code of conduct. He started it. I didn't kick him for no reason—I had to do it. Didn't have another choice. Don't think I was wrong either. This was what I'd been worried about: looking like an easy target. If I let some dude with one leg take my stamps, what could somebody with two legs take? In the Wild West, a farmer didn't expect the sheriff to show up every time somebody stole a cow. Sometimes he had to take the law into his own hands.

In the morning, a trustee gave us paper to fold into flowers. None of us knew how to do it. They brought a young dude from another cell to teach us.

"What's up, William!" he said with a grin. We fist-bumped.

"You know each other?" Broken Leg asked.

"He was my neighbor in Ren Wing."

Broken Leg looked at me. "I thought you said this was your first time locked up here?"

"It is. He's the cellmate of the guy who showed me how to make a lighter." I sparked it to show him I still remembered.

"That's right," the young guy chuckled. "It took him a while to get it too. He kept burning his fingers."

I laughed. "I don't anymore! The trick is to use your fingernails." I sparked it again.

Dude patted me on the back. "The first person to smuggle marijuana cookies into Taiwan. He's infamous. Everybody in our wing knows him. Hell, everybody in the country probably knows who he is."

"Fuck me," I moaned.

"Don't worry about it." He nudged me with his elbow. "Man, give it time and everybody will forget."

"I hope so."

He sensed the tension in the cell. I told him about the stamp incident, and he asked, "Is this true?"

My cellies nodded in silence. He kicked the thief's broken leg. I kicked it again, too, for good measure. Broken Leg shelled up like a turtle.

There was no bigger purpose, no overarching goal. I wasn't trying to help humanity or make the world a better place. I was selfish. All I wanted was to not get jacked. I'm not a saint, and I never claimed to be. I'm doing the best I can with what I've got. If the choices were to seem like a bully and keep my things or be a nice guy and get my things taken, well, what were they going to do? Lock me up?

Since Diao Cha was essentially prepping us for a factory, we didn't get to sit around. For cell work, each inmate had to make four paper flowers per day. They resembled golden chrysanthemums, and flower-folding time was 8:30 a.m. to 11:20 a.m. and 1:30 p.m. to 3:30 p.m. The prison would sell the flowers to temples, who marked them up, then sold them to worshippers to burn for funeral rituals. First locked in a cell forced to meditate, then they made me fold flowers. I wished they'd left me alone. I wasn't aware indentured servitude was part of my sentence.

Small Auntie came to see me again. To me, these weren't visits—they were lifelines. She put my mind at ease. The gulag was only fifteen minutes away from her. If something happened or if I needed anything, I'd be able to get it through her weekly visits. I had all the necessities and could keep her up to date on my situation and everything going on around me. I shudder to think about how bad this place would've been without my family.

That afternoon, I was leaning against the wall with one knee up and my legs crossed. The CO pulled me out and lectured me for acting too relaxed.

After my lecture, I noticed a full cell sitting on the floor, watching an old man get scolded. He'd masturbated in front of his cellmates. The CO smacked him upside his head, then got up and threw his chair at him! It broke, and part of it hit me.

"Pull down your pants," the CO commanded. He pulled out his taser, held it close to the old man's crotch, and said something in Taiwanese. I think he threatened to taser him if he did it again.

When I'd surrendered myself, the prison officials had said I'd stay in Kaohsiung, but all the inmates I came across told me I'd be transferred to Taipei. Somebody was lying, and the uncertainty was stressful.

Thankfully, paperwork came in that assigned me to Factory 2. I smiled as I signed it, happy they weren't transferring me.

CHAPTER 6
FACTORY 5

"But I don't want to go among mad people," Alice remarked. "Oh, you can't help that," said the Cat: "we're all mad here. I'm mad. You're mad."

—Lewis Carroll

September 13, 2016

Four days later, they transferred me from Factory 2 to Factory 5. One wasn't better than the other. I never even got to see Factory 2, nor was I given a reason for the abrupt change. It was just numbers. Whatever let me stay in Kaohsiung was fine with me.

I sat on the floor outside, looked around, and tried to soak in everything. The factory looked really clean.

"Close your eyes," shouted the CO. "If I see you look around again, I'll send you back upstairs."

While a trustee rummaged through my belongings, the CO bent me over and did his thing in front of the factory. "I have no problem having an American in my factory. ABC, doe ray me—it's all okay with me."

Dickhead had immigrant dad jokes.

"So . . . smuggling." He looked me up and down while I dressed. "Did you come into Taiwan with drugs strapped to your body?"

I get it. You see criminals every day, so you think I'm an average run-of-the-mill smuggler, but you need to stop talking to me like I'm some mule who swallows heroin balloons.

"Nah, how'd I hide seventy-six bags?" I asked. "I had it in my luggage beside my license. I didn't understand the laws. It's legal where I'm from, and I thought my license protected me."

"You have to obey the laws of the country you are in," he said with relish.

Even if I don't acknowledge the legitimacy of the justice system? Whatever. I nodded.

"Don't cause any trouble, and you'll be okay." His uniform looked freshly pressed.

"I'll do whatever everybody else is doing."

He surveyed the factory. "That's the right attitude." He waved over a guy who looked like Azn Vin Diesel. "Meet William. I'm putting him in your cell. Pick someone to kick out so he can take his place."

Azn, pronounced "Asian," are first- or second-generation immigrants or an Asian with questionable morals—gangsters, hustlers, dealers, smugglers. It's how we refer to each other. I use it as a compliment. Sometimes it's not.

"I'm Randy." He walked and talked. I trailed him. "There are two rows of six tables, six people per table. You are in row one, table two, seat four. Every table has a leader who's in charge of the table and a row chief in charge of the row. I'm your row chief."

The CO sat on an elevated desk in the front. They took roll every shift change, before and after meals. We counted off from 1 to 137 to take roll. Four restroom passes hung from the CO's desk. To use the restroom, we'd swap our IDs for one of them. We showered by table. They did everything in the factory. Before work, we got our electric razors and nail clippers and groomed. They let us put our heads down after lunch as commissary was distributed. We washed our own clothes, but at least they let us use the factory's industrial dryer. Towels hung high above the restroom.

An inmate was painting the bars of the factory windows. He looked like Beast from X-Men: stocky, well-built, and hairy. His eyebrows looked like a baby caterpillar chasing its momma.

"He's our room chief," Randy said, "and in charge of the cell."

We lined up in two rows in the center of the factory and squatted for medicine. The trustee called out our inmate numbers. When we heard our number, we'd say "Yo," and hold out our hands for medicine.

We wore shorts and undershirts. Tank tops were for cells only. At all times, we were to remain seated and working. We needed permission to get up.

Randy introduced an older man. "He's also in our cell. It's his job to periodically collect and refill our water mugs. They do their best to ensure maximum production here. Factory 5 has won multiple awards as best factory."

"What's 'best factory' mean for us?" I asked.

"Nothing. It's bullshit. Something for them to brag about."

It's strange to be a prisoner and not be called "inmate" or "prisoner." Officials addressed us as "students," and we called each other "classmates" (Tóngxué, 同學). COs were still guards, but counselors were "teachers" (Lǎoshī, 老師). It wasn't a gulag, it was a factory. Every morning we pretended we were going to work (Shàngbān, 上班), class (Shàngkè, 上課), and end of class (Xiàkè, 下課). Semantics.

The factory resembled an elementary school classroom. Pastel flowers were painted on the back wall above our cubbies. Trustees had desks in the front. Cabinets along the wall with motivational slogans above them. The desks had a space to put our bag and snacks, like a first grader's cubby.

By the time I settled in, the day was over. They assigned me to cell 15. It had ten people, including me. My cigarettes hadn't come yet. Randy gave me seven of his and told me what commissary I would need for the factory, schedule, and routines.

A celly called me an ABC. Nobody thought anything of it. All he said was, "Hey, ABC."

Randy chastised him. "Don't call him that. He has a name. It's William."

"My bad. Yo, William."

Randy was in for smuggling, six years. He was married with six kids, in his early forties, muscular, tattooed, and gregarious. He was a factory chief—and a shot-caller, I suspected, whether inside or out. He couldn't sit still—always needing to be busy.

The first pearls I ever saw were his. While I waited to shower, I saw him play with them, moving them around and arranging them.

"What's that?" I asked. I thought his cock had tumors.

"Pearls."

"What's a pearl?"

"It's like a piercing."

"Oh, shit."

"What? You thought I was sick? Like cancer or something? Nah, it's by choice."

"Is that what they're looking for whenever we get strip-searched? New tattoos and pearls?"

"Yeah, that's why you always show him your penis."

Pearling is also known as genital beading. The process involves permanently inserting small beads made of various materials beneath the skin of the penis's shaft or foreskin. It's an aesthetic practice, usually intended to enhance sexual pleasure. The best-known historical users of pearling are the Yakuza; each pearl supposedly symbolized a year incarcerated. Back in the day, they used actual pearls, hence the name.

✳ ✳ ✳

The next day, after breakfast, people sat around instead of getting ready. I shot Randy a quizzical look.

"Typhoon day," he replied calmly.

I didn't even know what typhoons were until I moved to Taiwan. "What's that mean?"

"No work. We stay in our cell the whole time." He seemed happy but sensed my anxiety. He lit a cigarette and took a puff. "Relax. They happen all the time. Nothing's gonna happen, and there's nothing to do. It's boring."

The typhoon caused two short blackouts. Both lasted less than two minutes, then the backup generators kicked in. When you're locked in a cell, typhoons feel like any other rainy day. At least, that's how my cellies and I treated it.

A trustee came by the cell after every meal with a jug of hot water to brew fresh tea. I wondered if they did this for everybody.

✳ ✳ ✳

Midautumn Festival. It's an East Asia harvest festival. Basically, this holiday is Thanksgiving without the genocide. If I were free, my family and I would've had mooncakes and an enormous meal. As it was, some of my cellies had visitors and I had outside food. Nonprison food is as good a holiday meal as they came.

The typhoon caused another short blackout.

"Does this happen regularly?" I asked Beast.

"Regularly?" he said. "No, but it happens from time to time."

I'd experienced three short blackouts, and it hadn't even been a month!

We got water for fifteen minutes after dinner. We washed our dishes as quickly as possible, then took one-minute showers. No soap, no shampoo, and we kept our shirts partially on. Even by their standards, this was craptastic, but we made the best of what we got.

*   *   *

My foot hurt. I only slept a couple hours because of the pain. Randy tried to get a painkiller for me from a trustee.

"I would if I could," the trustee said, "but the guy on duty is strict. Since he's not lying about his foot, you're better off asking yourself."

I thanked them both for trying.

"Why do you pretend like you don't speak Chinese to the guards?" Randy asked after the trustee left.

"You noticed, huh?" I smirked, "They don't know what I do or don't under—"

"Makes it easier on you because they think it's harder for them to communicate. They'll hassle you less."

I smiled. "There it is."

He lit a cigarette and offered me one. "Smart guy."

Randy told the CO about my foot situation. He looked me over and eyed me suspiciously. "If it still hurts tonight, I'll give you a painkiller."

Why'd I have to suffer a whole day? Why can't I get it now? The whole point of Friday was to prevent this! I wouldn't be able to see the doctor until Monday, and I wouldn't get medicine until Monday night. Four days!

At night Randy asked again. The CO relented and gave me a painkiller. Randy's the man. I wasn't even going to ask why they gave it to him but not me.

* * *

My first full factory day was Monday, September 19. I limped from my cell. Work was simple but tedious and repetitive. Nothing prison made is especially complex. It can't be; the only tools we're allowed are our hands. The cell were cramped, tedious, and repetitive but at least COs left me alone. I'd rather wither in a cell than be a slave. The factory was a little more spacious—but again, tedious and repetitive. The work never ended with even the supervised, timed breaks of an Amazon employee.

The punishment should reflect the crime, and no crime justifies the exploitation of prison labor. These mofos put me here, and they have made it clear I meant less than nothing to them. Why would I lift a finger to do anything that benefits them? I schemed up ways to dismantle this system and rebuild it from scratch. I'd rather let my talents rot in a cell than contribute one fucking cent to the prison's bottom line or Taiwan's GDP.

Each row was an assembly line. Boxes were stacked behind the rows, and every table had a job. When a task was completed, the product was passed down. Factory 5 made paper bags. Table 6 got the flat piece of paper, table 5 folded it, table 4 and table 3 taped the sides, table 2 taped the bottom, and table 1 put in the shoestring handles. In the front, they were inventoried and packaged.

Working with a swollen foot sucked. All I thought about was how much it hurt. At least it kept my mind off work.

I dropped off a letter for Small Auntie and finally saw a doctor. Before I left, the CO said, "It's not like we denied you treatment. Friday was a half day and for serious problems only. The doctor was in on Saturday, but the person on duty didn't know. Be thankful we let you see a doctor today. You need to do a better job of taking care of yourself."

You don't think I tried? I gritted my teeth. Mighty haughty for a police academy reject. The patronizing way the officials talked to me made me want to strangle them. I didn't know being a guard gave anyone moral authority.

I took a deep breath. Through a clenched jaw, I said, "Thank you, sir. It's not you fault. You weren't there. I'm salty at the substitute."

"It's not any of our fault. It's yours. Your health is your job, not ours."

When I returned from my appointment, the CO summoned me to his desk and whispered, "You're transferring. Don't tell anybody. Here's your letter." He handed me the letter I'd tried to send to Small Auntie.

I looked at it, then at him. I opened my mouth, but nothing came out.

"Mail it at your next stop. There's no point letting you mail it now because if they write back, you won't be here."

This was a worrying time for me, and it seemed like the Taiwanese justice system tried to make it more stressful. I was angry, sad, and frustrated. Angry because prison officials told me I'd stay in Kaohsiung. Why lie? Why couldn't they just tell me the truth? Sad for obvious reasons. I was being transferred away from my family to . . . I had no idea where. No more weekly visitors. My life would become substantially more difficult. And I was frustrated because it seemed as though they were making my life difficult as possible. It was as if taking away my freedom and treating me like a dog with rabies wasn't enough. Cruel and unusual was their goal.

Small Auntie usually came on Monday or Tuesday. I hoped she would come that day so I could tell her. I didn't want her to visit the next day only to discover I wasn't there. I worried for the rest of the morning as I packed.

To my relief, she came shortly after lunch. Hell yeah! I couldn't help but smile. On my way out, the CO said, "Don't buy commissary. You won't get it before you leave."

"I'll be transferred today or tomorrow," I blurted as soon as she picked up the receiver. "I'm not sure where, but I'll write to you as soon as possible."

"If it's someplace close like Tainan or Chiayi, I can still visit often. But if it's far like Taichung or Taipei . . ." She sighed. "Probably once a month."

"Don't worry about visits. I'll be fine. I'll write. Try not to worry too much." She brought Cantonese barbecue pork and *chow fun*.

When I got back to the factory, I gave Randy my food to thank him for everything. He refused at first, but I wasn't planning on taking it with me. He put his hand on my shoulder.

"You're going to another wing to sleep tonight and moving first thing in the morning," he said. "You'll be in for one year and about two months."

I looked down and frowned.

"It'll fly. Take care of yourself, brother."

75

We exchanged information as he helped me gather my things from the cell.

They moved me into a different wing and put in a cell with three others who'd be released the next day. Lucky them. It was the same size as my factory cell, but it had nothing: no soap, no shampoo, no toothpaste. Four people in a cell felt so spacious, but it was a little chilly.

I mentally prepared for the move. I'd be far from my family, adjusting to a new environment, and making new friends. What if the people in Taipei weren't as cool as the ones in Kaohsiung?

CHAPTER 7
TAIPEI FRESHMAN DORMS

For what it's worth, getting the shit kicked out of you? Not to say you get used to it, but you do kinda get used to it.

—Jesse Pinkman, Breaking Bad

September 20, 2016

The smoke woke me up. One guy took a puff and offered me a cigarette.

"Going to Taipei, huh?" he asked between drags.

"Yeah." I rubbed my eyes. "I thought I was gonna stay here."

"All foreigners have to. The government wants to keep them all in one place. Easier for them." He took a puff. "How long have you been here?"

"This time?" I sat up and lit my own cigarette. "Today is thirty-four days since I surrendered."

"I meant the factory."

"Oh, four or five days. Less than a week, for sure."

"You can have our meat bao. We're leaving. We'll eat outside," the guy said.

"Hell yeah, extra meat bao."

Meat bao is a variation of mantou. It has many variations of fillings, and they're most often steamed. Inside, meat bao was about as good as the food got.

A CO came to get me at 6:30 a.m. I told him to wait while I smoked one last cigarette. Little did I know it'd be my last for a month.

"What about breakfast?" I asked.

"We'll give you a sack breakfast."

There goes my extra meat bao.

In the intake room, a CO searched my stuff, bent me over and did his thing, then handed me a sack breakfast. "Don't drink too much. There's no restroom stops."

A trustee entered and shackled my feet together. One of the inmates was an elderly man who needed an oxygen tank to breathe. Seemed excessive to shackle him. How was he gonna get away? The shackles were heavy and needed to be hammered into place. There was no key, just iron bent with a hammer and wedge to lock and unlock it. How medieval.

Clang! My leg vibrated from the impact of hammer on metal. *Clang!*

"How many more times are you going to do this?" I asked.

"One more. Now shush, so I can concentrate."

I hoped his hammer stayed true. Didn't want him to miss and hit my leg. *Clang!* Phew! I touched my ankle. I'd made it with all my limbs intact. We got on the bus shortly after.

The transport bus was a twenty-eight-seater, yet there were only two prisoners, four guards, and a bus driver. I wondered how much of the penal budget went toward transportation.

When I sat down, a CO instructed another officer, "Put a face mask on him."

"Why?" I asked. "I'm not sick."

"Because you won't shut up."

Like a face mask was gonna stop me from running my mouth. My eyes bulged when I saw the "face mask." It was baby blue and resembled an N95, but it wasn't a medical mask because it had a hole with three bars between my mouth and nose to breathe. The mask was pulled so tight my mouth couldn't move. It was a muzzle.

"I'm in for smuggling, not cannibalism!"

I would've complained the whole way if the muzzle didn't do its job so effectively. It was too tight and smelled musty. I tried to speak, but nothing came out. It made my jaw hurt. The CO cuffed my hand to the bar in front of me. After a while, I lost feeling in my arm.

It was a great day to be out, even on a prison bus. I felt the wind and sun on my face through the window. I was used to the confines of a cell. The sights and sounds overwhelmed me at first. The AC even made me cold.

Taiwan's penitentiaries are overcrowded. Instead of addressing the actual issue, they transfer inmates to less-populated institutions. They could transfer anybody anyplace in Taiwan at any time. Not me, though. We foreigners all must be in Taipei. To be incarcerated was bad enough, but to not know where I was even going to sleep from night to night was stressful. Then, to be transferred far from my family felt like piling it on. It's cruel and unusual, a waste of time, money, and resources.

We got to Taichung midmorning. As we drove through the city, I stood up in my seat to soak in the ambiance. Crowded streets, cars honking, people talking. I'd forgotten how loud the outside world was. The smell of freshly prepared food and even the stench of smog were so refreshing. It was such a tease. Day to day, I tried not to think about the outside world. It made me long for the things I missed. I felt like Icarus. I saw the sun up close for a bit, but soon my wings would melt, and I'd crash.

"Sit down!" the CO shouted and banged on the gate.

We dropped off the old man and picked up another inmate—a kid a little younger than me, in for fraud. They'd drop me off in Taipei first, then him in Kaohsiung. All this driving in a big-ass bus for one person. They let me take a piss in the prison's office. It was hard to walk while shackled. They were heavy and made this loud clanging sound every time I took a step. Felt like a ghost or a fucked-up demon of some sort. My feet could only move so much, and the walk to the restroom took forever. It was tiring.

When we got to Taipei, an official said, "There's nobody to process you. The guards are on lunch." I waited on the bus for them to return. Between my shackles, cuffs, and muzzle, I looked and felt like Hannibal Lector.

After lunch, a guard pulled me out to get unshackled, processed, and placed in the waiting room—a windowless space the size of a walk-in closet.

It was a while before a CO escorted me to intake. Taipei's sprawl took me by surprise. The prison was the size of a city block and had multiple buildings. (It's not the biggest prison in Taiwan; that's Taichung.) The interior was lush, with flowers everywhere.

Taipei prison isn't even in Taipei; it's in Taoyuan. Kaohsiung had six factories; Taipei had eighteen. Because Kaohsiung was only one building, I walked little and rarely saw the sun. Visitation and the sick bay were near Taipei's entrance, closest to the street. I especially enjoyed visitation and doctors' visits because they were the longest strolls. Cell to factory was a five-minute walk.

Taipei had two exercise yards big enough for a basketball and volleyball court. I saw at least five in Kaohsiung, and they were twice the size. There was even an auditorium for special events. Kaohsiung just used the yard.

Kaohsiung was in a rural area with a school across the street. Taipei was down the street from Taoyuan International Airport, in a residential area surrounded by high-rise apartments. Imagine renting an apartment with prison views! Who the hell wants that?

The most intelligently designed part of Taipei was the plastic canopy over the walkways. It rained often, but the cover ensured we stayed dry and kept normal walking routes open—cell to factory, factory to doctor, cell to visitation, and so on.

At intake, my stuff was searched, then they bent me over and did their thing. Then I filled out the paperwork. They were the same forms I'd filled out in Kaohsiung. Why didn't they just get copies from them?

"Can you speak Chinese?" a trustee asked.

"Yeah, but my reading and writing aren't so good."

"No problem." He looked relieved. "I'll ask you the questions and write in your answers."

My new inmate number was 3443. Easy enough to remember, but all those fours are bad luck. The number sounds like the word for *death* in Chinese. I liked 4020 more; it only had one four and was weed adjacent.

They assigned me to cell 21 in Yi Yi wing. It looked like hobbit-hole, and was the dirtiest room I'd ever been in. Cockroaches crawled everywhere, and their audacity disturbed me. What respectable roach would go out and about in broad daylight? These weren't normal nocturnal roaches. These were *Blade*-type roaches. We had no supplies to clean, even if we wanted to. It was a newcomer's cell, and people constantly cycled in and out—mostly addicts without good hygiene habits. Half the time they were still detoxing when they arrived.

I thought Kaohsiung was bad, but Taipei took it to another level. The cell only fit three mats on each side, so we had to overlap them to squeeze in the fourth. Every inch of the floor was covered. The ceiling had a small fan, but it was low. If I raised my hands and jumped, I could touch it. It was packed; eight was the max. At least I slept next to a wall.

*   *   *

Different prison, same fucking gong. I wondered if they used a real one or a recording.

After breakfast, I noticed the daily schedule posted on the door. Twenty-four hours a day in a cell. No smoking in the Taipei dorms. Kaohsiung had only done meditation four times a day. Taipei required six times! I failed to understand how "meditating" on my crime was supposed to rehabilitate or change my behavior. What I did wasn't even a crime in my state.

The toilet was a squatter. At least they didn't turn off the water. It ran for twenty-four hours. Other than that, the bathroom situation was the same: faucet and buckets. The water bucket couldn't be reached from the toilet. You needed somebody to get it. There was a small wall dividing the toilet and the faucet, which didn't leave enough room for an adult and a bucket. The bucket couldn't be kept in arm's reach because there was usually a person or their mat in the way. Having somebody hand the bucket to you was, somehow, the only way. My cellies said it was supposed to teach us teamwork, but I think it was just piss-poor planning and overcrowding. At least in the other cells, I could flush by myself.

Some cells had windows, others didn't. Mine had one, but the view was of the penitentiary's outer wall. Like all the others, the cell had a hole in the wall beside the door to push things through. Instead of being handed bowls for meals, each cell kept a box. A CO would announce which ones we needed. We used, washed, and stored them. Didn't know why they made us deal with the storage; it was cramped enough as it was.

Exercise was at 11:00 a.m. I don't mean exercise in the traditional sense; they didn't let us outside or anything. English words don't mean what they mean in Taiwan. For our exercise, a recording played on the speakers, and we stretched in the cell. It got hot and stuffy. Proper exercise wasn't allowed. Most of the time, we stood around. "Exercising" was optional.

I found the commissary list posted below the schedule.

"Is this it?" I asked. "Where's the rest of it?"

"Unlike Kaohsiung, we don't have access to the full list," somebody replied. "Only if we have a visitor. We're allowed to buy the basics—undershirts, underwear, toothbrush, toothpaste, and two or three snacks. It takes two weeks to arrive instead of the usual week. Trustees and COs think it's too much trouble, so they don't do it."

If this was all we were allowed, I was screwed. Who knew when my next visit would be? I wasn't even sure anybody knew where I was.

Anytime the cell door opened, inmates were required to go to the back, crouch, and face the wall. It didn't matter if somebody left or came, or if the CO made an announcement. I rarely interacted with anybody. The door rarely opened. The trustees were assholes, they shouted all the time. Didn't understand why they were shouting. They were inmates like us. If they had talked normally, it's not like we wouldn't have listened—we had no choice. Seemed as though they thought they were better than us because of a vest.

A few days passed. They pulled me out of the cell to get blood drawn and X-rays from a mobile X-ray van. It was my first time outside in three days. It was the third time they'd wanted blood work. I'd had it drawn twice in Kaohsiung: once when they caught me, again when I surrendered. They'd rayed me during intake in Kaohsiung as well.

After my X-ray, the CO asked the usual questions: *Have you been to Taiwan before? Anybody visiting you? Education level? Circumstances regarding your case?* Yada yada yada.

When a trustee escorted me back, he asked, "So you can speak English?"

"Mm-hmm, I'm a native English speaker."

"I have a girl from California. If I write a letter in Chinese, can you translate to English for me?"

"I got you. I'm ready whenever you are."

He nodded and put me back in my cell.

"What'd the CO want?" my cellies asked.

I filled them in. "This seems to happen everywhere," I wondered aloud. "The CO pulls me out for the same questions."

"Because you and your case are unique," one guy replied. "They don't see people like you every day. They're trying to understand the situation."

The trustee with the Cali girlfriend stopped by in the afternoon and passed me a handwritten letter.

"Let me get a pen and some paper." I motioned around. "This cell has nothing."

I translated and handed it to him. He left but came back a few moments later. "No, I want this translated word for word."

"Translation doesn't work like that. If you want me to do it word for word, I can, but it's not going to make sense."

"Well, can you write it again? This time neater."

He wanted to copy it in his own handwriting. I put two fingers to my lips and pretended to inhale a cigarette. I don't mind being an Azn Cyrano de Bergerac, but I don't work for free.

Before dinner, I handed him his new letter. He thanked me. Once again, I put two fingers to my mouth and puffed air.

"I can't give you cigarettes, but I'll be right back."

He returned and threw a bag of seventy-seven chocolate candies through the hole.

That'll do.

* * *

September 27, 2016, was my thirty-second birthday. My first birthday incarcerated, and it wasn't even in an American prison.

* * *

We shaved on Wednesdays. For a lot of these tweakers, once a week was an upgrade. For me, it was a downgrade. Human rights and plain decency aside, I wanted to look my best so I could feel my best, so I could do my best. Taiwan treated me like week-old, rotten trash. I felt like Oscar the Grouch, and I didn't want to do anything. And dealing with Dumbass only made it worse.

Dumbass was the name I gave to the guy who slept next to me. He'd smoked so much meth he fried his brain. The dude was skinny, with shifty eyes and a face full of acne. He woke me up four times in one night. In the morning, I took my pillow and hit him in the head.

He felt his face. "Do it again, and we'll see who hits who."

Tweakers: the bane of my existence.

A few days was all it took for Dumbass to get under my skin. He kept waking me in the middle of the night. I couldn't take it anymore. He was dismissive when I confronted him the next morning. A mofo only knows what a mofo knows, so I shoved him into a wall. He took a few steps toward me, but suddenly jumped and grabbed the seat of his pants.

"Oh!" he squealed. "I think a little shit came out!"

First time I'd scared somebody so bad they shat themselves. He was probably still detoxing.

* * *

Medicine arrived nightly at 8:00 p.m. Dumbass got his first. Spaceman—who often zoned out and stared into space—went second. He had salt-and-pepper hair, wrinkles, and a few teeth missing. As a convicted smuggler, I had no mercy or compassion for my fellow criminals. If you do the crime, you do the time. Keep your mouth shut, stand tall, make yourself useful, and it'll all work out. Spaceman was the first (although sadly not the last) person I met that made me wonder why he was there. He seemed a few eggs short of a dozen. This guy shouldn't have been there . . . but if not there, where?

At first I was snotty toward Spaceman because he was a meth addict, and I thought the tweak had fried his brain. But then I noticed the Mentally Handicapped label on the back of his inmate ID. I felt like such a dick for being a dick to him. I wished people came with a thirty-second trailer so I could see what I'm getting myself into.

I didn't know where this sudden wave of empathy came from or why I even cared. He was a tweaker, and it wasn't like he made my life easier. Before him, I'd thought everybody I met was a predator. He was prey. This place doesn't end well for people like him.

Dammit, if I gave him a pass, does that mean I'd have to give Dumbass a pass too? Nah! That's taking it a little too far. But the fact that I'd reconsidered my utter disdain for tweakers boded well for his health.

Spaceman looked at the pills in his palm. "This isn't mine. Mine's is a different color. Where's mine?"

"What's in the bag is all there is," the CO asserted.

"Can you check again, please?"

He showed him the empty bag. "See?"

"May I see my medicine bag?" Spaceman paced back and forth. "I'm missing medication."

"You saw the bag. I can't give you anymore."

The rest of us prepared for bed, but Spaceman just kept pacing and mumbling under his breath. After lights out, I tried to sleep but heard light footsteps.

Guard came back and banged on the door. "Go to bed!"

Spaceman lay down for a moment, then banged his head against the floor.

Thud!

The sound woke everyone else up. "We're trying to sleep," somebody groaned.

Spaceman stood and paced silently. Suddenly, he threw up. We banged on the door to get a guards attention. One came and took him away.

The next day, a CO had us to put all of his things in a trash bag. I was pretty certain Dumbass "accidentally" took his medicine. Tweakers, ugh. One less guy in the cell.

*   *   *

"Pack up," a trustee told us during lunch. "You're all going to the sophomore dorms."

It was about time. I'd been there for thirteen days. Part of me wanted to go to the factory. I was curious to see what it was like, and staring at a wall had gotten boring quick. The other part of me just wanted to rot in a cell.

Trustees took our things out of storage, gave them back to us, and herded us across the hall. I walked maybe fifteen yards before being instructed to put my stuff down. COs searched my belongings, bent me over and did their thing, then threw them back in storage. I'd get everything when I went to the factory. Fucking security theater. It was all for show—pointless and a waste of time. No boxes, bags, or plastic allowed in the cells. However, I kept my notebooks, pens, and envelopes. A journal made a big difference in my quality of life. They placed me in cell 41.

As I sized up my cellies, a middle-aged man came and shook my hand.

"You know President Tsai?" he asked. "She's my girlfriend."

I snickered. "Does she know?"

"Not yet."

I chuckled.

"Don't listen to him," said the guy beside him. "He's full of shit. I'm Tofu."

"We all throw in 200 NTD to buy communal things for the room. Soap, shampoo, toothpaste, et cetera," said Prez Tsai's boyfriend.

Finally, people who cared about hygiene! "When?" I asked.

"Now," said Tofu. "Fill out the form. You submit commissary the same day you're placed in the cell to ensure it comes when you're still here."

"What'd you do?"

"Meth sales. Four years."

The cell was half-capacity, and the trustees and COs weren't as strict. They let us lie down on breaks, to my relief. It hurt to sit on the floor for so long.

"Mondays and Thursdays are when people cycle in and out. After this, you get your factory assignment," said Tofu.

Don't know why I didn't get my factory assignment sooner or why they didn't put me into a factory the day I arrived in Taipei. They'd even pulled me out of a factory. It would've made the most sense to place me in another one ASAP. I don't know if it was perplexing on purpose or just poor management. What ground my gears was how bad these people were at their jobs. They oversaw people locked in a room. The minute Skynet goes live, these jobs are the first to go.

It was a trip coming from America, whose prisons are multibillion-dollar, lean, mean machines, to . . . whatever fuck this was. As a red-blooded American, I can tell you we are imperialist, capitalist bastards and have been since day one. I'd prefer we didn't commit crimes against humanity, but if we did, we shouldn't half-ass it, at least. Taiwan's violating all these human rights and leaving money on the table.

* * *

In the middle of the morning, two weeks after I arrived, a trustee handed me a note through the hole. It said that Big Auntie, who lived in Taipei, had tried to visit last Sunday. The person in intake didn't believe we were related since she didn't bring her ID, so they wouldn't let her in. I hated this place so much. She'd put 8K NTD into my commissary on her way out. My family was good to me; I made it through because of them. Don't know what I would've done without them. Other inmates didn't have funds and were never visited. I was lonely and depressed enough as it was. Couldn't imagine what it would've been like to have never heard my number called for visitation. I'd prepared for people to be assholes, but not for the kindness. Why? They didn't know me. Other inmates didn't get treated like this. Even some Taiwanese inmates didn't get treated like this. Why was I so special?

* * *

On October 4, Small Auntie visited from Kaohsiung. She'd left home at 8:00 a.m. to come see me. I felt like trash. She threw another 2,000 NTD into my account. These numbers may seem large, but 2,000 NTD is a little over $71. The exchange rate is about 30 NTD to $1. Eight thousand NTD, the daily max, is a little over $285. When Kaohsiung was fifteen minutes away from her, she'd come weekly. I didn't need that much because she was close. Taipei was five hours away from her. My visits changed from weekly to monthly. Eight thousand NTD seemed like a lot, but it's the same as 2K NTD weekly.

"How'd you know where I was?"

Her glasses sat crookedly, and she straightened them. "We received a letter in the mail a few days after, informing us you'd transferred and where."

"It's far. You don't have to come all the way up to see me." I couldn't look her in the eye. "I'll be fine."

"Your grandma always taught us that if you don't have family, you don't have anything. We're here for you. You are far, so I can't come as often as I'd like, but I can make it about once a month."

I hadn't expected them to show the love and support they did. It's not like I had come back to visit all the time before this. I'd seen them maybe two or three times in my life. They could've easily left me hanging.

"I appreciate it." I sniffled. "I want you to know I'm sorry for all the trouble. But it's nice to see you."

"It's okay. Just don't get into any more trouble. Do you need any commissary?"

I waved her off. "I already submitted the order for everything I need."

We chatted until the line disconnected. I watched her walk away and thought about the people who didn't have anybody to visit. I slouched and started counting down the days until next month.

In Kaohsiung, whenever somebody wanted to bring me a book, they brought it during visitation. It'd get searched, and I'd receive the next day. In Taipei, I submitted a request, then mailed the approved form to Small Auntie. She mailed the books with the approval form. Only three books were allowed per month.

In Taipei, commissary from morning visits arrived by the afternoon. Commissary from afternoon visitors came next day. Kaohsiung was always the next day.

During breakfast, the cell divided into "tables" based on how much we'd chip in. The money went into a pot used to buy food and condiments for the table. We had a 300-NTD-per-month table and two 600-NTD-per-month tables. I was originally going to sit at the 300 NTD table, but I saw another table open a pack of preserved eggs. I love preserved eggs, so I sat at the 600 NTD table. What did 600 NTD a month get me? A lot of condiments for breakfast. We ate mantou and soybean milk. We had peanut butter, butter, meat floss, and jam for the bread; oatmeal, brown sugar, and black sesame mix for the soybean milk. We had canned goods for days, we ate *zhou* (congee), eel, tuna, beef, and instant noodles for seasoning. It was filling and tasty. Breakfast was the best meal of the day because we bought most of it.

The biggest change was water. I never had to drink Kaohsiung's water because I had visitors weekly. I only drank bottled. In Taipei, I was forced to conserve because I didn't know what to expect and needed a rainy-day fund. Bottled water was a luxury I could no longer afford. Shortly after I began drinking the prison water, these strange rashes and blisters appeared all over my legs and torso. Now I needed money for the doctor and medicine.

Putting money into another inmate's commissary is illegal in Taiwan. In serious cases, it can get extra time added to one's sentence. Officials assume the only reasons you're putting money into another inmate's account is because you're being bullied or gambling. A few commissary items were as good as cash: stamps, tea, batteries, and cigarettes. Tea may be surprising to include, but all Taiwanese love tea. The good stuff is always in demand. Batteries were only good in packs of four because they're a fixed rate, like stamps. A 12 NTD stamp is a 12 NTD bill.

People worked out all kinds of side deals for cigarettes. They were, without a doubt, the most sought-after thing. Most of these dudes smoked two packs a day on the outside. They couldn't get by on fifty per week. The easiest way to get more was to put money into a broke inmate's or nonsmoker's account and have them buy for you.

In Factory 11, three guys washed while another three guys dried the dishes. The people rotated weekly. It happened about once a month. There was an ecosystem. If I didn't want to do laundry, the laundry service was 1,000 NTD during summer, more in the winter. For chores, it was 100 NTD to wash and 300 NTD to dry.

Everybody threw in 200 NTD a month for communal items. Two guys had no money or visitors; they washed dishes for 100 NTD a month. Any chore I didn't want to do, somebody would for a price. Six hundred NTD for breakfast, 200 NTD for cell items, 100 NTD for dishwashing, and 1,040 NTD for cigarettes is 1940 NTD. Existing cost at least 1,940 NTD ($64) per month.

* * *

A fight occurred a few days later in the cell across from mine. At least Kaohsiung separated people on trial from those sentenced. Taipei mixed us all together.

I felt so cooped up. Twenty-four hours a day, seven days a week. Hadn't left my cell in three weeks. Or had any exercise since I'd surrendered over two months before. I needed to get out of this godforsaken cell. It was suffocating. It was a surprise that there weren't more fights.

Tension, stress, and arguments happened because inmates had no outlets. If we had something, anything, that allowed us to blow off some steam, a lot of fights could've been avoided. Familiarity breeds contempt; insignificant problems festered until they became enormous problems. Resentment built. Eventually, it exploded. Sometimes I wondered if executions for prisoners with long sentences would, in a fucked-up way, be more humane.

* * *

The water was filthy. The government used water directly from the ground and didn't filter it. It gave the inmates who did the most chores blisters on their extremities. Veins around the blisters turned a swollen red. One guy said it hurt to walk. Once I saw it, it concerned me. I hoped I wouldn't catch whatever they had, but I didn't know what to do to prevent it. Blisters and scabies were common reoccurring issues among inmates. A running joke was whoever showered first that day yelled out the water color. It never looked like water; sometimes it was yellow, sometimes it was black. We used it no matter what color it was. It was that or nothing.

We received hot water for tea. Tofu filled a thermos, folded his clothes, then rolled it over them back and forth.

"Whatchu doing?" I moved closer.

He looked up. "Ironing."

I whistled. "Prison ingenuity."

He held up his ironed shirt. "Just because we're locked up doesn't mean our clothes have to be messy."

All dressed up with no place to go.

* * *

Early in the second week of October, a trustee came and handed everybody a bundle of clothes: one thick jacket, one thin jacket, two gray short-sleeved button-ups, two light-blue shorts, two dark-blue long denim pants, and two dark-blue denim long-sleeve button-ups. We traded among ourselves. I ended up with an 6XL top and 3XL bottom.

They asked if I wanted to buy a newcomer's kit for 1,000 NTD. It'd been almost two months, and I'd been in Taipei for a few weeks. What did I need a newcomers' kit for?

The next day, a trustee brought me the letter I'd tried to mail the week before. They wanted to censor some parts; I couldn't talk about the conditions of the penitentiary or my cellies. If I wanted to mail it, I needed to make the adjustments.

One of the new guys was doing twelve years for meth sales. His girlfriend mailed him a letter saying she wanted to get married. She looked cute in her picture. I thought he should do it. Taiwan allows inmates to marry. It was just signing a piece of paper. A CO would be present, and both were allowed two witnesses, usually the mother and father. Incarcerated people get married and divorced all the time. It sounds like a good idea at first, but then reality sets in. Some guys get married so they'd have somebody to visit them. That's a fucked-up reason. What happened to love?

CHAPTER 8

FACTORY 11

Show me a hero, and I'll write you a tragedy.

—F. Scott Fitzgerald

October 20, 2016

My number got called for Factory 11—the drug and DUI factory. Outside was a small garden and a little pond with turtles that trustees tended. They'd decorated the pond with Pokéballs, dolphins, and temples. There were also classrooms where the bananas went for Sex Ed. *Bananas* is a catchall term for sex offenders—because *rape* in Chinese also sounds like the word for *banana*.

Guards searched my belongings before I entered. Inside, they had me strip down, then bend over so they could do their thing while the factory watched. The CO said, "Dress in the back."

While I organized my belongings, a young, skinny, bespectacled man approached me. His two front teeth were missing. "What's up, brother? I'm Tom. You doing your own laundry?"

"Yeah," I sized him up. "Why do you ask?"

"I'm the boss of the factory's laundry service." He helped gather my things. "Anyway, I'm in your cell. I'll introduce you to everybody."

Factory 11 had four rows of tables. Underneath was a cabinet for each person, just like Factory 5, and a cubby along the factory's back wall. I didn't have a cubby yet, but under my table was space for a box to store my stuff. The box sold in Kaohsiung was bigger than the ones in Taipei, and I'd have to buy another anyway. The list of things to buy was long: clothes hangers, soap, shampoo, face wash, and laundry detergent. My new cellies loaned me what I needed until commissary came.

Tom pointed at a rotund, balding, middle-aged man with glasses. "That's Dave. He's our room chief." Then he pointed at a skinny young adult. "Bruce, the room accountant."

"What's that?"

"He tells you what to buy for the room and stuff. Go to him if you need anything. He'll take care of you."

"Cool." I looked Tom over. "Whatchu in for?"

"Meth use. Thirteen months."

Showering and laundry were at the same time. Four tables, twentyish people. I raced to a faucet. The factory only had fifteen. Some shared if they couldn't get to one. I showered from a big trough. I scooped water from the trough and onto my head with buckets. It was crowded. People bumped into each other and splashed water everywhere. It was a hassle and disturbing; asses bumped into asses, and penises brushed against legs.

I signed a form to shave my head. No point in having hair. One less thing to worry about.

The first factory day was tiring. I nodded off around lunchtime.

* * *

Official wake-up time was 6:45 a.m., but we got up around 6:20 a.m. Otherwise, there wouldn't be enough time for all of us to wash up before breakfast since there was only one squatter and no sink. We used three buckets as spit buckets, huddling around them as we brushed our teeth. All meals were eaten on the floor, which we wiped after.

"I know you're not doing it on purpose, but you're saying my name wrong," a dude said over breakfast.

My head snapped back. I thought I knew how to say his name. "Huh? Isn't it One?"

"Yeah, but you say it like *won*. Your tone is wrong."

It was true. I knew how to say the words, but my tones were all over the place. I had a good feel for the language. I understood that I could get away with speaking in one or two tones if I said a full sentence or phrase.

"One," I tried again.

He sighed. "Now it sounds like *Juan*."

Everybody looked at me. I awkwardly chuckled. Felt like a dumbass foreigner. I took a deep breath. "One."

He threw his hands up. "Why was that so hard?"

"At least he knows your name," said the guy across from me dryly. "I know he knows Bruce's name, but I bet he doesn't know mine." This guy was shorter than me but more muscular. I could take him, but he'd do damage.

I struggled with the Chinese names. All of them kind of sounded similar, and a lot of them had characters I'd never seen. With so many names to remember, until that moment I'd just said "aye" or pointed at them. It was rude, and I wasn't thinking. No wonder they were annoyed.

"I don't know your name in Chinese, but in English it's James." James was only a year older than me, but he looked ten years older due to his balding widow's peak.

"I bet he doesn't know my name," said a kid whose teeth were wrecked from betel nuts.

Damn, these dudes are ganging up on me. "True, I don't, but your last name is Wong. I nicknamed you Prince."

He tried to hide a smile behind his resting bitch face. "Works for me."

"You work for the teacher?" I asked, having heard one of his previous conversations. "Where? What's he do?"

Prince nodded and lit a cigarette.

"I thought we couldn't smoke in here?"

He looked at me like the question offended him. "They ban smoking in the freshmen dorms but not here. We're not supposed to. Just don't make it obvious. Smoke in the restroom, or at least facing away from the peephole. At worst, we'll get a warning and a frown."

"Ah." I lit a cigarette. "It's not illegal. It's frowned upon."

He hid a grin. "The teacher's office is in a small room outside the factory. He informs inmates about their points, parole, and any other odd details. I input data and handle paperwork."

"Points?" I took a few puffs. "What's that?"

"Taiwan has a point system for inmates. Authorities say it rewards good behavior, but truthfully, it's based on nothing more than the time served." He took a couple drags. "Points only start when an inmate arrives at a factory. No points for the freshmen dorms. If they transfer, there are no points for that month, and they must go through the dorms all over—"

"How come I haven't met the teacher yet?" I interrupted.

"You just got here." He took a puff. "Within a week of arrival, the teacher will summon you for a meeting, and again when you're about to be paroled."

I scrunched my face. "Do points matter?"

"Only when applying for parole. They don't guarantee early release. They're just a prerequisite."

I maintained eye contact, but my gaze became glazed.

"If you need to speak with him in between, you can submit a written request."

* * *

On my sixty-seventh day, I exercised for the first time.

A guy commented, "I've been here seven months, and it's my fourth time exercising."

The yard was a basketball court surrounded by fences—hardly enough space for a full factory. Half the guys sat around. The other half walked around the court. Basketballs, volleyballs, badminton rackets, and baseballs (no bats or gloves) were available. Even though exercise time lasted only thirty minutes, it felt good to stretch my legs.

This was the second factory day without work. I sat at my desk, bored, and wondered aloud, "What kinda work does this factory do?"

"What'd you do in Kaohsiung?" Bruce replied.

I folded an imaginary bag.

"Same," Tom chirped. "Paper and cloth bags. Although, this factory is known for not working a lot. It's mostly DUI and drug offenders. We have class most days."

I didn't know what "class" meant, but anything that avoided work was cool with me.

* * *

Every Saturday between 7:00 and 8:00 a.m., we cleaned the cell. We washed the restroom, took apart and dusted the fans, wiped windows and walls, and mopped and bleached the floors. Our mats were down by 6:00 p.m.

"You're an American?" One asked as we cleaned.

I nodded.

He wiped the walls. "You're my first American friend."

"For real? That's kinda cool. I wish I could say you were my first Taiwanese—"

"I'm not Taiwanese. I'm Hakka."

"Hakka?" I stopped cleaning, "what's that?"

He wrung out his towel. "*Hakka* means 'guest people' in Mandarin. They're called guests because they migrated to southern China from the Yellow River to avoid war and disasters."

"Well, then you're my first Hakka friend." I picked up a fresh towel and wiped again.

"There aren't a lot of us down south. Mostly north and northwest."

"Do you speak Hakka?"

He shook his head.

"Very few speak it anymore," Bruce added. "It's dying out."

Tom interrupted to tell One, "Go wipe that other wall again. You missed a spot." He turned to me. "Why were you talking about the Hakka?"

I half shrugged. "I learned something new today."

"Wanna learn another thing?" he blurted before I could answer. "Since you're American, you get to go to a Christmas party."

"Bullshit," I scoffed. "Taiwan wouldn't do shit to hook me up."

"Christian missionaries throw it for foreigners only. No locals," said a tall, balding, middle-aged guy.

I nodded, but it seemed ridiculous.

"What's my nickname since Chinese names are so hard?" the tall guy asked.

I chuckled because he knew I had one for him. "The OG."

"OG . . ." His eyes narrowed suspiciously. "What's that mean?"

"Original Gangster," I said proudly.

He smiled. "I like it."

"Did you turn yourself in?" James asked.

I nodded. "Mm-hmm."

His eyes bulged. "Very few Taiwanese surrender when they're supposed to because there are no consequences if they don't. All they lose is bail money. If you're looking at five years or more, may as well run."

I looked him over. "How come you didn't run?"

"I'm just a heroin user, I only got twenty-one months."

"I got arrested at a hotel," One said. "I switched daily, hustled, and lived out of hotel rooms. One morning, I stepped out to get breakfast when I heard somebody call my name behind me. I turned around, and a cop grabbed me and said, 'Are you One?' 'No.' Then, he hit me. 'What are you doing here?' 'I'm getting some breakfast.' The police couldn't figure out what hotel I was staying at, so they beat me on the way to the station." He sighed. "I got five years for ketamine sales."

"So did I," Bruce said. "They arrested me at an elementary school when I dropped my oldest off. My son saw the cops take me away, and I told him, 'Daddy's going out of the country for a little while, for work.'"

Of all the people in the cell, only James and I had surrendered on time. We're a couple of stand-up crooks.

* * *

A couple days later, they added a new guy to my cell. He was the tallest person I'd met inside—six foot six.

"What's up, man?" Bruce asked when the cell door slammed shut.

I shot him an inquisitive look.

"He's my neighborhood friend, David," he said, then turned back to him. "Whatchu doing here?"

"Ketamine sales." David sat next to him. "Two years nine months."

Even though I'd been incarcerated a while, I still considered myself new. Seniority goes hand in hand with the length of an inmate's sentence. The goal was to be in and out. I only got two years—a short time. I may have been Taiwanese, but I wasn't born there. I was always going to be a foreigner.

I'm too Asian for America and too American for Asia. I don't belong anywhere.

My cell (any cell in Taiwan really) was not big enough for eighteen grown men. I'd say they treated us like animals, but if you put eighteen pigs in a room that small, they'd die. Mats were a constant source of conflict. People fought over a couple centimeters because everything needed to overlap. Some guys got upset. Others didn't want to do it. Everybody was miserable, and it was easy to understand why.

The restroom was another source of conflict. Half of the cells had restrooms in the center of a wall—the best layout. Even though we slept shoulder to shoulder, there was a path to the restroom that didn't bother anybody. It was easy and caused minimal conflict.

Mine had the other format. Even for a cell, it had to be one of the dumbest layouts I'd ever seen. The restroom was in the corner. There was no walkway, so we created one. In order to access the restroom, a dude slept in the middle. Two dudes—whoever slept closest to the restroom and the one next to him—were constantly disturbed by guys stumbling in the dark.

The faucet wasn't accessible from the restroom. Nearby, we kept two buckets of water to flush. There were eighteen people, so two buckets never lasted the whole night. Mornings smelled like urine. Once our mats were down, we couldn't refill the buckets because the mats would get wet—especially the ones near the faucet or restroom.

We showered and shat as soon as we returned from the factory. My towel saved my place in line. We brushed our teeth immediately after dinner, before our mats were down. It was impractical and time consuming to brush individually.

When it was time to masturbate, we hung a curtain over the restroom for privacy with a turned-over water pail as a seat. In the summer, there'd be a small fan. People didn't masturbate on their beds because there was no privacy and it made a mess. It was easier and cleaner this way. Porn is illegal in Taiwan, so we used whatever we could find. Most of the time it was *SexyNuts*, a magazine that advertised Japanese Adult DVDs. We went one by one. The line was usually six or seven dudes long. Whoever set up the curtain went first. I nicknamed this Seven Minutes of Heaven.

Some guys, especially the older ones, did weird stuff at night. The old man next to me did leg lifts, opened and closed his hands, and sat up for no reason. One guy stood up and meditated. I wasn't getting a good night's sleep. Once I was stirred, the light—which was constantly on—kept me awake.

* * *

On my fifth day in the factory, a trustee told Dave the factory was having an inspection soon.

"What's that?" I asked.

"We organize our cabinets so it looks nice and neat and fold all our clothes and clean the factory." He pointed in their direction, "Wash the shower area, restrooms, et cetera."

"What for?"

"Think of it like a contest between factories to see who's the cleanest and most organized," Bruce said.

"What do we get if we win?"

"Us? Nothing," Tom chimed. "BaiMao gets a plaque."

Our CO was nicknamed BaiMao ("white facial hair") because he had a protruding mole with a single hair growing out on his chin. The hair was long—he probably never cut it. I've been told it's bad luck to do that.

"What happens if we do poorly?

"Nothing." Tom pushed his glasses further up his nose. "More bullshit."

Heads nodded.

Two days later, the morning of the inspection, we cleaned the factory. For inspection six polo-shirt officials entered, looked around for a moment, and left. We cleaned all day for this?

The prison made us buy the cleaning supplies. Every even month, each inmate threw in around 200 NTD for factory commissary. I paid 180 NTD for October even though it was my seventh day in the factory.

Trustees assigned me cubby 49 in the back. Finally, a place to put my factory clothes. I did nothing to earn it. A cubby freed up because a guy left and I was next. Getting more storage space made me smile even though I wished I had more food or snacks. My stomach growled all the time.

Blisters and rashes appeared on my shin and forearms.

* * *

Over a week after I arrived at the factory, the teacher summoned me for an afternoon meeting. Two trustees were inside. Files and folders were everywhere. I sat on the other side of his desk. He held out his hand, and a trustee handed him my dossier. He thumbed through it.

I held my breath.

"You're eligible for early release on May 18, 2017."

I exhaled. "That's not too long from now." I looked around but didn't see Prince. "I was worried I'd have to do a consecutive year before parole."

"Do you want to stay in Taiwan after your release?"

I sucked my teeth. "Hell no."

"You have family here." He closed my folder and leaned back in his chair. "You can stay if you want."

"I want to go home to Los Angeles."

I got up and left.

Back at my seat, as I was telling people how it went, One and James made me a chart that tracked my point progression. At month's end, a trustee posted a spreadsheet with everybody's inmate's number, crime, monthly and points total on the factory's back wall. I rarely thought about points until I saw the printout. It was a reminder of how far I'd come—and how many more miles to go before I could sleep.

Every Friday, we'd have karaoke on the factory TVs and mic from two to three. It was mostly Chinese music, but they had a few English songs. When a younger guy sang, it could get pretty lively. It was a morale booster. We did karaoke more regularly than exercise.

* * *

Small Auntie visited. It was a pleasant surprise. I hadn't expected to see her for a while. It was bittersweet; I desperately needed it, and loved it when she came, but I felt guilty about the five-hour drive each way.

"I met with the dude who tells me about parole," I said nonchalantly.

She pushed her glasses further up her nose. "What'd he say?"

I grinned from ear to ear like Sylvester when he eats Tweety. "May 18th, 2017."

"Great news." She smiled slightly. "What happens after?"

I titled my head. "What do you mean?"

"Do they take you directly to the airport or what?"

Good question. I didn't know. I was so focused on the date I forgot to ask about a timeline. The line disconnected after I told her.

When I got back to the cell, Dave came up to me.

"You're on water duty this week," he said.

"Oh shit." I facepalmed. "I forgot."

He sighed. "Look, man, I don't want to hold your hand through this."

I rolled my eyes so hard I saw my brain.

"If you don't want to do chores, it's only 300 NTD to pay somebody. Your irresponsibility is delaying our schedule."

"My bad." I went and got the water.

This time went well, but the next might not. Things could escalate so quickly. I tried to minimize opportunities for conflict. I usually vegged out after slaving. The last thing I wanted to do was more work. 300 NTD ($10) to avoid the possibility of a lecture, conflict, and chores was cheap.

* * *

Commissary arrived in the morning. I forgot how convenient next-day commissary was. Waiting a week sucked.

The scabs and bug bites all over my legs were getting worse since arriving at the factory.

BaiMao summoned me to his desk.

I hoped he was going to tell me my doctor's visit had been approved.

"I'm enrolling you in this factory's Chinese class."

I couldn't help but grin as I shook my head. *This place juked me again.* I stared at his mole hair. "Really? Why? I speak Chinese." *We're fucking speaking Chinese right now!*

"Doesn't matter." He waved dismissively. "It's required for all foreigners."

I bit my lower lip and plodded back to my seat.

"Why'd he call you up?" the OG asked.

"Fool just enrolled me in a Chinese class." I huffed.

The table laughed.

"Maybe he believes your bullshit about not speaking Chinese," he joked.

One looked confused. "Whatchu mean?"

I looked between them and smirked, "Anytime I talk to a guard, official, in court, or someone like that, I say I can't speak—"

Dave interrupted, "Is that why, whenever he talks to you, he asks for another guy?"

"Yup," I chirped. "You're there to trans—"

"But you don't need one." He shook his head in disbelief. "I'm just standing there—"

"He does it so they don't bother him." The OG smiled. "If they think he can't speak Chinese, they'll leave him alone as long as he's not causing trouble."

I nodded. "What tipped you off?"

"A few days ago, somebody tried to talk to you. I watched you shrug and say, 'I don't understand,' then they walked away."

"I didn't even notice—"

"It's not a bad thing. I think it's smart and smooth."

We bumped fists.

"I'm not talking about you, but we think ABCs are all the same."

I cocked my head. "I don't think we're all the same, but what do we look like through your eyes?"

"All ABCs are a 'little bit.' Do you come to Taiwan often?" Tom mockingly said.

"Little bit," the OG replied, not in his normal voice. He'd put on this weird accent.

"Do you understand Chinese?"

"Little bit," One replied in the same weird accent.

Tom pushed his glasses further up his nose. "Can you read or write?"

"Little bit," James replied with the weird accent.

"You're not a little bit," the OG said. "You're not a little anything. It's different and takes time to understand but . . . you are you."

"What's up with the weird accent?" I asked.

"It's what ABCs sound like to us. We thought if we talked like you, maybe you'd understand us better," he joked.

I chortled. "Dicks." The table laughed.

The OG elbowed me. "I'm just fucking with you."

There needs to be a certain level of understanding, trust, and history to joke with someone. I could say we were boys, but doesn't mean shit if they don't feel the same way. It's a two-way street. Before this, I'd never said my cellies were my friends—never even thought it. We had to share a cell, but we didn't pick each other. That's why I call them cellies. Most of them were more like work acquaintances. Guys only joke with their friends, especially in prison. Who knows how they'll take it—also, optics. Who wants to be the butt of a joke or look like an easy mark?

"I know," I said, "but I also have a heavy accent. Sometimes hearing you guys talk makes me self-conscious because I know I don't sound like that."

"Everybody has an accent," James said. "It's not like we don't understand you. I'm impressed by your vocabulary."

We fist-bumped.

"This isn't a knock on your Chinese," said Tom. "I think it's interesting is all. Most ABCs claim they speak Chinese when they can't. You lie the other way. Makes me wonder —"

"They can't prove I know it," I interjected. "My Chinese does suck compared to yours."

"Compared to us, yeah, but we're from here," James reassured me. "You're not."

"When I was younger, I wanted the ABC accent so people would think I was rich," Tom confessed.

I thought about my first night in the factory cells in Kaohsiung, when Randy had checked a celly for offhandedly calling me an ABC. It had caught me off guard at first, and seemed excessive. I didn't really understand, and nobody explained it. I benefited—that was good enough— but I hadn't gotten why he would defend me. We'd just met. After this, I got it. He was the man, and he didn't want other people thinking less of me.

"I'll trade you," I chuckled.

"Next time, I'm going to get locked up in America," One said with a grin.

It saddened me he knew he was going to get arrested again. "Why would you say that?"

"So I can learn English." He looked so confident in his answer.

I missed being young and knowing everything. I clicked my tongue. "You know I didn't learn Chinese here. I've spoken it my whole life."

"But it got better in prison, didn't it?"

"It did."

He nodded. "See?"

It's not what people say, it's who says it. How am I supposed to run with wolves at night if I play with puppies all day? The fact that locals saw me as one of them and complimented me on my Chinese was an eye-opening surprise. It felt great to be accepted.

* * *

After two weeks, it all felt routine. A few cellies said I'd gained weight. Gulag food was still putrid, but more visitors meant more outside food and full commissary access.

The first day we folded and inventoried bags, I'd frowned the whole time.

"You look like you're going to cry," James had teased.

"I forgot how much I hate this," I muttered sotto voce.

"You're hard to please." He'd looked at the bags. "Do nothing, you're bored. Work, you hate it."

James had a high efficiency rating. He didn't say much, but when he did, it hit. This dude was the buffest heroin addict I'd ever met. The most muscular guy in the cell. Only he and Carmelo worked out in their spare time. The rest of us sat around, watched TV, read, or played chess.

As I walked back to the cell one day, the wing chief pointed at me. "Your pants are too baggy"

I looked down. "These were prison issued."

"Get smaller pants ASAP," he said.

Taiwan wasn't down with my style. Too groovy for them.

* * *

A guard caught Tom, David, and the OG gambling. He warned them to be more subtle. Asians love to gamble. It's in our blood. It was strictly prohibited, but that didn't stop anybody. We were criminals. If we followed the rules, we wouldn't have been here. We wagered the only thing we could: commissary. People gambled on basketball and baseball. Most of the time they weren't able to watch the game, only check the scores in the next morning's paper. They also gambled on Chinese chess and a stupid page-opening game. In this game, we found the thickest book we could and randomly opened to a page. Then we added the digits of the page numbers together for a point total—9 was the highest, 10 equaled 0. For example, page 199 would be 1 + 9 + 9 = 19, which was worth 9 points. Page 109 would be 1 + 0 + 9 = 10, which was zero points. It was a mix of baccarat and lucky nine.

I understood why people did it, though. The boredom was so real. We had nothing but time. I wondered what God did to occupy his time in the infinite eons before the creation. It was on us to find ways to keep busy. Some were constructive; others weren't. Some guys did standards like *fo jing*. Lots of guys read. Each factory had a library of books that rotated every two months. I read a lot in Kaohsiung, but not so much in Taipei. Some of the younger guys practiced their characters. What an excellent use of time. The younger generation's Chinese characters are ugly. Nowadays, everybody uses smartphones. Nobody writes anymore. Calligraphy is becoming a lost art. The people who spent time on letters sketched and made sure their characters were neat as possible.

I learned how to play Chinese chess. That and go were the only games allowed. In Kaohsiung, they hadn't allowed any. I first saw them in Factory 11. Commissary sold the game pieces but not the boards, strangely enough. They used to, but they didn't anymore. The factory had a few lying around. Often, the loser shared a cigarette with the winner.

A few guys, such as David, were learning English. They were pretty good at reading and writing, although their listening and speaking skills were lacking. I want to say it was because they had nobody to practice with until I arrived, but I think it has more to do with Taiwan's educational style. Whenever David or anybody else wanted to learn, they'd never even try to converse with me in English. They'd ask me for definitions or translations of words. It was as if they thought rote memorization was how to learn. It's not. Language isn't vocabulary words—it's a way to communicate. What matters is getting my point across, not how many words I know. Take my Chinese, for example. I'm not a native speaker, but I speak it at home. It got better when I moved to Taiwan and took Chinese classes. I can read a comic book and about 60 percent of a newspaper. It didn't improve by studying, only by interacting with people—learning how people talk, what to say, what not to say.

Nobody doubted my ability to speak English until Taiwan. There's this weird assumption that Asians can't speak English as well as a white dude. It was jarring and strangely offensive. A few times when I talked to a (white) inmate, a dude would come by and ask the white guy, "How's William's English? Do you understand him?"

I was once called a fake ABC at a bar. I'd gotten into an argument with a local dude, and he'd shouted, "Fake ABC!" Was that an insult? I am an ABC, but he'd used it like a slur. It was confusing. I offered him a drink. He looked at me like I was crazy and walked away.

I asked my grandma about it the next day.

"Were you arguing in English or Chinese?" she replied.

"Chinese."

"You're ABC, American-born Chinese. Born in America and Chinese. You speak English and Chinese."

I nodded.

"Speaking English is a way of showing status here. The better your English is, the richer people think you are. Kids think ABCs are cool. Most of the young celebrities are ABCs like you or went to school in America somewhere, usually along the West Coast."

"Yeah, we've talked about English equaling money in Asia before."

"Here, some people who study abroad for a year or semester only learn a phrase or two in English but will pretend to be ABCs for the status."

I laughed.

"Those are fake ABC's. They'll order a drink in English at a bar or at Starbucks, but the rest is Chinese." She chuckled. "They used up all their English."

* * *

The morning of November 7, I arrived at my factory seat in the morning to find roaches all over my desk. This was their house. I was only a tenant.

We had a book fair. A bookseller came twice a year and set up shop in the auditorium. Each factory had thirty minutes. It felt rushed. They had books, notebooks, magazines, pencils, envelopes, and so on. I asked the guy working there if he had any English books. He pointed to a Chinese-to-English dictionary.

"No, no, no." I looked in the dictionary's neighborhood. "I mean like novels."

He had a puzzled look. "We only have these," he said, pointing at the dictionary.

"Huh." I stroked my chin and looked around.

I spent 1,862 NTD—which was considered low—on a couple of coloring books, markers, envelopes, paper, and a stack of notebooks. Some guys spent over 8K NTD buying an entire series. They searched everything overnight, and we received them the next day.

After lunch was the first day of Chinese class. The teacher was a banana. Four Vietnamese, two Malaysians, a dude from the mainland, and I were the students. These fools made a native Chinese speaker from mainland China attend! Now I didn't feel so bad. Class was half an hour starting at one every Monday. "Good morning, good afternoon, good evening" was today's lesson. At least I wasn't working.

It was One's nineteenth birthday, so he bought the cell a cake. I wished I could've spent my birthday in the factory instead of the freshmen dorms. Shit, I wished I'd spent my birthday free.

"You look so sad," James said as we ate.

"I am." I slouched in my chair. "I wouldn't recommend this place to a rat."

"I'm the opposite." He leaned toward me. "I think I'm happier inside and sad outside."

"Why would you say that?" I stuffed cake into my mouth.

He put his fork down. "Every morning," he exhaled, "I'd cry as I stuck the needle in my arm."

"How'd you get hooked?"

"I went through a nasty breakup. My friend said, 'This will help,' and gave me a heroin-laced cigarette." He took off his glasses to wipe down.

"Damn," I said between mouthfuls.

"It felt amazing and took my mind off my ex. I kept smoking my friend's cigarettes, and by the time I knew what it was . . ." He wiped a lens and sighed. "I was hooked."

I shook my head, "Could've happened to anybody."

James needed help, not punishment. I wished people like James wouldn't get hooked on intravenous drugs, but if they did, it should be a problem for health care professionals, not the judicial system.

* * *

"I'm gonna fuck with Shithead," Tom said as he sat in the empty seat next to me shortly before dinner.

Shithead sat two tables down. A bigger guy with beady eyes and a square face, he looked like Fred Flintstone.

"How'd he get that nickname?" I asked.

"Before your time, he used to be here but transferred." Tom leaned in and whispered, "Sometimes, I don't know why, he shits his pants. When it happened at the next factory, they sent him back with a new nickname."

I snickered. "What'd he do?"

"Statutory rape."

"Oh." My face changed. "He's one of *those* people. Is that why we don't like him?" I opened a bag of rice crackers, ate a couple, and offered him some.

"Nah, I don't think it's like that." He grabbed a handful and popped a few in his mouth. "He slept with a sixteen-year-old who lied about her age. Her mother reported them."

"So he's one of the weirder ones then." I dusted a piece of cracker off my pants. "Do you believe him?"

"He's naive and a little slow, but he means well." Tom shrugged. "Divorced, with a daughter. And it's his first time, like you."

I nodded, then threw a cracker in the air and caught it with my mouth.

"Watch this." He looked around and whispered, "I told my trustee friends to tell him he's transferring soon."

I side-eyed him.

"We're just fucking with him." He grabbed a handful of crackers and watched Shithead like the show was about to start. "Play along."

The trustees summoned Shithead and spoke to him for a few moments. He plodded with slumped shoulders back to his seat, put his head down, and teared up.

The entire table laughed. Harder we laughed, the more he cried. I felt like such a dick, but it wasn't every day I bullied a statutory rapist. Waterworks were off and on the rest of the afternoon and even through dinner. The rest of the factory got in on it, too.

After dinner, while Shithead washed dishes, another cell's dishwasher asked, "How much money you got in your account?"

He bawled.

Some trustees overheard, looked at each other and a guy said, "Hey, we're playing. You're not transferring."

Shithead shook his head and silently wept.

Before we went back to the cell, a group of trustees came by. "Look, man, we're joking," one of them said. Seriously, you're not transferring."

"I'm not crying because I'm transferring," he explained. "I'm crying because if I transfer, it means my daughter won't be able to visit anymore."

At the factory the next morning, two guys from another cell came to Shithead's table. One guy said, "Hey, you're still here."

"You okay now?" said the other.

Shithead mumbled something under his breath. They laughed and walked away. He turned to Tom. "This is all your fault."

"It was a joke." Tom laughed. "Look on the bright side, you're factory famous now."

"Yeah, as the crying guy," Shithead whimpered.

Everybody laughed.

"It's not funny."

"It kinda is," I replied. "It's a tragedy when it happens to you, but it's comedy when it happens to somebody else."

* * *

Exercise! The second time in twenty-two factory days.

Saw the doctor nine days after I submitted the request. I left at 8:30 a.m. The sick bay had sixty seats—twelve rows of five. Almost every seat was taken.

"How come there's always so many people here? You guys need to take better care of yourselves," the sick bay CO scolded. He was middle-aged and chubby, with a droopy face, and complained a lot. He was right to. His job was one of the worst; this place was a petri dish, and he dealt with all the sick ones.

I found a seat with a view of the monitor, which displayed the next five in line, and relaxed. Two people talked in the row in front of me.

"Keep talking, and I won't let you see the doctor," Droopy-Face warned them.

I didn't know withholding treatment was legal or an appropriate punishment for talking.

The prison provided two doctors, one free and one you have to pay for. When I was up, the trustee asked, "Which one do you wanna see?"

Nobody had asked this before. I'd only seen one and didn't know which one it was. "Is there a difference?"

"A difference in care?" He looked up from my paperwork. "Yes."

"When you say it like that, I'll pay for better treatment."

The doctor was sixty or older and didn't speak a word of English.

I handed him my doctor's paperwork. "I want these medicines."

He took my paper and jotted some notes.

I lifted my shirt. "What's this?"

He looked for a moment. "I'll prescribe a few ointments."

"What's this?" I pulled down my pants to show him a rash on my scrotum and penis.

He glanced. "I don't know."

"What?" I pulled my pants back up. "Whatchu mean you don't know? Why don't you know?"

"You should submit a request to see the dermatologist," he replied calmly.

"You mean wait another week or two?" I ran my fingers over my scalp. I looked around the office for degrees or qualifications of any kind. I didn't see any. "How come you don't know? Are you even an actual doctor?"

He didn't look at me. He didn't even look up from the paperwork. "Do you have any STDs?"

"No," I replied tersely.

He tapped his pen against the table. "What about AIDS?"

"No."

He looked me over. "How're you so sure?"

I made eye contact. "I get a check-up every six months, and an STD test is included."

He eyed me suspiciously. "When was your last check-up?"

"Right before I surrendered. If I caught something"—I pointed my finger at him—"you people gave it to me."

He tapped his pen against the table. "When's the last time you had your blood drawn?"

I put my hands on my hips. "A few weeks ago, when I arrived. Before that, a month ago, when I surrendered at Kaohsiung."

"Are you sure you don't have AIDs?"

I ran a hand down my face. "How can I make this any clearer? I don't have AIDs. If I did, wouldn't it show up on my blood work?" I gestured to stacks of paperwork around the office. "Or other tests?"

He clicked his tongue. "It's probably nothing, but just to be safe, I want to get your blood drawn again."

I was a little worried. I'd always used protection—no glove, no love. This quack had Leonardo DiCaprio'd me, he'd *Inception*'d me, put the idea in my head, and now I couldn't stop thinking about it. Did I have AIDS? I ran through all the ways I could've contracted AIDS here. Unprotected sex? Nope, not a chance. Shared needles? Here? Never. Contact between open wounds? Huh. I thought for a moment. I hadn't had any open wounds yet, but a few of my cellies had. They hadn't pressed their open wounds against my skin or anything. Pretty sure none of my cellies had AIDS, or else they'd have been flagged when they arrived. At least, that was how the system was supposed to work.

Medicine didn't come immediately. The quickest was later that day, but usually next day. We weren't allowed to hold our own. Officials kept it in a locked box. I had to write out a report for it every time. Medicine was handed out four times a day on factory days. Short days, holidays, or weekends were in our cells.

* * *

I'd used to dread the factory, but now I looked forward to it. Brewed some tea, walked around, chatted, zoned out during "class." Better than being in a cell twenty-four hours a day.

A Buddhist monk came and talked about giving back.

Mid-class, BaiMao summoned me and asked, "Are you Christian?"

I furrowed my brow. "No."

"I thought all Americans are Christians," he replied smugly.

There's no point arguing. I took a deep breath. "All right, sir, I'm Christian."

"Good. A Christian Bible study class starts in five minutes. You'll attend."

Bible study had five students: a Taoist, a Buddhist, a Christian, a Muslim, and me. I wondered if BaiMao picked people at random. The preacher was an ex-con who'd found God inside and changed his life. Now he went around spreading the Word. He read scripture, and we listened. He sang hymns, we sat there. It was an hour and a half and ended with a prayer. He told us we'd meet twice a week and passed around a sign-up sheet. Nobody signed up.

* * *

"Do you really have AIDS?" Tom asked while we were smoking after dinner.

I took a puff. "No, dick."

"Then," he took a few puffs and looked at the wall, "why's the doctor think you do?"

I told him the story and lifted my shirt.

"Looks like AIDS."

I slouched and hung my head.

"I'm kidding." He elbowed me.

"That's not funny." I stared at the floor.

James was nearby, overheard, and came to look me over. "It's scabies. You'll be fine. Maybe, since you're a foreigner, he wants to be safe."

I knew I'd be fine, but dammit, this doctor *Inception*'d me. I'd stopped thinking about it until Tom brought it up. Now it was all I thought about.

* * *

I skipped breakfast because of the morning blood test. Hoped it was nothing and the doctor was just an idiot. It wasn't even the sick bay; it was just a big room. Most of us sat on the floor because they only had thirty seats. The guards wouldn't let us use the restrooms. When it was my turn, I got up, had my blood drawn, then sat back down.

For class, they played a video about bullying that some high school students had made. That meant it wasn't about bullying in prison, but in an elementary school. Did this count as rehabilitation? What was I supposed to learn? Don't bully little kids?

* * *

"Body checks today." A trustee announced the following week as I sat at my desk, waiting for work.

"What's that?" I asked Dave.

"We strip down to our boxers, and BaiMao inspects us."

"Oh, I did that when I surrendered." I smirked. "I'm good."

"No." He chuckled. "You're not. They do it when you arrive and about once a month."

"That's right." I sighed. "New tattoos or pearls."

The time for body checks arrived. I cringed as I stripped. A line formed, and I dawdled to the end. I hunched over to look shorter while I waited.

"Why haven't you seen the doctor?" BaiMao asked when he saw my skin.

"I did," I growled.

"What'd he say?"

I stared at his mole hair. "He doesn't know what it is."

He rolled his eyes. I scoffed at him.

"Everybody who has rashes or scabs, come to my desk," BaiMao announced after the checks were done.

Including me, forty-five people went up. Forty-five out of 184! I bet there was actually more, but people were too embarrassed to go.

BaiMao did a double-take when he saw how many there were. "You need to take better care of yourselves!" He scolded, then sighed. "I'll bring a doctor to the factory to treat you."

A few days later, he summoned everybody who weighed over a hundred kilograms to put their names on a list. "Everybody who's on this list needs to see the doctor," he said. "If it isn't cured in one month, I'll put everybody who has it in the same room."

People looked at me. I was only eighty-nine kilograms. Dicks.

* * *

During class, a lady played movies. We watched the last twenty minutes of *Avatar* and the beginning of *The Judge*. Movie lady was my favorite because

114

her class felt the least like incarceration. I love going to the movies; they take me away to another place. Whenever she came, we'd dim the lights and put the movie on a projector pointed at the front wall. Most other classes were religious and taught by missionaries or priests of some sort. All she did was show movies with no judgment, guilt, or expectations. Every time she left, everybody applauded.

After class, BaiMao announced, "Chinese New Year is coming up. People who are level 1 and 2 are eligible for face-to-face visits. The rest are allowed a three-minute phone call."

"It's mid-November. Isn't Chinese New Year months away?" I wondered aloud.

James nodded. "This year it's late January."

"Then how's it coming up?"

"Paperwork," Tom replied. "They start the process three or four months before the holiday."

I submitted a request for a phone card.

Some guy came in the afternoon to show another movie, this one in Chinese. I was pulled out mid-class to see the doctor. It was a different one this time.

I pulled down my pants. "What's on my penis?"

He glanced at it. "Scabies"

I exhaled and lifted my shirt.

He prescribed medicine and ointments. On my way out, he said, "I'm going to give you a shot."

I stopped and turned. "Do I have to come back?"

"No, we're going to do it right now."

The nurse produced a vampire harpoon and stuck it in my arm before I could react. It hurt a little. I hoped it was penicillin.

I knew I didn't have AIDS, but it was reassuring to receive confirmation. Getting a full physical and updating my booster shots before my surrender had seemed like a good idea, but after this, I was so happy I had. Getting everything documented gave me peace of mind. If I hadn't, I would've been going crazy thinking about it. I wondered if the doctor before was fucking with me or if he was just incompetent. I'd splurged for the "good" doctor too. What would the free one have said?

CHAPTER 9
THE HOLIDAYS

This is extremely important. Will you please tell Santa that instead of presents this year, I just want my family back.

—Kevin McCallister, Home Alone

November 24, 2016

Thanksgiving. It had completely slipped my mind, and nobody mentioned it until I realized Christmas was almost here.

My Russian video game arrived. I'd submitted the request a few weeks before, and I was so thankful when it came. I didn't expect much from it, as it was only 310 NTD—a little over $10. I love video games. The first arcade game I remember playing was *Street Fighter II*. Growing up, I had a Sega Genesis and a Nintendo 64. I'd hoped the Russian game would be Tetris, but it was not. It was a different kind of block-moving game. Tom, James, and I took turns. We played for about a week, then got stuck on a level and couldn't figure it out. Nobody touched it again after that. I understood why so few people bought these.

* * *

We had reached the winter of my discontent. I thought winter would be the best time to do my sentence because it wouldn't be as hot and humid. Now I realized there was no good time. Prison sucked, no matter the weather. Winters in north Taiwan were a lot colder than the south. I wore three layers. The cold didn't come gradually, it arrived as suddenly as police when they shout, "He's resisting arrest!" and assault an unarmed "suspect."

It excited me when BaiMao announced we'd finally use warm water. "Each person is allowed four buckets to shower. No more standing. From now on, squat and shower."

I didn't know how he intended to enforce that, but it wasn't my problem. I was grateful for the warm-water showers. Or I thought I'd be. After I dried myself, I itched all over—and I wasn't the only one. After two or three days, I switched back to cold. I'd rather be cold for a few moments than itchy for the rest of the day.

Never got a legitimate answer for why the hot water made us itchy. I assumed it was sewage.

* * *

December 2. Tom's last weekend. He'd be released on Tuesday, having served his full sentence. He gave everybody in the factory a cigarette—over two hundred of us! Back in the cell, he handed each of us an extra cigarette and a green tea. We opened whatever snacks we had and threw a little party. I played the book gambling game, and I won ten cigarettes.

"Make sure you know how phones work," Dave advised Tom.

"Whatchu mean?" Tom asked.

"When I got out, I was at a poker game. My friend went to the restroom, and his phone rang. I picked it up, hit the answer button, and nothing happened. I hit it again—nothing. He came back and showed me how to slide to answer."

Everybody laughed.

Dave sighed. "I didn't know how phones worked."

"By the time we get out, cars will fly," the OG joked.

"You're the first friend getting released," I said. I couldn't stop smiling. "I'd be lying if I said I wasn't envious. I wish I was the one going home."

Up to that point, nobody I considered a friend had gone home. Home was still far, far away for me. It felt bittersweet.

"It's not only you," Tom whispered. "It's why I'm not constantly talking about it. Feels like I'm rubbing it in everybody's face."

That was pretty cool. I didn't feel that, but I could see how some people would.

"Just behave yourself. Keep doing what you're doing, and you'll be home soon." He wrote down his information. "Look me up when you get out."

"Hope you don't come back. I wouldn't recommend this place to a cockroach." We shared a cigarette.

On his way out, Tom stopped by the restaurant across the street and bought food for us via visitation. Ex-cons can't visit the day they're released; they're only allowed to send food. I planned to do the same when I get out. These small gestures meant a lot. They made us feel less forgotten and discarded.

*　*　*

Went back to the skin doctor and ordered more medicine, but the rash wasn't going away.

"Fuck this place," I lamented back in the cell after my appointment. "My skin used to look like porcelain. Now it looks like a heroin addict's."

"That's not true," James quipped. "I do heroin, and my skin looks better than yours."

I groaned. "Heroin addicts have better skin than me."

"Your skin is more like a meth addict's."

I lit a cigarette and ranted, "Skin's all fucked up. Dumping water on my head for showers. Sleeping on Japanese mats—"

"You don't know why we sleep on tatami mats?" the OG interrupted.

I shook my head and passed him my cigarette.

"They're leftover from Japanese occupation and World War II. Originally used for prisoners of war." He took a puff. "When the Kuomintang came over, they kept them and built more of the same." The Kuomintang was also known as the Chinese Nationalist Party.

I gasped. "I never thought we'd be treated the same as World War II prisoners."

"You need to understand two things about Taiwan. First, when the Kuomintang came over after World War II, they weren't interested in how to properly run a country. They tried to make as much as they could and regroup because they all thought they were going back to the mainland." He took another few puffs, "Second, there's not a sector of Taiwan that *isn't* falling apart from negligence, incompetence, or corruption." He flicked away the cigarette and frowned. "My country has been left with too many problems, for too long, with too little being done."

* * *

I received my first "salary." I made 6 NTD in October and November—$0.02. They did not make it clear whether we were paid hourly, per box we made, or what. Every paycheck was different, but they were all sad to look at.

A new guy arrived at our factory—a Malaysian serving eight years for heroin smuggling. He couldn't speak Chinese. Trustees used me to translate. During the teacher's meeting, the guy complained that they'd held him at Bei Shuo for 496 days, but they'd only credited him 486. Four hundred eighty-seven was the magic number for him. If you're held for one-sixth your total time, you entered at level 3 instead of 4. It was a big difference. At level 3, he'd be eligible for parole at exactly 50 percent of his time. Still, he had to wait an extra six months for his points. The rules say first-time offenders are eligible at 50 percent, but nobody got out at 50 percent. Usually at least 60 percent, sometimes 70 percent. People either had their points but waited for time or had time but waited for points. I was time waiting for points.

"It's common for the prison to underreport time served," Bruce told me.

* * *

Another celly—nicknamed Crazy-Eyes because his eyes went in different directions and were constantly darting around—hadn't been eating. During breakfast, Bruce repeatedly offered him food, to no avail.

"What's up with him?" I asked Bruce once Crazy-Eyes was out of earshot.

Bruce looked around, then whispered, "His uncle and cousin passed away yesterday. He's taking it pretty rough."

I looked over at Crazy-Eyes. "What should I say?"

"You?" James said. "Nothing. He doesn't want a lot of people to know."

"That came out wrong." I scratched my head. "What I meant was, what's the translation for 'my condolences'?"

"Don't bring it up unless he does!" James snapped.

"He's had a bad few days," Bruce said. "At least he'll be released soon."

During class, a teacher said he would play us a movie called *Actually Love*. I wondered what the hell he was talking about. Turned out to be *Love Actually*. If that's a Christmas movie, then so is *Die Hard* because they both happen around Christmas. *Love Actually* was a pirated Chinese version with bad audio and a shaky camera. It even had shadows whenever people got up to use the restroom. These bastards were downloading and showing pirated movies, and they were the ones who incarcerated us.

* * *

One of the first things my cellies had told me about was the Christmas party. I always thought they were fucking with me, but it was true! Most foreigners were in for drugs, specifically smuggling. Many got fifteen years or more. Taipei had a lot of them, over four hundred. They split the party into two, morning and afternoon. There was a priest from Pasadena, California, as well as ones from Vietnam, Thailand, and Malaysia.

I attended the morning party. An orchestra played Christmas music for about an hour, then two ladies sang carols. After they finished, the missionaries set up food: fried chicken, pizza, Indian curry, pho, salad, cookies, chocolate, and brownies. They had a lot of food; it was pretty much all-you-can-eat, and they gave each inmate a one-liter bottle of cold Coke. I drank mine and half of another dude's. I went back for fourths and fifths. I ate so much I skipped lunch and dinner.

I'd always been skeptical of missionaries. I could never understand why they'd go to another country to help the less fortunate. Now I know. It was a powerful thing, being in a room with complete strangers and reminding us of our humanity. I appreciated what they did for us so much. It made that Christmas unforgettable.

The prison gave each foreigner a Christmas present: an undershirt, boxers, Lays potato chips (spicy tuna flavor), a bag of instant coffee, crackers, and strawberry waffles. I kept the undershirt and boxers and shared the food with my cellies.

Christmas incarcerated wasn't as sad as I thought it'd be. It felt like any other day. I knew it was coming up because of the holiday theme bags.

Work was nonstop around the holidays. Fucking holiday bags. Fucking commercialization of Christmas. I felt like an elf in Santa's sweatshop. I didn't usually feel homesick, but I did around the holidays. The whole month of December, I looked at my pictures every morning. It helped nobody talked about it. I imagined they'd feel how I felt around Chinese New Year.

* * *

A few days after the party, shortly after we arrived at the factory, the trustees told one of my cellies to pack up his things. He'd be transferring. At least this time they didn't come in the middle of the night as if it were a raid and wake everybody up.

Spaceman transferred to the factory midmorning. He looked sedated but better and had a thousand-yard stare. I watched him meander around in a daze. Whenever I heard him talk, his speech was slurred. He didn't recognize me, and I didn't say hello. I don't know how long I gawked at my old celly.

I saw One coming back out of the corner of my eye, holding his mouth and looking pissed.

"What happened?" I asked.

"I saw the dentist for a toothache, and the bastard drilled a hole in the wrong tooth!" He opened his mouth and pointed.

My eyes widened. "The fuck? What now?"

He shrugged. "Now I have two problems instead of one."

* * *

Prince pulled me aside for a before-work smoke. "Don't tell anybody, but you're gonna be transferring factories pretty soon."

"Wha—" My cigarette fell out of my mouth. "How soon is soon? You know where?"

He picked it up and took a puff. "Probably before Chinese New Year. And they didn't say."

That year, the New Year would be at the end of January. That wasn't much time. It felt like anytime I became acclimated to my surroundings, they switched it up. This place was the bane of my existence.

"I'm gonna talk to the teacher and ask if I can stay," I said.

Prince flinched. "Don't. You'll get me in trouble. People aren't supposed to know they're transferring, for security reasons."

"Don't worry, man." I smirked. "I'll keep you outta it. I wanna double-check my points and parole date anyway."

He rubbed his temples and took a puff.

Until this factory, I'd moved every two weeks, and my cell spot had changed regularly. Not knowing where I was going to lay my head at night was unsettling. Even parking lots have reserved spaces. I couldn't even reserve a spot on the floor. Bastards treated a Mercedes better than humans.

Days after, I was still riding a high from the party and wanted to do something nice for my cellies. I bought a pack of smokes on the black market and gave everybody a cigarette as a Christmas present. Cigarettes were 60 NTD ($2) regularly. On the black market, they tripled. Still cheaper than Cali.

On Christmas Eve, I passed out a cigarette to everyone. *Merry Christmas, ya filthy animals.* Seventeen of them, and two didn't smoke. I had five leftover. It was satisfying to see them smile, even if some of those bastards got on my last nerve. Sometimes, when you're not getting the love you want, giving makes you feel like you will.

* * *

A Buddhist monk came and showed slides of his trip to Hong Kong. Not a religious trip—his vacation, and the slides were of tourist sites he'd visited. Some of these "classes" made me wonder what the fuck was happening. Then again, anything was better than making paper bags.

My old celly, Tofu, transferred to the factory.

"Did he leave the sophomore dorms after you?" Bruce asked.

I shook my head. "I left after him."

He looked over at Tofu and scratched his chin. "He must've gotten into some trouble."

"How do you know?"

"You've been here for a while, a little over two months now. If he left before you, then he went to another factory before here. They wouldn't transfer him for no reason. I bet he got in trouble."

"He doesn't seem like the type. I'll find out what happened."

I found Tofu in his seat. He followed me to the restroom, where we shared a cigarette.

"What's up, man!"

He smiled. He looked older than his years due to drug use. When he smiled, his wrinkles had wrinkles. "William, how're you?"

"I can't complain. This place is all right. We don't do much work." I took a couple puffs and passed the cigarette to him. "Where were you before?"

"Factory Seven." He took a puff. "We made tea boxes."

"You got any more?" Inside, tea boxes doubled as cigarette boxes.

He looked down. "Ah, no. I used to have a lot, but I didn't know if I could bring them." He took a few puffs and passed it back. "I gave them all away."

"No worries." I shrugged and took a puff. "So, what's up? Whatchu doing here? What happened?"

"I ran into a hater. This guy was a jerk, and one day he attacked me. I didn't fight back, but I had friends who did. He got sent to the black room, and they sent me to Ping Wing. Spent a couple of weeks there, then transferred here."

I nodded. "At least you're all right. On the low, I'm gonna be transferring factories soon. I got the word from my celly. I'm gonna ask the teacher if there's any way I can stay. If not, I'll introduce you to my boys here." I took a puff and flicked the cigarette into the squatter. "They'll take care of you."

In the cell after work, Crazy-Eyes gave everybody a cigarette. He'd be released tomorrow.

I woke up to piss in the middle of the night and heard heard One say, "Fuck!" He stood up, walked to the restroom, looked at his pants, shook his head, washed his leg, and took a piss. Then he hung his pants up.

He'd had a wet dream. He looked at me and put a finger to his lips. I mimed zipping mine. Tom saw the pants drying in the morning, put the pieces together, and gave him shit the rest of the day.

✳ ✳ ✳

Just before lunch, a week after Tofu arrived, the teacher summoned me. Prince was outside when I arrived, and he followed me in, I assumed to eavesdrop. The teacher's desk was a mess. How could his desk be messy when he had access to slave labor? He moved folders around to get an unobstructed view of me as I sat down.

I chose my words carefully because I didn't want to burn Prince, who stood in my peripheral. "There are rumors people are going to be moving factories."

Prince handed him my file and scowled at me on his way out.

I avoided eye contact, waited for him to leave, and cleared my throat. "I don't know if I'm moving or staying, but if my opinion means anything, I'd like to stay. I can help translate for foreigners."

"It's not up to me. BaiMao gives us the names, and I process the paperwork." He opened my dossier. "I have already submitted yours. You have no choice."

I slumped in the chair. "Okay. Last thing, I'm eligible for parole on May 18, 2017."

"Yes, if all your points are in order."

"I meet the requirements May 1." I leaned forward.

"You have to maintain the level for three months, then you're eligible the following month. Parole applications are only at the beginning of the month," he replied matter-of-factly.

"So I'm eligible—but I won't be able to apply until—" I counted on my fingers. "May, June, July . . . August?" I practically shouted, "The beginning of August!"

"You need to fulfill the prerequisites and maintain them for three months." He rustled some papers and closed my dossier. "Just keep doing what you're doing, and you'll be fine."

I pointed at it. "How come I didn't get any points earlier?"

"You only get points from the factory. You didn't receive any in Kaohsiung, from your trial, or in the freshmen cells."

"None of it counted?" My body went limp in the seat.

"It counts toward the end of your sentence, not the beginning. Two years is twenty-four months. We held you for three months, your sentence is now twenty-one months."

"So I still need to do a year before I'm eligible for parole?" I groaned.

"Yes."

"Why d'you guys gotta lie to me?" I threw my arms up. "Why say I'm eligible for parole after a year when you mean a factory year?"

"Well . . ." He leaned back in his chair and crossed his leg. "You are eligible after fifty percent of your time, as a first-time offender. Whether you can apply is different."

If I had a parole date, they couldn't delay it without cause. Seemed like the Taiwanese penal system looked for reasons to keep people in rather than help people get out and stay out.

CHAPTER 10
FACTORY 15

Don't interrupt a man when he's giving himself hell.

—Elmore Leonard

January 1, 2017

I dreamed in Chinese for the first time. I woke up middream. It tripped me out. Until then, I'd always dreamed in English. My dream Chinese was better than my real-life Chinese. How does that work? We're the same person!

After breakfast the next day, one of my cellies handed me a pill—Xanax. Narcotics were impossible to find, but apparently they handed out prescription drugs like candy. A pill could be bartered for two cigarettes. The next time I saw the doctor, I ordered medicine for my skin problems, Xanax to help me sleep, and codeine for a cough. I wouldn't take all those pills. Whatever I didn't use, I'd barter or stash for a rainy day.

I was hazy all day. It felt amazing to self-medicate, and I did my part to share the love. I wrote the pill names in English on a piece of paper for my people. All they had to do was tell the doctor their "symptoms," show him the paper when asked, and he'd sign. It worked every time. All the government seemed to care about was if we'd pay or not.

Silly me, I was naive enough to think the point of health care was actually a person's health. I wonder if this burgeoning prescription pill problem was a bug or a feature of Taiwan's health care system. If I could take a pill and sleep my two years away like Sylvester Stallone in *Demolition Man*, I would.

* * *

January 3 was the first factory day of the new year. I applied for a TV. Prince informed nine of us we'd be transferring.

He took me aside during a work break and quietly said, "Best case, you'll be home in September. Worst case, December."

My eyes widened.

"How come you're not happy? It's good news."

"Sure. Thanks."

* * *

I washed an undershirt in the factory and hung it to dry, then it disappeared. I suspected somebody stole it, but it was old and torn. I was going to throw it away anyway and already had a new one prepared. As James helped me sew a button onto the fresh shirt, a trustee pulled him away. Another trustee offered to help, and his friend gave me an apple. The VIP treatment. I was transferring right as I was getting settled in.

My number was called. Moving day was tomorrow. I'd be transferred to Factory 15, the old people's factory. Factory 11 was said to be the drug offenders' factory because we attended class instead of work, but they stuck all kinds of people here. Nobody stayed permanently. They moved people biannually, like the Quarter Quell in *Hunger Games*. They had no reason to rotate people in and out in a janky version of musical chairs. The prison probably got bored and wanted to shake things up every six months.

The OG would go to Factory 1. Dave to Factory 2. Factories 1 and 2 were for those with long sentences, ten years and up. One was headed to Factory 13. Factories 13 and 15 were the old people's factories, sixty-five and older, and they were side by side.

The last hour was hectic. People ran around and gathered all their things. All personal items had to go with us. If we forgot anything, too bad.

Back in the cell was a party. We opened the rest of our snacks, and a couple of guys'd had visitors earlier. People exchanged information.

"Tell me about Factory 15," I asked nobody in particular.

"Factory 15 is the best place to be," Dave replied as he opened a candy bar. "You sleep in the factory, spots are bigger, it's not as crowded, and everybody gets at least one mat. None of this overlapping shit." He took a big bite. "You don't do much hard work because everybody's old. Job can't be too complex or difficult. You know what it is?"

I shook my head, then opened a bag of corn chips.

"You know the shoestring bags? Your job is sticking the string in the shoestring bags. I wanna go to Factory 15, but I'm too young."

"I thought you were going to Factory 1 or 2," the OG said to me, offering a milk tea. "Who knew you'd be going to 15?"

I opened it and took a sip. "Either I got lucky, or my grandma's prayers are still protecting me."

"Justin Lee is there. Look for him." Bruce sat along the wall and jotted his information to hand to people. "He speaks English."

I put my drink to the side and lit a cigarette. "Who's that?"

"You don't know who Justin Lee is?"

"I didn't grow up here." I half-shrugged and took a puff. "I don't watch a lot of news."

"His family is ballin'. He drugged and raped a bunch of models, singers, and famous people and secretly recorded himself."

My head snapped back. "For real?" I took a few puffs and passed it to him.

"Yeah, it was a big deal when it happened. He was all over the news."

"The Banana King," Shithead said from the corner, his mouth full.

I looked for my drink. "What's that mean?"

"You know how we're bananas? He's our king,"

"All his videos are online too." Bruce puffed and handed the cigarette back to me.

I took a puff, then flicked it into the squatter. "Online?"

"Somehow, they leaked during his trial."

These guys weren't angels. Some were far below that. They had some problems, and many of them clearly didn't have their priorities straight. But all things considered, these guys weren't so bad. Taiwan's penitentiaries were filled with not-so-bad people, especially considering the heavy penalties for drug use. I'd miss some—One, Bruce, James, the OG, and Carmelo. Thinking about the transfer, I felt a tinge of sadness, like you feel at the end of something. I popped more pills, or else I wouldn't have been able to sleep.

* * *

"Why do they have young people in Factory 15?" I wondered out loud during breakfast the next morning.

"There's a group of kids there," the OG replied between mouthfuls, "to help the old people. Do their laundry, move heavy things, wash dishes— that kind of thing. 'Kids' means under forty."

"Wonderful." I groaned. "I'm a slave to a slave."

"At least you'll be comfortable."

"I'm a house slave." I shuddered.

The OG and I popped leftover pills after breakfast. I wanted to be on a good one for the rest of the day. James helped me carry my stuff to the factory.

It was pandemonium after the prison song. Trustees ran around to get everybody's paperwork ready, and those of us moving were double-checking we'd packed everything.

We left in two groups. Those in the front factories (1 through 8) left first. I felt hazy from the pills and had this dopey look on my face. The morning passed in a blur. Soon it was my time. James and Bruce helped me carry my stuff to the cart. We embraced.

The guard sat me outside the wing chief's office. Chief came out, introduced himself, had us introduce ourselves, then gave a speech. I stopped listening after, "I hate drug users. You know why? Because drug users will kill their families. Not metaphorically. They will actually murder their parents, brothers, and sisters."

It was like Charlie Brown's teacher talking. All I heard was "Wah, wah, wah."

He inspected me as he walked by. "Is this a tumor on the back of your head? You should get it checked out."

I've had a big, protruding bump on the back of my head since I was a kid. It doesn't hurt or anything, but it looks strange.

"It's bone, sir." I touched it. "Feel it."

He felt it. "It's bone."

Patronizing dick.

After his rousing speech, the chief herded us to our factories. I arrived around mid-lunch. Newcomers sat at a small table to the side. Prez Tsai's boyfriend came, shook my hand, and handed me a cigarette. I'd forgotten they had transferred him here from the freshmen dorms. I was thankful he remembered me.

"I'm in the back of row one," he said. "Find me if you need anything."

After lunch, the factory CO—nicknamed Sunshine because his surname means *sun* in Chinese—announced, "Congratulations on coming to Factory 15. This is like heaven compared to the upstairs cells. Factory 13 and 15 both sleep in the factory, the only two who have this privilege, but here is better. Follow the rules, don't cause any trouble, and we won't have any problems. Any issues, and I'll send you back to the cells. Once you're gone, that's it. You won't come back."

During individual questioning, Sunshine asked something I was unsure of, but an athletic, balding kid appeared and helped with the translation. "My name is Justin. Let me know if you need anything."

After they searched everything, including my cavities, the five row chiefs went to the front to pick the newcomers. It was a meat market. The rows with no kids had priority. It was down to me, and another dude, my future row chief, said, "I'll take the big one. You're in row two, table two."

I shouldn't have taken those pills. I felt so groggy. Then again, moving was a bitch.

After I settled in, I found Justin in his seat. "Yo, thanks for earlier."

"No problem." He got up. "Do you smoke?" I followed him to the restroom, where he offered me a cigarette.

I took it and lit it, then lit his.

"So"—he took a puff—"you're an ABC, huh?"

"Yeah." I took a puff and sized him up. "How come your English is so good?"

"I went to high school in Virginia."

After that, he introduced me to his friend, Stanley—younger than both of us, pale-skinned, and husky—who was serving eleven years for meth dealing.

I'd made some friends on my first day. Maybe this factory wouldn't be so bad after all.

Over the course of the day, I got to know the guys at my table. I think one of them, Yohey, had early onset dementia. His mind wasn't all there. The man was a boss. He had people filling out his commissary, retrieving his mat, and rolling and unrolling it for him. He even had a dude scrub him down when he showered. The oldest person in the factory was an eighty-eight-year-old who I ironically nicknamed Junior. There was another inmate I called Mumbles because he talked to himself. I think the joint had broken him. My table was next to Heisenberg's.

My row chief, Heisenberg, was a bespectacled, heavy-built guy, bald up top with gray on the sides. On my left was Sosa, who was in for insider trading—seven years four months. He'd been locked up for a year, and it was his first time too. Other than the hair, Sosa was Heisenberg's physical opposite: short, hunchbacked, skinny, and frail. Howard (five years, ketamine sales), Heisenberg, Sosa, and a fourth guy sat at the first table, the head table. Howard looked out of place at the table. Like a grandson visiting a grandpa.

There was also a guy who resembled my grandpa. It was uncanny. He could've been his doppelgänger. But my grandpa was no heroin smuggler.

I slept in the last row, fifth from the corner by the restrooms, in front of windows. Big Face, another heroin smuggler, slept on my right. He was in his early forties, skinny, and balding, with black hair that had specks of white. He, Sosa, and Heisenberg had friendly smiles.

The rumors were true: the sleeping spaces were bigger. Everybody got at least their mat. I even had a few inches between my mat and the people next to me. Felt like the penthouse at the Ritz.

* * *

I nicknamed Factory 15 the Taipei Retirement Castle because it reminded me of Grandpa Simpson's retirement home. My first impression when I got here was this place was like heaven. So much more space. It was the third of Taiwan's gulags I'd been in, and all things considered, I liked this one the best. But a golden cage is still a cage. Factory 15 had its drawbacks.

This place got up early. People stirred as early as 5:00 a.m.—and they weren't quiet. They coughed, gargled, and spat. The noise woke me. There were over a hundred men yet only four sinks. Most guys squatted where they could and spat on the floor.

The factory's restroom had eight toilets: six thrones and two squatters. Each toilet had a small hose on the side, which we used as a ghetto bidet. We kept a bucket close by for the squatters. It was common to see people read a newspaper or magazine while they sat on the throne. Just like home, ain't it? There was also a trough urinal and a sink with soap on a rope. We needed to get restroom badges, but they had more badges than toilets. Nobody waited for one during factory hours. There were only ten badges after hours, so sometimes there'd be a line for the restroom.

No guard after hours. He clocked in at 8:00 a.m., out at 5:30 p.m., and padlocked the factory when he left. Every night, a different volunteer (inmate) patrolled every couple hours to make sure nobody died in their sleep. He slept in the factory's front. If an old man didn't have his blanket on, he'd put it on for him. Any issues, the volunteer got the attention of the watchman on duty. Usually, he waved his arms.

They strictly controlled the factory's population. The most I saw was 130. Factory 15 was for sixty-five-or-older, white-collar criminals and people with serious medical conditions. One guy had only one leg, the other one amputated at the thigh. They allowed him to have crutches in the factory.

"Do they still shackle you?" I once asked him.

"Yeah," he grunted. "I hold the other shackle in my hand."

The kid nicknamed Wintermelon only had use of his right arm. His left was smaller, shriveled, and hung lifelessly by his side. He used a wheelchair outside the factory. Two handfuls needed wheelchairs. One guy needed an oxygen tank to breathe at night. Many couldn't see or hear well. They needed people to read things to them or repeat instructions. The senile ones needed people to fill out forms. A few guys needed daily insulin shots. They got them every morning and after dinner. Almost the whole factory had medication.

Laundry service was 800 NTD for summer and 1,000 NTD in the winter. Four dishwashers were the factory's janitors, garbage collectors, and handymen. Everybody called them the water company. Big Face was the shot-caller of the dishwashers, and most slept to the right of me in the corner. I was lucky. A dishwasher left the day before I came, and the space was open. It was prime real estate because it was in the corner, in front of windows, and away from heavy foot traffic.

Every morning, we rolled up our beds as we had in the cells, but we put them in our kit bags. Then, a trustee called us by row, and we stacked them in the corner as tall as the cabinets. After dinner every night, a handful of the kids threw the sacks into the center and called out the number on the bag as they chucked it.

During factory hours, we'd eat breakfast, lunch, and dinner at our workspace.

Four big-screen TVs hung from the ceiling. Sometimes, during break or when we were done with work, they turned them on to let us watch the news or a movie. On Fridays, we did karaoke from two to three. After hours and weekends, they'd put on whatever channel we wanted. No need to buy a TV here. However, from my spot, I didn't have a clear view of any.

At the end of the workday, we stacked all the tables and pushed them to one side of the factory in front of our cabinets. The tables were bound with nylon rope to ensure they didn't accidentally fall and hit someone.

Then there were chores. We swept and mopped, then put down a tarp, which we put our mats on. Chores were done by row, and there was about a month between each session. I moved furniture and mopped. Tarp duty depended on your sleeping spot. It was about five weeks between turns. I paid somebody to do mine. It cost 100 NTD or ten cigarettes.

Weekends were different. We didn't need to move furniture, and they kept the TVs on most of the day. I was thankful for the space to walk around.

Winter had two shower times: 9:00 a.m. for cold water and 1:00 p.m. for hot. I still showered with cold.

"Are you going to be arrested when you land in America?" Justin asked as I admired my mat one night.

"Shit, I didn't think of that. I don't think so. It's legal there, but I don't know. Since you mention it, I don't know what's going to happen with my visa either." I unmade then remade my mat. "I entered on a ninety-day visa, so it's expired by now. Wonder if they'll let me leave." I wanted to get my mind off it and went to go smoke a cigarette.

He caught up to me a little bit later and gently elbowed me. "Don't worry, bro. I'm sure it'll be fine. Ask AIT when they visit you."

* * *

Carmelo unexpectedly arrived before lunch. As soon as I could, I pulled him away for a smoke.

"What a pleasant surprise!" I said.

"I know, right?" He took a puff. "Everybody from Factory 11 says hello. James is the accountant, and Bruce is the chief."

We fist-bumped. "Good for Bruce!"

Stanley and Justin saw us talking and came over. I introduced them. Carmelo introduced us to the people he arrived with. Fat Tiger was in for a parole violation. He'd gotten eleven years for armed robbery, did seven years and ten months, was out for eight months, then caught another charge. Lion was in for K sales, five years. Fat Tiger was the tallest, Carmelo the shortest, but they were both husky with barrel chests. Together, they looked like trolls, the mean kind from *Lord of the Rings*.

Later that afternoon, I arrived at the sick bay as they were closing. I told the trustee, "I'll pay to see the good doctor."

He looked at the clock and shook his head. "There's not enough time."

Free doctor, then. I showed him my blisters, rashes, and scabs. They'd never completely gone away.

"You have allergies—"

I scoffed. "I'm not allergic to anything," I gestured around. "This place is filthy."

He waved dismissively. "I'll prescribe allergy medicine. If the problem continues, come back in a week."

Charlatan.

* * *

Received my level 3 badge. I felt a sense of accomplishment, which quickly made me depressed. All we did was make bags.

Sunshine summoned me to his desk during work. "Do you know your passport information?"

"Uh, no." Strange. Nobody had ever asked before. "But inside my bag is a photocopy of my passport." I went to retrieve it. I was glad I'd kept a copy in case of an emergency. But that was my only one. I handed it to him.

"That's good enough." He jotted some notes. "Get back to work."

He never gave it back. I didn't even have time to ask why he wanted it.

Factory 15 had six foreigners: me, a Thai, a Japanese, a Malaysian, a Brit, and a dude from Denmark. I got to know the Brit. His name was Peter, and he was serving thirty years (a life sentence) for heroin smuggling. I also got to know the dude from Denmark, whose name was Erik. He was doing nine years, also for heroin smuggling. They both spoke English, so it was easy to get to know them. I never spoke to the Japanese guy. The Malaysian was also in for smuggling.

Thailand got fifteen years for murder. "I got into an argument with some guy and used a knife to gut him like a fish." He gestured. "From stomach to chin."

I cringed when he told me. I'd never heard someone talk about murder so nonchalantly.

Peter had done fifteen years and was up for parole soon. He was short, round, blue-eyed, and wrinkly with white hair. Heisenberg had known him that whole time.

"When Peter and I were in Factory 19," he said, "which was the old people's factory back then, he had a bad temper and argued with people all the time."

"With other foreigners or Taiwanese?" I asked, looking over at Peter.

"Both. Everybody. He was always complaining to the guards. Then he learned Chinese. He slowly learned to control his temper."

"Being able to speak and understand Chinese helps."

"Absolutely. It's a big difference if you can't speak the language. It's going to be tough."

One of the first times I spoke to Peter, he told me about his friend Zane Dean. "He accidentally killed a Taiwanese national, borrowed somebody's passport, and fled the country back to England. He refuses to return because Taiwanese penitentiaries are inhumane—"

"He's right."

Peter nodded. "Zane was supposed to surrender in September 2012."

"2012? Before my time. No wonder I've never heard of this guy."

"He fled the month before. Both the Taiwanese and English governments kept quiet about it until January 2013. The Taiwanese government kept it a secret because the UK prosecutor and judge wouldn't send him back if they knew about the conditions. The two countries have no official extradition agreement, but they have a one-time memorandum of understanding to send him back here. But they have to be careful because Taiwanese prisons don't follow EU regulations."

Sounded like my old celly Nigel. I like how a white guy can borrow another white guy's passport and skip town because they all look alike to Taiwanese authorities.

Erik looked like a heroin-smuggling Viking: tattooed, tall, blue-eyed, and broad shouldered. He was in his late forties, and his white hair had started balding. His story sounded like an alternate reality version of mine, but worse because he didn't speak Chinese. I asked him about his holding cell.

"Taoyuan had five people in a small cell," he told me. "One point eight meters by three meters, with no windows. And I'm on hundred eighty centimeters."

"What was your interrogation like?"

"When they interrogated me, I received no lawyer, no embassy, and a useless translator. I signed a confession without translation."

I shook my head. "They did the same to me."

"It's what they do to all foreigners."

I sighed. "USDA grade-A bullshit."

"You know what's bullshit? After the interrogation, the police took me outside the station where the TV crews were for a perp walk, put me in a cop car, and drove me around the block and back to the same station so the reporters could get more footage."

I snickered. "My bad, I'm not laughing at you, but the lengths these Mickey Mouse cops go to put on a show to make themselves look good."

"It's pathetic, isn't it?"

I nodded. "How was court?"

"Court was when I discovered my confession had been doctored. For my trial, they used the doctored confession and refused to change it."

"It's eerie how similar our stories are. Where's your embassy or family during all this?"

"The government took forty-eight days to notify my family and only allowed embassy contact in court."

"I wish I had an embassy to help me."

* * *

During work, a trustee told Junior they had denied his parole. He stopped what he was doing and cried. Sunshine told him to go outside and play because his crying was a distraction.

"Junior's in for murder," Heisenberg explained when I asked what they had convicted him of. "When he was eighty, he had a thirty-year-old mistress he bragged about. He thought she loved him, but she only loved his money. He threatened her with a knife. 'I want you to give me my money back and go back to China.' She's originally from China but has ROC citizenship. She reported it to the police. They did nothing. He stalked, confronted, then stabbed her seventeen times. Immediately after they arrested him, he signed over all his money and assets to his wife so the victim's family couldn't sue. His friend visited and said his wife and their next-door neighbor ran off with his money. 'I'm going to murder both of them when I get out.' During the trial, his wife told the judge not to release him because she's scared of what he might do. They only gave him ten years."

How could they treat a murderer better than a smuggler? I understood the culture showed deference to their elders, but I didn't think it applied to a place like prison. I thought we were all pieces of shit here. Every time I left, they shackled, cuffed, and muzzled me, and yet this geezer got to go outside and play when he felt sad. Maybe I'd been thinking of this all wrong. At first, I'd thought it was a justice system. Then, I'd thought it was a gulag. Now I think of it as a Chinatown version of *Animal Farm*— "Where some are more equal than others."

I tried not to look at him the rest of the day. It made me grit my teeth.

* * *

They approved my call home. Officially, I was allowed a call every three months. Unofficially, it depended on how they felt. I'd been in custody five months, and this was the first time. It was a few days late too. I was told my call would be January 9; it was the twelfth. Each inmate needed a phone card, and we couldn't share. In Factory 11, the trustees held our cards. Here, we held our own.

After work, guards took out the group making local calls, then the international callers. Pay phones were set up in the auditorium. It looked like an Indian telemarketing center. There must've been at least fifty phones, but there weren't enough seats. We waited outside in the grass.

Foreigners had a separate, shorter line than locals. Locals got five minutes, but foreigners got just three. Why'd foreigners only get 60 percent of what locals got? It wasn't like the cost had anything to do with it. We used our own phone cards.

"You sound okay." Mom sounded worried.

"I'm all right." I tried to sound cool. "Has Small Auntie been filling you in?"

"Yes, she calls after every visit to update us."

"Good." My lower lip quivered. "You know, I'm not a bad person. I made a mistake." I don't know why I felt the need to say that. Maybe because this place treated me like I was as dangerous as a Bond villain.

"I totally understand what you're saying. I know you're not a bad person—"

I sniffled.

"—but you should learn from this mistake. Sometimes I think about you and wonder if I did something wrong. Maybe I should've spent more time with you when you were younger."

I bit my tongue to keep from showing emotion. I didn't want to look like a punk.

"But I needed to work and hoped you understood how hard your parents worked and would learn to work hard yourself. Work on being a better person. It's not too late. You're still young."

I didn't know what to say. I sat there, holding the phone. Then the line disconnected. I was relieved I didn't have to hear any more, but it was reassuring to chat with my mom, if only for a little while.

I'd never given much thought to how my time affected my family and friends. I'd done the crime, I could do the time. They weren't the ones in there, I was. But now I realized how wrong I was. The emotional toll had to be overwhelming. My mom was probably worried all the time, and I was sure I'd contributed to Pops's heart attack. It wasn't their fault, it was mine. I felt so guilty, selfish, and immature. Such a piece of shit.

A CO came over, took the receiver from my hand, and hung up. I'd only spent 15 NTD of my 200-NTD phone card, so I don't think I even got my full three minutes.

* * *

In the morning, Factories 13 and 15 met in the auditorium for a Korean Christian missionary show. Midshow, a trustee pulled me out. I thought I was going to the doctor.

Instead Sunshine said, "AIT is here."

The US has no embassy in Taiwan because there are no official diplomatic ties due to the One China policy. Unofficially, the American Institute in Taiwan (AIT) was the embassy. This was my first visit.

They put me in the closet that passed for a waiting room with the rest of the Americans. There were only five of us. I recognized one of them as another Taiwanese-American, Nicky, from Factory 16. He was in his late thirties and skinny. His hair was black and blended with the frames of his glasses.

I sat next to him on the floor and asked, "Is the water dirty?"

"Yeah, but think of it this way. You grew up in LA, right? We're not used to it. It's like when you go to Tijuana or South America on vacation, they tell us not to drink the water because we'll get sick." He mimed vomiting.

I nodded. "But that doesn't explain all the other inmates who grew up here and have the same problems." I pointed at the door because there was no window. "I lived in Taiwan for three years before this and didn't experience any problems with the water until prison."

"It takes time for your body to build an immunity to it. I was like you when I arrived. It takes about two or three years." He lifted his pant leg and shirt. "Now? I'm fine."

"Two or three years? I'll be gone." I sucked my teeth. "Do you know if we're going to be arrested when we land in America?" I didn't give anybody a chance to respond before blurting, "And what's up with our visas?"

Nicky shrugged. "Ask them." He jerked a thumb toward the door.

I was last to be seen and searched prior to entering the meeting room. A female intern and a white-haired Asian guy in a suit sat at a table. I looked around the room and sat in a foldable chair across from them.

"State your name in English," the man said.

"William Tsung." I titled my head. "Why'd you wanna know?"

He scribbled in his notepad. I tried to peek, but I couldn't read what he wrote. "Because you entered under your Chinese name, you're not in our database. We weren't sure if you were a US citizen." He made eye contact. "Sometimes people lie."

I leaned back. "I'm an American citizen with a valid passport. It's practically brand new."

"What's your crime?"

"Smuggling, two years." I folded my arms. "Why didn't you visit me in Kaohsiung?"

He jotted down something. "These visits are biannual. Were you locked up for over six months?"

I shook my head.

"That's why."

"Will they deport me when this is over?" I leaned forward in my chair.

"Yes."

I sighed in relief.

"Unless you want to stay in Taiwan. Then you'll need to fill out an application."

"No, I wanna leave." I held up two fingers and rubbed them against my thumb. "Do I have to pay for my ticket?"

"Yes. If you are destitute, you can apply for a loan from the US government, but I don't recommend it." He looked out the window, then at me. "You'll be held in immigration until we approve your application."

"Will they arrest me when I land?" I tapped my foot.

"Allow me to be frank." He put his pen down. "No. You committed a crime and were punished in Taiwan. This has nothing to do with the US Justice Department."

"Great." I grinned. "I'm eligible for parole soon. I should be home by year's end."

"Be aware parole isn't automatic," he cautioned. "It can take between one and ten applications."

"Are you reading from a script?" I tried to sneak a look at his notepad in case he was. He pulled it away. "Ten times?" I scoffed. "Worst case, I apply twice. I only got two years." I side-eyed him. "What about my visa?"

"They froze your status the minute they arrested you."

I exhaled. One less problem to worry about.

"How often do you exercise?"

I held up two fingers.

He wrote something. "A week?"

"No." I laughed. "Twice since I've arrived, about five months."

"How much do you work?"

I could see a factory from the window. Not sure which one it was, but I looked at it sadly. "Monday through Friday, 8:30 a.m. to 11:30 a.m., then 1:00 p.m. to 4:00 p.m."

"Do you have any medical conditions?"

I lifted my shirt and pant legs.

He wrote *rashes and scabies*. "You have a short sentence. We hope next time we come, you won't be here."

Nobody hoped that more than me. I shook his hand and told the guard I was ready.

Shortly after I returned to the factory, a trustee handed me some English magazines, courtesy of Nicky.

* * *

I had a blister on my ass the size of a golf ball. I asked a trustee if I could see the doctor. Sunshine summoned me to his desk, did a quick glance, and scowled.

"Doesn't look serious. It's unnecessary."

I looked at my blister for a moment, looked at him, then moved in so close I was practically in his lap.

The head trustee laughed. Sunshine flinched, then quickly looked away.

"Pull up your pants," he grunted. "I don't need to see. Submit a report, and I'll let you go."

The head trustee pulled me aside and whispered, "It's infected."

I felt so weak and tired all the time from the diseases.

Sunshine and the teacher held an "open forum" for any problems or questions we had. Trustees set up a table in the center of the factory, where they sat. "Does anybody have questions?"

Only Junior did. "I'm eighty-eight. I can't see or hear well. What can I do?"

"You can sweep and clean the factory," Sunshine replied.

The night watchman said our factory was too loud and wanted us to be quieter. There wasn't much he could do about 130 unsupervised adults locked in a forced-labor camp. I didn't see him telling the crazy people in the wing next to us to quiet down. They yelled for hours. Sometimes I heard one nut in particular shouting nonsense at the top of his lungs.

"He's been shouting for over a year," Big Face said, then gave me an antibiotic and a painkiller before bed.

* * *

I didn't leave the factory for days or sometimes weeks. The only time I saw the sun was through a window. At least in the cells, we walked to and from the factory daily. It wasn't much, but I was outside momentarily.

We showered in front of an open window. Some folks chose not to at all or went as long as they could between showers. You'd be surprised. It wasn't uncommon to hear about dudes going days or even a week between showers. Usually, they only took action if their neighbors complained about the smell. We couldn't wear socks with flip-flops because the restroom floor was usually wet. My feet were cold all the time. It was a bitch taking shits, especially in the morning or at night. We stripped down to our undershirts, and the toilet was below a window.

My body felt like it was disintegrating. My blisters and infections leaked blood, pus, and a clear liquid. Open wounds all over my extremities. Rashes and scabies. I couldn't believe these diseases were normal Taiwanese penal problems. This was cruel and unusual punishment. Sunshine said my skin problems were because I wasn't getting enough sun. During lunch, he sat me outside for twenty-five minutes. As if a half hour of sun would be a cure-all. But he meant well, I had to give him that.

* * *

Big Auntie, who lived in Taipei, visited a week before Lunar New Year. On the way to visitation, I saw inmates from Factories 1 and 2 practice a dragon dance with a CO overseer. It was the first time Big Auntie had gotten to see me. They'd turned her away last time because they didn't believe we were related. That was early October. I was so happy to see her.

She has short Mary Tyler Moore hair, fierce eyes, a short nose, and an authoritative voice. "When the official weighed the food, I saw it was less than two kilograms. I went back and bought more so you'd have enough to pass around to all your—"

I beamed.

She chuckled, then zipped her jacket up. "Are you cold? Do you have enough winter clothes and blankets?"

"I'm good on those, but I wanted to stock up for the New Year."

"That's why I came. I figured you'd be running low with the holiday."

"Thanks. You saved my ass, coming today."

She understood. I was blessed to have family.

Looking at an empty drawer on an empty stomach was disheartening. I kept opening it, wishing food would magically appear. When I received the afternoon commissary, I wanted to jump for joy, but I realized where I was.

My TV arrived, and Nicky sent some books from upstairs. This piece-of-shit TV improved my quality of life so much. I turned on and tuned out.

Big Face saw me watching TV after work, sat on his mat next to mine, and asked, "What do you watch?"

I sat up and took a headphone out, "Sports, when it's on. The news. Music videos. Mostly local TV."

"Local TV isn't good." He rummaged for his TV, found it, and unrolled his headphones. "It's mostly game shows where the contestants are D-list local comedians, models, and influencers doing ridiculous, repetitive tasks."

I nodded. "I watch *Kangsi Coming* (康熙来了), *The Hunger Game* (飢餓遊戲), *Mr. Player* (綜藝玩很大), *Genius Go Go Go* (天才衝衝衝), and *Super Followers* (小明星大跟班). My favorite is probably *Rap of China* (中国嘻哈)."

He chuckled, "That's not even a Taiwanese show. It's from the mainland. Any girls catch your eye?"

"I like Albee (劉璟瑩) and Ah-yuan (郭源元)."

"You have eclectic tastes, and women like that—"

144

"We can't live on love," I interrupted.

"Ah-yuan, she's a model for Breeze department stores. Breeze is the best—"

"Why are they the best?"

"They're the only department store whose bags we don't make." We chuckled.

I sniffled. "When do we close these windows?"

"It's been cold this past week, huh? We only close them when Sunshine says. All I can tell you is wear more layers or buy extra blankets."

*   *   *

The factory had a Secret Santa gift exchange for CNY on January 25— four days before the new year. The commissary limit was 200 NTD, so I threw in a bag of black sesame mix. Best gift was a pack of cigarettes from Sunshine. Lucky that Big Auntie had come two days before, or I'd have had nothing to contribute. My name was called third, and I picked the biggest bag left. I got a bag of crackers and a box of Choco pie. I shared it with my row. Everybody did the same when they received theirs.

As I watched everybody eat, I suddenly felt homesick. I didn't expect to be locked up for one, let alone two CNYs. It's a time to be with family. I wished I were eating with my family instead of a bunch of lowlifes. This second CNY showed me the importance of family and what the holiday truly meant. I felt like crawling into a hole whenever my family visited because the government had moved me so far. It took them all day, and I didn't want them to waste a holiday visiting me—even though I needed them desperately.

Some of these guys weren't so lucky. I saw envy in their eyes whenever their buddies had visitors and they didn't. My family and I didn't always see eye to eye, but I couldn't imagine them forgetting about me, letting me rot. Hard to feel blessed in a place like this, but meeting people who had it worse than I did made me count what I had, instead of what I didn't.

It looked festive after the trustees finished decorating. Outside, one of the old guys did calligraphy. Sunshine had him work on scrolls to hang on the walls. The scrolls were pink because they ran out of red paper. This was the Year of the Rooster. Paper roosters were all over the walls, and

Sunshine taped a sequined rooster on his desk. The crème de la crème was a twenty-foot dragon made of paper, cardboard, wire, and cloth that hung from the ceiling. The tail obstructed my seat's TV view.

Stupid dragon. I didn't know why they decorated. It was such a tease. Like setting up for a party we couldn't attend. I couldn't wait for them to be taken down. The decorations just reminded me of the things I was missing out on. I tried not to look.

* * *

The next day, dragon dancers came to the factory: two dragons, two dancers in each dragon, inmates from Factories 1 and 2, accompanied by guards and inmates banging drums. The dragon dancers were for good luck and prosperity and to ward off evil spirits. They entered and danced in the middle and on tables. When they finished, Sunshine put a red envelope and a pack of cigarettes in the dragon's mouth. They danced from factory to factory.

* * *

CNY Eve. The prison passed out buckets of candy and snacks to each row that morning. I felt like a kid on Halloween. I stuffed a bunch of goodies in my pocket and searched for extras. People walked around and handed out gifts to their friends. I received cigarettes, a file folder, and a jar of hot sauce. It was weird to get gifts instead of red envelopes, but fuck it—it felt good to receive anything. I gave milk teas in return; I had nothing else. I wasn't prepared to give or receive anything.

Sunshine let us karaoke for the rest of the day.

That whole week, but especially those two days, people had lots of visitors. I ate outside food for lunch and dinner every day. People wanted to make sure their loved ones behind the walls had everything they needed. Most of all, they wanted us to feel love and compassion. If loved ones couldn't visit, some sent food.

Sosa received a letter from his son with pictures of his grandson's third-place finish at a tae kwon do tournament. His grandson had written a note that said, "Happy New Year, Grandpa. When you gonna come home so you can play with me?"

Tears ran down Sosa's cheeks as he read it. Was this how I made Pops feel? After reading, he put his head down and wept silently.

Yes, we committed crimes and deserve to be punished, but our families aren't guilty.

Everybody broke into groups with their friends, opened snacks and drinks, and had a party. I was on some painkillers I'd taken earlier. Right before dinner, the watchman on duty wished everybody a happy New Year, good health, parole, and the promise we'd never come back. Then, he randomly pulled numbers out of a hat and gifted the raffle winners a cigarette. My number was called. I was on fire. The watchman knew I was an ABC because when I collected my cigarette, he wished me a happy New Year in English. I wished him good health.

That night, I ate so much junk food I got a stomachache. One guy ate so much he threw up. I was surprised we had so much left over, so we saved it for the next day. I couldn't see the fireworks, but I heard them. It sounded like a war zone.

* * *

On Lunar New Year, I used the restroom in the middle of the night. I noticed Howard crouched in a squatter, pretending to pee, but silently weeping. He was young, and it was his first time. He probably missed his family. I understood; I missed mine too. It'd been over two years since I'd seen my mom. We made eye contact, and I put my hand on his shoulder as I walked past, like Randy had done for me.

Growing up, I was a shitty big brother. Too young for so much responsibility. As I get older, I feel like I'm getting the hang of this mentor thing. I didn't expect an award, but it felt good to console him. I thought I was doing a good deed.

He wiped a tear and looked at me.

I nodded on my way out. I'd been in his shoes. Shit, I still was in his shoes.

* * *

"You passed out with your TV on," Big Face said when I woke the next day. "I turned it off and put it away for you."

I smiled. "Thank you, and my bad, man. You're a stand-up dude." I offered him a cigarette.

Heisenberg invited me to chill with him and his friends that night.

I was reluctant. "I feel bad because I don't have anything to contribute. We ate all my commissary over these past couple days. I didn't know we'd planned to eat and drink so long. I would've bought more. It's bad manners to come empty-handed."

"Think of it this way: if you were locked up in the US and a Taiwanese guy was there, would you give him food if he didn't have any?" He opened his arms.

"Of course." I straightened my posture. "There ain't that many of us, and we gotta stick together."

"Atta boy. So come, eat up, and don't be polite. We have plenty. We won't finish it all."

I went, and Heisenberg handed me a sandwich—black sesame, ground beef, tuna, strawberry jam. I took a big bite. It tasted as strange as it sounded.

He stared at me. "How is it?"

I gulped. "Good." It was the only thing to say.

There was one other kid among the group, Heisenberg's friend. He was a nice guy but had a mean-looking face. I nicknamed him Kung Fu Guy because, every night before bed, he did whatever old Asian people do in the park in the mornings. Some kind of martial art. He was half a head shorter than me, in his midtwenties, polite, and shredded. Think Bruce Lee's body with a six pack instead of an eighteen pack.

As we snacked, I asked Heisenberg, "How long you been here?"

"Thirteen years, with another five or six, at least, before parole."

He'd be over seventy when he got out. "You don't seem like a meth cook. How'd you get started in all this?"

"My family supplies the chemicals for manufacturing, among other stuff. At first, some new clients asked for chemicals. After a while, they asked for a warehouse to make it, then they taught me how to make it. By the time I knew what it was, I was in too deep. Been doing this for thirty years since."

I nicknamed him Heisenberg out of respect and affection. He gave me Randy vibes. Leadership isn't talk—it's action, it's influence, its accountability. But that's not all. It's kind and generous as well. I don't think it's hard, but people make it harder than it has to be. Randy and Heisenberg were in charge. Any problems went to them. Credit or accolades went there too. Too many people want to be Big Brother without being a big brother. You can't have it both ways. That was me when I was young. I wanted all the good and none of the bad.

Heisenberg wasn't the first meth cook I'd met inside, and he wouldn't be the last. But he was the only one who talked about warehouses and wholesale ingredients. I bet he was one of the first guys who'd done it. He was almost seventy. Thirty years ago would have been the '90s. No wonder he knew so many people. He'd probably hooked up most of them. I was fortunate to have him looking out for me.

CHAPTER 11

TAIPEI RETIREMENT CASTLE

Whenever we submit our will to someone else's opinion, a part of us dies.

—Lauryn Hill

February 1, 2017

The last day off for Lunar New Year. Almost had a week off for the holiday. It was great. I dreaded every factory day. I didn't understand why this factory did more work than Factory 11, which though it was full of kids. The seniors didn't have the eyesight or coordination to do the more demanding jobs. To do the work, I felt like I had to take my brain out of my head and put it in my drawer. Mostly, we folded paper bags, but there were different ones.

Sometimes we cut loose threads off the bags, and they had loose threads all over. They handed out scissors, usually just to the kids and non-senile. The scissors sucked anyway. They were dull and rusted and didn't cut cleanly. Sometimes I needed to stab a thread three or four times.

Often a few bags arrived inside out. Those were a hassle. We flipped them back then folded them. The bag-flippers wore gloves because the bags gave them rashes; they were cheap from China. I didn't know what material gave people rashes. These bags were for everyday citizens. I wondered how they took care of the rash issue before getting them into the hands of customers. Or maybe they didn't, and people just didn't notice.

The biggest bitch, by far, was the drawstring bags. We hand-drew the strings, one by one, with a tool that looked like a chopstick with a bent top. A shoelace was hooked to the top and stuck in until it came out the other side, then tied into a knot. Only the young and middle-aged could do this job. It was tedious and time consuming. Three or four seniors per row (at least) sat to the side and tried not to get in the way.

We attached tags to the handles and folded the handles into the bags. We stuck stickers on the tags. They were often started at another factory, and we put on the finishing touches.

Being a slave was draining. The focus was production. Work was non-stop, with people yelling at us to go faster and faster. If I was tired after a long day of slaving, the relics I slaved with must have been exhausted. Everybody was older than Mr. Burns. I thought the retirement age in Taiwan was sixty-five. If these geriatrics were past retirement age, why'd they still have to work? Was working them to death the goal? In Taiwan, once we commit a crime, are we not people anymore? It was unfair; we all got paid the same amount, but we did an unequal amount of work.

The senile inmates frustrated me. I did more to cover for them—I double-checked their work. When these geezers messed up, they refused to apologize or accept responsibility. They'd yell at us for yelling at them. These dudes had to be constantly reminded of what they needed to do and how to do it. Overlords accommodated those who couldn't work fast or see well; they collected our finished bags, swept the floor, or did whatever menial task needed doing. Junior collected the finished bags. He accidentally dropped them sometimes, so we'd have to refold them. One of the slower guys sat on the bags so they wouldn't rustle. Old dudes couldn't work fast. We were backed up often; it resembled the chocolate factory scene from *I Love Lucy*.

Instead of stools, we sat on benches. They were uncomfortable and, even worse, inconvenient. Some guys tripped and fell because they couldn't lift their leg over the bench. It caused a lot more noise and arguments over how far or close it should be. I thought because most of them were old, it'd be more peaceful, but what did I know? People argued all the time. Mofos never wanted to admit when they were wrong, so they'd yell louder. The more wrong they were, the louder they yelled.

It was noisy at night. These dudes smoked their whole lives, so come bedtime, it sounded like they coughed up a lung. Made me want to quit. And the snoring! Some of these mofos snored so loud it put me to shame. The key was to fall asleep first. Whoever fell asleep first won.

I wished there were more kids. These old folks got on my nerves. Half needed a nurse instead of a CO. If there were any justice, they'd be released on "medical grounds." They couldn't even go about their day without help. How dangerous could they be? Taiwan's solution was to have young prisoners care for the old in place of actual caregivers. Old prisoners shouldn't have been there if Taiwan knew it couldn't take care of them. The kids there were janitors, dishwashers, cleaners, movers, caregivers—whatever they needed. All unofficial, of course.

I felt taken for granted; a simple thank-you would've gone a long way. I was tired of cleaning up after them. Tired of dudes leaning on me because they couldn't walk on their own. Tired of pushing wheelchairs. Tired of being woken up at all hours of the night. Tired of smelling urine when I woke up in the morning. Tired of being expected to be a caregiver for cantankerous old men. Tired of doing the government's job for them.

* * *

On February 9, I had court. They only told me about it the day before. I expected them to bus me to Kaohsiung for court, then bus me back to Taipei for my sentence, but I suppose common sense prevailed in Taiwan for once. I didn't know what the right way was; everything they did to me seemed wrong.

When I received my clothes in the morning, I asked the trustee, "Are they washed?"

"They are."

My court clothes were a light-tan short-sleeve polo, dark-gray track pants, a gray windbreaker, and a pair of worn, dirty slip-on shoes. "Am I going to get picked up before or after breakfast?"

"After." He turned and walked away.

At least I got to eat breakfast. Courthouse food was terrible.

Court was in the afternoon. There was a judge, a court secretary, and an officer. The judge showed me the evidence and asked, "How do you plead?"

"Guilty. What's the point of this if I already pleaded guilty in Kaohsiung?"

"That was a Kaohsiung police station. This is Taoyuan court."

"I want a translator."

"You don't need one."

"Do I get a lawyer?"

"You don't need one for this case."

"Are you sure? Feels like I should have one."

"Do you want to settle out of court?"

"How much to settle?"

"Over one million NTD."

"I don't have any money."

"Okay."

"Will there be any more court dates after this?"

"No. This is your first and last court appearance. Do you have any final words?"

"No."

And that was the end of that.

We left as soon as I returned to the cell. Guards cuffed us in pairs. Two of the guys were accomplices and weren't allowed to be next to each other. Four dudes sat in the second compartment, and I sat with one accomplice in the third. As he pulled out of the garage, the driver scraped the bus against the wall. I kept my mouth shut. I wasn't in the mood to be told to shut up.

The dungeon was only a ten-minute drive from the courthouse. On the way back to the factory, some guy from Factory 13 was with me. I told him to say what's up to my friend One.

Jurassic World was playing when I walked in. Justin gave me a curry pastry and an instant noodle. My people told me they'd had a full day of work and that the movie had just begun. At least I'd missed work.

I handed my court clothes back to the trustee. He looked at them like they were rotten. "Wash them first."

"Oh!" I put a hand to my head. "That's why they were clean when I received them."

He nodded. "Whoever uses them has to wash them, then give them back. Return them tomorrow or the next day."

I didn't know why the government was hellbent on fucking with me. Didn't they have real criminals to catch or better things to spend their time and resources on? They didn't have money for this. I chuckled, imagining Taiwan going into debt just so they could harass me. They don't fuck with nobodies.

*   *   *

Since last month, I'd been complaining about my skin to trustees and officials whenever they'd listen.

"The prison didn't cause it," Sunshine told me. "A lack of sun did." I disagreed, but now and then he'd let me sit outside for twenty-five minutes after lunch.

Lately, I'd stopped complaining because my skin had improved. I didn't think the sun had anything to do with it, but I wasn't going to complain about sitting outside. After lunch, Sunshine summoned me, looked at my skin, and said it was beautiful. I didn't need to sit outside anymore. I showed him my penis.

"You'll need to see the doctor."

Good news: I received letters from a bunch of my people back home. I got five all at once. It was nice to know my friends hadn't forgotten about me. It was easy to feel forgotten here. I felt like something on the bottom of somebody's shoe. And the worst part? It wasn't even somebody interesting.

Bad news: no money in my commissary. My seven doctor visits cost a total of 6,392 NTD, which was finally deducted from my account all at once. It was almost a month after my first one. I wished they did it after each time instead of all at once.

*   *   *

I received a letter from my mom that said she was coming to Taiwan. She'd be landing in a week, on February 26, and intended to go directly to me from the airport. I'd told her before I surrendered that I didn't want her to visit. It could only be a five-minute visit. All the time on the plane, train, and automobile wasn't worth it for five minutes. I'd be fine. I was happy to see her. It had been over a year.

Justin came by after work. He looked over my shoulder. "Whatchu doing?" He sat in the empty seat next to mine.

I didn't bother looking up. "Jotting some notes in a journal. I'm going to write a book about my experiences."

Justin sighed. "Honestly, I was like you. I didn't know how they lived until I experienced it. I mean, yeah, it's fucked up, but once I leave, I'm never coming back."

I shook my head.

"Most Taiwanese people will think it's good. That we're criminals and deserve what we get."

I posed like Obama did in his hope posters. "I'm out for the noble causes of truth and justice, on some Captain America–type shit." I looked around. "I'm also out for the not-so-noble causes of dicking people who dicked me along the way."

He grinned. We chuckled.

I smirked. "I'm the carnival barker from hell."

"I bet Taiwan didn't think you'd respond like this." He stood up. "Let's go smoke a cigarette, Captain ABC."

* * *

The scab on my penis broke open. It fucking hurt. My poor penis. It didn't commit any crime, so why was it being punished?

My time in Factory 15 made me think about my health and mortality. Part of the reason I was in this mess was thinking rules didn't apply to me—that I was young and invincible. I wasn't. I drank, smoked, and did drugs. At some point, all of this was going to catch up to me. Being in prison was proof actions have consequences. These old guys made me want to change more than any lecture or punishment ever would. Some of these dudes would die here.

I wouldn't say this place scared me straight. I don't think prison scares anybody straight. These geriatric career criminals were the Ghosts of Christmas Future, and being around them put a fear in me like I'd never felt before. It was hard to explain; being there didn't scare me, dying didn't scare me, but the possibility of dying there put the fear of God in me. The Ghosts of Christmas Future weren't death. They were unfulfilled potential.

* * *

My cigarette requests were voided because I had no money. Being incarcerated without money reminded me of my humanity. To shower, you needed soap and shampoo. Things to write, you needed things to write with and things to write on. If I couldn't pay for stuff, I'd be the one doing chores instead of hiring. This was the first time I'd contemplated being broke. Wasn't a good feeling.

Before lunch, I had a visitor. It was a name I didn't recognize in Chinese, and I wondered who it could be. Turned out to be my friend from Monterey Park, Kobe. He'd put his cousin's name, Josh, on the visitor log. What a pleasant surprise.

I smiled when I saw him and sat down. "Whatchu doing in Taiwan?"

He grinned from ear to ear. "Visiting family."

"How'd you know where I was?"

"I got ahold of your mom," he said proudly. "She gave me the address and told me to tell you she's coming next week."

"I got her letter." I nodded at his cousin. "You brought Josh with you?" Both were wide-eyed, like deer in the headlights.

"Yeah, but I didn't tell him where we were going." He laughed. "I said, 'Let's go here,' and gave him the address. When we rolled up, he asked, 'What are we doing here?' We're here to visit Will."

I looked at the floor. "Hate to ask, but you got some ends you can throw in my commissary? I'm short on funds because of doctor visits."

He smiled. "Bruh, it's already in."

"Thanks, man." I beamed. "I'll hit you back when I'm in LA"

He waved me off. "Don't worry about it."

"Did you bring any food?"

On cue, an official came by and dropped off a big bag of food. My eyes lit up. Then the line disconnected.

I couldn't stop smiling the rest of the day. He brought fried chicken, a burger, a pork sandwich, and some much-needed cash. He didn't even know what it meant for him to take time out of his vacation to visit. Commissary came in the afternoon. I didn't have room for it all and had to give some away.

* * *

The last week of February, the avian flu spread throughout Taiwan. The prison had lots of chicken and duck because nobody else dared to eat it; they got it cheap. We had chicken wings for dinner. Each person was allowed one wing, but a bunch of people didn't touch theirs. I ate seven. *I ain't a bird. I ain't scared of the bird flu.*

My diet had changed since I arrived at this factory—since I'd first surrendered, even. At first it was hard to get used to the food because it was so terrible. But I didn't want to drink soda, eat chips, and instant noodles all day every day. They didn't give us a lot of meat. My diet was mostly vegetables (they provided) and fruit (we bought) based with meat and carbs whenever I could. I used to eat until I was full. In prison, I ate until I wasn't hungry. At first I was hungry all the time. It wasn't so bad anymore, but I could always eat. A fruit and vegetable diet is the way to go for a long and healthy life.

* * *

"What's up with you? You've been out of it all day," Heisenberg said as he lit his cigarette after dinner.

"My folks were supposed to land today." I said in between puffs.

"Ah. Be patient and relax. They'll come."

"I know. I'm excited to see them. It's been a while. Felt like our relationship has changed since I've been here." I took a few puffs. "Before, every time we talked seemed to end in a fight. Maybe it's a turning point. If so, that alone would be worth the two-year sentence." I flicked the butt into the squatter.

My parents never came. I wondered if something happened. I was so worried I had to take some pills to calm down before bed.

"You acted like a fool last night," Justin said the next day during the after-breakfast smoke. "Brushed your teeth for fifteen minutes."

"Because of the pills." I shrugged. "Maybe a little nerves."

He took a puff. "I had to come tell you to stop."

"I blacked out. I passed out with the TV on again. Big Face put it away for me." I looked in Big Face's direction. "What a stand-up crook."

* * *

"You talked in your sleep." Big Face said the following morning when I woke up.

I rubbed my eyes. "What'd I say?"

He shrugged. "It was in English."

"Did I wake you up?"

"Nah, I was already awake. You were probably thinking of your mom."

I wondered why they hadn't come yet. They should've landed already. I hoped nothing had happened. If the plane crashed, I'd have heard about it on the news. I felt helpless.

During a break, I'd just put the last of my snack into my mouth when Sunshine announced, "Break's over."

Howard strutted over to me and snickered. "It's work time, not eating-bread time."

I was working. I don't know about him, but I could work and chew at the same time. Not sure if snark translated into Chinese, but I replied, "Yes, boss. Sorry, boss."

Later, during work, I noticed Howard eating. I went up to him and mocked, "It's work time, not eating time."

"Yeah, so?" He scowled. "We're not the same."

Fucking Howard. Didn't know what I ever did to him. I think when I saw him cry during Chinese New Year, he thought I thought he was a punk, and I did. I'd tried to help, but he took it the wrong way. Meh, whatever. I'd tried to be nice, but if that was the way he wanted to handle it, so be it.

I held my fist to my eye and pretended to cry. He walked away in a huff.

* * *

After class on March 3, Small Auntie visited.

"Don't worry, your parents are fine." She pushed her glasses further up her nose. "Your maternal grandpa passed on February twenty-second. Your parents were supposed to fly out on the twenty-fourth, but because of his passing, they never boarded the plane. They refunded their tickets and planned for the funeral. I came to tell you as soon as possible. I knew you must be wondering why they never showed up."

I couldn't believe he was gone. My eyes watered, and I hung my head. I didn't know what to say. There was nothing I could do in here. Was ignorance bliss? Would it have been better to not even know until I was out? I wanted to do some drugs.

"Okay," I said, and sat with a thousand-yard stare for the rest of the visit.

I felt bad for Small Auntie; she was always the bearer of bad news. My mom was a soldier: her oldest son was locked up abroad, her husband had recently had a heart attack, and her father passed away. Sometimes I wondered how she did it. I got my strength from her.

My grandpa and I were close. He used to own a beef-noodle soup restaurant called Noodle King. When I was a kid, every Saturday morning, I'd work as a busboy, mopping or sweeping. As I got older, I learned how to use the cash register. At that time, he'd beaten prostate cancer. For the last few years, he was bedridden in a hospice after suffering a stroke. His passing was for the best. Spending all day in a hospital bed was no way to live.

Other inmates told me a death in the family was the worst thing that could happen while inside. I'm inclined to agree. I remembered how bad Crazy-Eyes was. Felt wrong to say, but I was a little happy when I heard. I hated seeing him laid up in the bed all the time. It wasn't how I wanted to remember him.

After hours, Justin and Carmelo came by to console me.

"If a family member passes, they usually let you call home," Justin said. "Submit a request tomorrow, and see what happens."

It'd be nice to speak to my mom again.

I couldn't sleep. I needed pills to self-medicate.

* * *

"Do you regret what you've done?" Sosa asked during a snack break.

I shook my head. "Not even a little. It's legal in my country, and I don't understand Taiwan's laws. It was a miscommunication." I opened a milk tea and took a sip. I offered him one.

He waved it away. "Too sweet."

"Only got two years. So be it." I opened a bag of crackers. "I won't do it again, but I don't regret it. Do you?"

"Yeah, I do." He slumped in his chair and rested his hands on the table. "Every day."

He was the only person I'd met in prison who told me he regretted it. A few told me they were innocent. Others had said it was a matter of wrong place, wrong time. Then, there were people like me: guilty as sin and proud of it.

"Why?" I asked.

"Because I got too big. I couldn't supervise or control everybody under me." He stared at a stain on the wall. "I regret getting too big."

I nodded, pretended to understand, and took a sip of my milk tea.

"You know you're lucky it's just you. I have a wife, kids, grandkids—a lot of people who depend on me. I have things to do when I get out." He stared out the window. "You just have to worry about you."

"True." I looked around at all the dinosaurs in the factory. "Seen some of you guys worry, and it must suck." I threw a cracker in the air and caught it with my mouth. "Suppose I'm lucky."

"How old are you?"

"Thirty-two. By the time I'm out, thirty-three."

He lifted his hands. "About time to settle down and get married."

"My grandma said something similar. 'If you had a wife and kid, you wouldn't have time to be out causing trouble.'"

"She's right."

Old-people logic.

Because of the culture, most kids lived at home until they're married. Guys went from being taken care of by their mom, to their girlfriend, to their wives. Boys were treated like princes and preferred over girls. Some of these dudes had zero hygiene or life skills. It was a huge disservice to them. They didn't know how to do the most basic chores because they'd been taken care of their whole lives. If they had money, it'd be okay—they could pay somebody. But if they were broke, they'd better learn quick.

One dude who didn't wash his clothes said he didn't have extra to wear while washing. He was the same size as trustee #1, so the trustee gave him clothes. Turned out the dude soaked his clothes in water and dried them, no soap. "See, there are bubbles. I'm washing it."

* * *

Reporters came to do a story on the Taipei Retirement Castle. Sunshine proudly displayed the plaques on the wall and told them a bunch of propaganda. "They love it here. It's like heaven. They love doing work; it keeps them busy and from getting bored. Plus, they're moving all day instead of doing nothing."

I didn't love work and didn't know anybody who fucking did. I'd rather rot. They took a few pictures and left. We weren't allowed to talk to them.

I itched all over and scabs randomly appeared on my back and legs.

* * *

March 10 was Sunshine's last day! Huzzah! On Monday, he'd transfer to Factory 6. He gave a long speech about the importance of health. I thought we'd throw a party because it was his last day, but no. Business as usual—work all day.

Grandpa's funeral was the same day. No chance the Taiwanese government would let me attend; I didn't even ask. Hopefully they'd let me call my mom. It'd be the least they could do.

* * *

The Pimp—guess what he was serving time for—made his special noodles: milk powder, corn chowder powder, two cans of beef, one can sweet corn, and eight packs of instant noodles. Tasted like alfredo sauce. I liked it when the Pimp made noodles. The menu was always different—like a pop-up restaurant.

It was a weekend. I had a nice dinner with my friends, did some pills to put a cherry on top of a not-so-bad sundae.

I overindulged and woke up with two ID badges. Must've taken the extra one by mistake when I'd grabbed mine from the restroom. It was an old man's level 2 badge. I hoped nobody found out I took it. Didn't want to get yelled at.

I wasn't sure what to do with it. I couldn't keep it, and I couldn't put it back. People would wonder why I had it. The more time passed, the more trouble I was going to be in. I put the badge in the palm of my hand when I moved tables before breakfast. When I finished, I walked away, and it looked like the badge had been left on the table overnight. Weird that nobody tried to look for it. He probably didn't even know he'd lost it.

* * *

While Big Face and I unrolled our mats for the night, he whispered, "My parole was granted."

My eyes bulged out of their sockets. "For real?"

He nodded.

"That's huge! Congrats!" I was getting louder and louder. "You know when you're getting out?" I patted him on the back.

"Thanks, and keep it to yourself. I don't want a lot of people to know because I have to do another six months for a use charge. They made me change numbers too. It was 781. My new one is 5888."

I rubbed my chin. "At least all those eights mean it's good luck!"

"Well." He sighed. "They also demoted me from level 1 back to 4 and are trying to take away my TV and radio."

I didn't understand the logic behind him switching numbers or demoting him to level 4. Wouldn't that mean extra paperwork?

"Sunshine probably would've let me keep my TV"—he looked toward the guard's desk—"but Monkei doesn't know me and is a real stickler for rules."

CO Sun was nicknamed Monkei because the Monkey King's name is Sun Wukong (although this guy was more cannon fodder than king). He was from the freshmen dorms, and this was his first time supervising a factory. I hoped he wasn't a total dick. Then again, even if he were, there was nothing I could do about it. He seemed by the book, and he took the time to interview everybody individually on his first day.

While Big Face figured it out, I loaned him my TV.

* * *

I bumped into Bruce, one of my old cellies from Factory 11, while waiting to see the doctor.

He sat next to me. "I'm in Factory 14 now. BaiMao sent everybody in the cell to different factories on his last day. David's the room chief, and the only one left. James is in the kitchen, making bread."

I nodded. "Good for him. At least he gets to keep busy."

"He sent me to Factory 14 and transferred there himself." Bruce slouched in his seat and sighed. "We're in the same factory again."

"Shitty luck. Still, it's not a contest"—I showed him my rashes—"but I win. This place gave me scabies."

"Ah, it's no big deal." He elbowed me. "Everybody gets it eventually. It'll go away."

I frowned. "It doesn't make it okay."

When I saw the doctor, he didn't even look up from his paperwork. He said, "Okay, okay, okay," and gave me whatever I asked for. It can't be drug abuse if a doctor prescribes it.

Took some Codeine to help me sleep, courtesy of the quack.

* * *

They approved my call home. Realizing I'd get to speak to my mom made me smile.

I called, but nobody picked up. Tried three times, then left a voice mail. They'd taken me to the phone at 3:30 p.m. Taiwan time, which was 12:30 a.m. back home. They didn't consider the time difference.

When I got back to the factory, I asked Monkei, "I'd like to call in the morning, which is nighttime in LA."

"You get two more attempts," he grunted. "If you can't get ahold of them, you have to reapply."

Yeah, that sounded about right.

CHAPTER 12
THE DAYS ARE JUST PACKED

If there's a heaven, I can't find the stairway.

—Tariq Trotter

April 1, 2017

"You bumped into me when I was sleeping," said the old man who slept across from Howard.

Whenever Howard got yelled at, his face turned red and his eyes watered. Looked like he was trying to hold back tears. This time, he could've apologized and it would've been the end. Instead, this fool picked up the old man's glasses and threw them across the factory.

The old man's friend retrieved his glasses while Howard tore into him, and the commotion woke everybody else up.

The kerfuffle was the talk of the factory the rest of the morning. I was quietly pleased the ruckus had nothing to do with me, for once.

"What happened between you and Howard?" the Pimp asked me during a smoke break.

Dammit, spoke too soon. All roads still led back to me. I chuckled. "We had a moment."

"Something happened between you and Howard?" Justin chimed in. "How come I'm the last to find out?"

"Because there's nothing to tell." I shrugged. "We got into an argument about work a few weeks ago. It is what it is." I took a puff and flicked the butt into the squatter. "He's a kid. If I fucked him up, it'd be child abuse."

Anything involving Howard made my blood boil. I wished I could be the one to remind him of his place, but I had enough problems. Pills calmed me down.

Whenever anything good or bad happened, pills had become my go-to. Self-medication, addiction, call it what you will. I put it on the list of things to worry about when I got out.

*　*　*

Justin came by during work. "Kung Fu Guy is in the black room."

"What? Since when? Why?"

"During his banana class. For class, other people question you about your case."

"Doesn't seem helpful." I thought about it. "Sounds like a ticking time bomb."

"It is. Anyway, Kung Fu Guy was talking, and this guy was talking shit to him, like, 'Who do you know? Where you from?' Tempers flared, they yelled at each other and needed to be separated. Now he's in the black room."

"Shit. Can he come back?"

"Yeah, when he's done. It'll be about a month."

"If he's going to the black room regardless, he may as well have socked the dude." I mimicked a haymaker.

Justin pretended to dodge. "That's what I said! As long as he's getting sent, he should've hit him. It's not worth it for yelling."

"Didn't Monkei say if anybody gets sent to the black room, they can't come back?"

"It's what he says." He rolled his eyes. "But trust me, he'll be back."

I wished I'd gotten to know Kung Fu Guy better, but he didn't smoke. Most of our interactions happened when we hung out with Heisenberg or when all the kids shared food.

After we put the tables away, I was called for visitation. Big and Small Auntie had come. Great! I needed commissary and money. They deposited the max into my account and maxed out commissary too. I'd be good until next month. It was great to see them both. This time away had shown me how much my family cared and how selfish I'd been.

* * *

"It's time to switch to short-sleeve shirts and shorts," Monkei announced shortly after he arrived.

Finally! It was too hot to be in denim long sleeves and jeans. It was annoying carrying them around when not worn.

"There's a job opening at 7-Eleven, moving boxes."

They have a 7-Eleven?

"The requirements are less than one year remaining before release, no infractions, and no drug-dealers or sex offenders."

Oh shit, I qualified! I applied, of course—anything was better than making paper bags. The rest of the day, all I thought about was how sweet a job at 7-Eleven would be. Toward the end, however, I got depressed about how sad my life had become if I was wishing for a job at 7-Eleven.

* * *

"Do you know you're singing the prison song wrong?" Sosa said one morning.

Every penitentiary had a song. We'd learned it upon arrival at the factory and sang it after the first roll call in the morning. Some inmate wrote it.

"I don't know the words." I smirked. "I make sounds and try to sound like everybody else."

He scrunched his face. His wrinkles had wrinkles. "Nobody ever showed you the lyrics?"

"They did, but I just move my mouth. As long as it sounds like everybody else, I'm okay." I rubbed my chin. "How can you hear me over everybody else?"

"You're right behind me. You sing into my ear." Sosa was kind enough to write the lyrics. I looked at them for a moment, to be polite, then put them away. I didn't give a fuck about the song.

* * *

At night, Justin and I smoked and listened to his radio. Hip-hop was on, and he loaned me an earpiece. I forgot how much I missed music.

Never thought I'd be friends with a serial sexual predator, but there we were. Back when I was on trial, I was pissed they'd put me in with a rapist because it felt like they'd tried to take advantage of me when I didn't know any better. "Oh, let's put the rapist in with the foreigner." I was also a little scared to be in a cell alone with a rapist. I was constantly looking over my shoulder. This place was weird, and it was getting to me. It made for strange bedfellows. Meth users got on my last nerve, yet Heisenberg was a meth cook. I was mad the prison put me in with a dude who did one rape, but here I was, listening to the radio with the Taiwanese Bill Cosby. Simply being friends with him made me a piece of shit, I know that. But it was nice to have somebody to converse with in English.

I'd worry about morals and character when I wasn't surrounded by lowlifes. I needed all the allies I could get. It was like the War of the Roses.

* * *

I applied for a radio the following Monday. I don't know why I didn't buy one when I'd bought my TV.

After work in the morning, trustees collected the scissors. Row 4 was short a pair. They searched and searched, emptied their drawers and moved the tables. Justin had handed out and collected the scissors, so they pestered him. "Are you sure you counted right?" The row 4 chief said one dude hadn't given them back. Monkei tossed his drawer and didn't find them. The wing chief checked the cameras.

The wing chief came back an hour later, scolded the row—specifically the row chief—for twenty minutes, and left. A mob of guards congregated outside the factory shortly after.

"Stop what you're doing, line up, and exit the factory single file," Monkei announced.

On the way out, a guard ran us over with a metal detector. He was a moron. Every inmate set off the metal detector because he accidentally swung the wand by his waist, so his own belt set it off. Another CO frisked those who set off the detector.

When they finished, an official announced, "Line up in rows of two to be searched again before you enter."

I stood behind the row 4 chief. There was blood on the seat of his shorts. It looked like Jack the Ripper had killed a whore in his pants. The old man next to me noticed it too and told a guard, "Look at all the blood." They pulled the chief out of line, cavity searched him, and found the scissors. He'd had them the whole time and keister'd them when guards showed up. One escorted him to the black room while another ordered an inmate to pack his belongings. I never saw the chief again.

Because of his age (midsixties) and severity of crime (kidnapping), the two dominant theories were attempted jailbreak or suicide. How bad are conditions when people would rather kill themselves than be here?

* * *

I received my parole paperwork. Since I couldn't apply until August, and today was April 25, it felt early. The whole thing was eight pages long. Heisenberg filled it out for me because it had to be written in Chinese, and I didn't want to take any chances.

* * *

I cut the loose threads off the bags and finished work early. Howard counted the finished bags and asked for help. I was in a good mood, so I went. When we finished, I went back to my seat for a few moments, unsure of what to do next.

He came up to me and sneered, "Why're you sitting there, you lazy fuck?"

"Pardon me?" I wanted to yell at him, but I was in a good mood because I'd hit level 2 and would receive my badge in a few days. "Wasn't sure what to do. Awaiting further instructions."

"Locked up all this time, and you don't know what to do? You're fucking lazy."

I nodded exaggeratedly. "Sorry, boss. Won't happen again."

After work, Justin came over for a chat while some guys swept. "How're you doing, bro?"

I exhaled. "Howard was nagging me about some bullshit."

Howard, who thought he understood English, overheard from his seat and yelled, "So? Whatchu gonna do about it?"

I held my fist to my eye and pretended to cry.

He slammed his fist on the table and stood up. People stared as he walked toward me. Fat Tiger and Justin got between us.

Justin pulled me aside. "Just let it go, bro. You're leaving soon—don't fuck it up. It's not worth it. You saw what happened to Kung Fu Guy. Ignore him."

I shook my head, grabbed a cigarette, and left.

"Don't take it personally. I'll talk to him later," said Fat Tiger when he found us smoking. Justin was still calming me down.

I took a puff. "You don't need to do that. It's nothing."

"It's a recurring issue with him. He needs to learn how to deal with people."

I nodded, flicked the butt into the squatter, and went back inside.

At my seat, I overheard some of the old guys talk back to Howard.

"We're not working slow on purpose," one said. "I'm old. I can't see well. Yelling at us to hurry does nothing. You get mad for no reason."

"I'm not yelling at you. I'm yelling at everybody."

"We can't work any faster," said the guy across from him.

Viva la revolution! Howard slithered away and was unusually quiet for the rest of the day.

* * *

During lunch, I bit on a stale dumpling and heard a crack. I touched my tooth, and it wiggled. Dammit. Another problem.

I was rubbing my cheek when I saw Kung Fu Guy walk in. He'd been gone for a month. His muscles were gone, and he looked malnourished.

"What's the black room like?" I asked. Felt like paparazzi, interviewing him while he was working out, but it was the only time I could get away.

"The room is small—smaller than the cells. Sleeps six people, but the guards will stuff up to seven." He horse-punched the air. "It's so crowded you can only sleep on your side."

I nodded and took notes. "Hate that. I slept on my side in the cells."

"It sucks. The first stop is pre-black room, while they review your offense." He stopped for a water break. "No pillows, blankets, or pads allowed. The prison only provides dirty, unwashed blankets. The trustees will hold your toothbrushes for you and give them back when it's time. Each cell gets a box with toothpaste, soap, shampoo, et cetera." He started punching air. "No pens allowed, only the ink from the inside. People will take the inside ink and wrap paper around it to create a handle. They kept the lights on in the cell twenty-four hours a day."

"It's hard to sleep, huh?"

"I know! It's annoying enough sleeping on my side all the time." He swung his arm in a broad sweeping motion. "The trustees take all the pots and pans and give them to the cell when it's time to eat. They're filthy. There are roaches on them when the trustees pass them out."

It felt awkward standing there, taking notes while he exercised, but I was a muckraker. The public had a right to know.

He stopped the workout and shrugged. "No slippers. We walk around barefoot, hands stuck to our sides like glue. You get to wear your own clothes, but nothing else. Shackles on whenever we're out of the cell."

I touched my ankle where they'd shackled me. "Fuck shackles. Did yours have keys?"

"They did. The next stop is the actual black room. The room has nothing, not even a storage box. No underwear allowed." He lay on the floor and did crunches.

"So you're walking around naked?" I joked and sat next to him.

"They give us clothes with no buttons. It's all one piece, like a sweater. They're dirty and unwashed. No towels either. When it's time to shower, the trustees will give you everything— soap, towels, et cetera. Then, you give it back to them when you're done. Six men share a small bar of soap. Each inmate gets two bowls, one to drink water out of and one to shower with. When it's time to wash the dishes, they'll give you laundry detergent." He started doing sit-ups. This dude hadn't broken a sweat.

I glanced toward our restroom. "What's the toilet situation like?"

"It's metal, not porcelain. They're scared we'd break it or more likely use it to commit suicide. Medicine and lotions were squeezed on the wall and used. No tubes allowed. The cell is filthy, there's nothing to clean it with. The black room is where they stick all the mentally ill."

I looked at factory's back windows. "Are those the people we sometimes hear screaming at night?"

He took a water break. "No, we hear the *really* mentally ill wing."

I felt bad for doing this when he worked out, so I gave him a milk tea and beef noodle ramen, the good stuff that came in a bowl, as a thank you. He refused, but I insisted.

The black room was just solitary confinement. However, in Taiwan, *solitary* meant confinement with other people. Basically, a smaller cell with fewer amenities. Whoever thought of that wasn't even trying. What would happen if people fought in the black room? Did they have a blacker-than-black room, or did they just shuffle them around the black rooms? They could have avoided a lot of these fights with better conditions, beds, higher pay, and more exercise. Instead of getting counseling, offenders went to the black room, then returned to gen pop angrier than ever. No wonder the black rooms were always full. It was an ouroboros of human misery.

* * *

Monkei didn't like us watching TV or movies. Instead, he put on a DVD of old people speaking to an audience of old people. I was unsure of what it was. I'd been told it extolled all the benefits of traditional Chinese culture. It couldn't be ignored because he had the volume turned all the way up like a half-assed attempt at brainwashing. He said we didn't have to pay attention, but it was so loud that, no matter what I did, it always pulled me back in.

The hardest part of being in prison, skin problems aside, was the psychological torture.

* * *

I complained about my toothache to Erik and the Malay, who was in his midforties, missing teeth, and balding with salt-and-pepper hair.

"I had three teeth pulled out by the dentist so far," Erik said. "Used to laugh at all the people with no teeth here. Now I'm one of them."

"These people came in with all their teeth. They lost them here," added the Malay.

I touched my cheek and frowned. Taiwan's health care may be world class, but her dental is not.

* * *

Received my level 2 badge. I was supposed to swap badges but kept my level 3 and told them I threw it away. I wanted to use it as my book cover.

Stanley saw my new badge when he came in to handoff paperwork. "You're level 2. Congrats! You're earning days now."

"What's that mean?" I looked down at it. "How do you know?"

"For every month here, you'll get four days off your sentence. I know because I just did your paperwork. The biggest perk of level 1 and 2 is the earned days off." He patted me on the shoulder.

Ideally, I'd be paroled before days off affected me, but good news didn't come around often, and I wasn't sure when she'd be back. I smiled. "Thanks."

The good vibes only lasted a few hours. The ointment the doctor gave me turned my testicles a strange color. I hated this place. It gave me these weird skin diseases and then some "cure" worse than the disease. Felt so tired and beaten down. I slumped on my mat and didn't get up for the rest of the day.

* * *

Monkei made us recite traditional Chinese culture teachings before lunch. We used to have fifteen minutes before lunch to ourselves, but not anymore. In the whole gulag, only ours did that. Factory morale was at an all-time low.

I received a letter from the prosecutor. I'd been given three months for vandalizing the snitches' car but was allowed to pay 1,000 NTD per day instead of prison time. Just what I'd hoped for. Three months would only cost 93K NTD.

The snitch had originally asked for a million NTD to settle. I thought, *fuck off,* and told the judge I'd take the time. One million minus the 93K for the fine, and I'd saved myself over 900K NTD. Justice, Taiwan-style.

Don't hate the player, hate the game.

* * *

My radio came. It was awesome to hear music again. Music heals the soul. It could stir up memories or help me forget.

After dinner, a few of the kids snacked together.

"What do you listen to on the radio?" Carmelo asked.

I stirred my instant noodles. "The local station: 107.7, 99.9, 92.9, and 98.1."

"Do you understand what they're saying?" asked Fat Tiger, his mouth full.

"Nope. Music in Mandarin is over my head." I slurped a noodle. "I get the gist of what they're talking about, but I couldn't tell you for sure, especially with the metaphors they use."

"Anybody you like?" Lion asked as he prepped some instant noodles.

"I like FIR. They're like a Taiwanese No Doubt." I sipped a milk tea. "Mayday is cool too."

Carmelo pushed his glasses up his nose. "How about rap?"

"Honestly, they go too fast. I catch every fifth word."

Whenever I went into a streetwear store in Taiwan, they'd often be playing '90s hip-hop. But I always wondered if they understood what these rappers were saying. I know I do, but did they? Or were they playing it because it was "cool"? (And it is!) I feel what they feel when I listen to rap in Mandarin, just nodding my head.

I looked at Carmelo—"I know you like Underlover"—then, at Lion—"GUTS is your favorite." I nodded at Fat Tiger, "You like 911."

They looked at each other and laughed.

"How'd you know?" Fat Tiger asked.

"Those're the ones you guys always pick during karaoke," I said proudly.

Lion grinned. "Good eye for someone who doesn't speak Chinese."

At first, my friends would ask me about America, or I'd ask them about Taiwan. We mostly talked about drugs, women, or how craptastic the prison and justice system was. Since then, I'd been trying to find more things in common. It made me feel like one of them instead of an outsider. Music is a powerful language we can all understand. It enters through our ears but touches the soul.

* * *

My table had finished for the day and was hanging out before dinner. Howard walked up and ran his index finger along the tabletop. "You guys didn't clean good enough. Your table is sticky. Why's it sticky?"

"What are you?" I asked. "A butler? Get the fuck out of here, Lilliputian."

He mean-mugged me, mumbled something under his breath, and slinked away.

Later, I was chilling next to Heisenberg for after-dinner smokes when Howard walked up to him. "Tell William's table to clean their table better. It's sticky." He side-eyed me. "Oh, but don't tell William to do it because he's the boss. He doesn't do anything."

My heat vision was burning holes through him. I took a puff and blew the smoke in his face. "Damn right," I growled.

Heisenberg looked at him, then looked at me. "I'll take care of it."

Howard smiled and slithered away.

"Fuck him, for real," I huffed.

"Why do you treat him like that?" Heisenberg calmly replied between puffs.

"We started off good, then he became an asshole and . . . well, turnabout is fair play." I took a couple of puffs. "I treat him how he treats me, and some people get mad when you treat them the way they treat you."

He put his hand on my shoulder. "We're all friends here."

"No," I rasped. "We aren't."

"If you can't be friends"—he took a few puffs—"at least don't talk down to him."

"I can't. Either I listen to his nonsense and get mad, or I ignore him and he throws a tantrum."

"Well." Heisenberg sighed. "It's annoying for me when he keeps complaining about you."

I lowered my head, so nobody could see me grin.

He relented. "Give me some face, and pretend like I talked to you, okay? Make me look good."

I flicked my cigarette into the squatter and nodded. "You're the man. My bad. Next time, I'll make sure I don't hurt his feelings too badly."

*   *   *

My old friend Gonzo visited shortly before dinner. He grew up down the street in Monterey Park. A year after I'd moved to Kaohsiung, he moved to Taipei for work. Outside, we'd meet whenever we were in the same city. I was surprised to see him, but it's always nice to see an old friend, regardless of the circumstances.

I smiled. "Thanks for coming."

"Hey, no sweat, man." He looked as wide-eyed as all the others. "I brought you fruit."

"You're the man. Can you buy some commissary?"

"I got you." He had a pen in his pocket. Homeboy came prepared. "What do you want?"

"Instant noodles, rice crackers, milk tea—"

"Slow down." He wrote franticly. "You look good, man."

"I'm on a prison diet: the food is terrible, so I don't eat." I lifted my shirt to show my abs. "I'd rather starve."

He whistled. "I threw 3K into your account."

I thanked him, but the line disconnected. Why'd visits always seem so short? I wrote him a thank-you note and sent it out the next day. Just because I was locked up didn't mean I'd forgotten my manners. He'd brought me a big bag of fruit: apples, bananas, pears, and blueberries. The officials cut all food in half. I guess they were looking for guns, drugs or filers. They even cut my blueberries in half. Every single one. The fuck was I going to smuggle in a blueberry?

*   *   *

I woke up in a foul mood. It was May 18—my parole date, or it would have been if it weren't for this nonsensical, arbitrary point system. I wanted this day to end. Didn't want to speak to anybody, do anything, or eat anything. Tried my best to keep my mind off it, but whatever I did, it was always there, in the back, marinating. I thought about what it'd take to start an anti-Taiwanese government terrorist organization and call it, like, the Human Liberation Front, with me in a Che Guevara–type role. Maybe we could secure a Good Friday–type deal for better conditions. I'd have penitentiaries full of recruits.

So . . . this is how terrorism starts.

I ate a bunch of pills. It was Saturday, which helped soften the blow. I wouldn't have been released that day anyway. It'd most likely have been Monday. Plus, no work. Taiwan was the antagonist in my life's story. Anytime there was a fork in the road, Taiwan went with whatever that dicked me most. Her priorities were a rich tapestry of fucked-up.

* * *

Small Auntie visited.

"Had court for the vandalism charge in February. I'm waiting for paperwork." I blurted as soon as she picked up the receiver.

She pretended like I'd never said it. "Do you know when you're going to be released?"

"I don't know when, but I'd like a ticket ready the same day. I'm trying to avoid going to immigration and go straight to the—"

"Tell them you have family in Taiwan that can buy you a ticket."

I nodded. "I don't want to give immigration any reason to hold me longer than necessary." A CO walked by, hovered over my shoulder for a moment, then walked away. "I'm concerned I'd be held there indefinitely."

"Just tell them you have family. We can buy you a ticket," she repeated.

"The problem is, I don't know when I'm leaving." I sighed wearily. "The government doesn't even know."

* * *

I received a letter from the court that said the snitch appealed my sentence. His reasons were I hadn't given him any money, I'd never apologized, and—this was my favorite—I'd hurt his feelings. He was lucky I didn't hurt more than his feelings. All this for petty vandalism, which I'd already plead guilty to. What a waste of the government's time and resources. He used the system against itself.

I showed Heisenberg the letter for his opinion. "Hurt his feelings? You've been a bad boy." He laughed. "You'll be all right. It's a nothing case. They probably won't add more time to your sentence, but don't go running your mouth and talking back to the judge. Say whatever you said the first time."

I showed Big Face the letter for a second opinion. "This may not even be anything. Just because the snitch wants to appeal, doesn't mean they'll let him. You'll get more paperwork in the mail in a week or two, then you'll have a better idea. This informs you the snitch doesn't accept the sentence. Fuck this guy, though."

* * *

The work was endless in the afternoon. Worse, Heisenberg was out for a doctor's visit, which made Howard and the fourth guy at the head table the de facto chiefs. Howard set an excellent example by eating instead of working. Half the row followed his lead and did their own thing. Sosa and I worked; this shit needed to get done. Howard and the fourth guy passed out the paper and told us to "hurry the fuck up." No further instructions.

We bundled and folded the paper wrong. They blamed us for doing whatever we wanted. Everything went to shit whenever Heisenberg left. Howard and the fourth guy passed back the work for Sosa and me to fix. We grudgingly fixed it. While fixing, Howard was over my shoulder, repeating, "You gotta fix it. You gotta fix it. It's not fixed yet."

Micromanaging wannabe alpha male. Taiwanese people think leadership is top down. They want to say, "I told him to do that" or "It was my idea." But it's never their fault when things go wrong, only when they go right.

"How about you help instead of standing around?" I snarled. "If you had given instructions when we started, none of this would've happened."

"A mistake is a mistake." He straightened his glasses. "Don't blame me for your mistakes."

"You suck at this leadership thing."

I unfucked the fuckups as fast as I could and went to smoke a cigarette. Incompetent leadership is the worst, especially the when the leaders don't know they're incompetent.

After work, the wing chief entered. "Later today, we're going to blow a whistle. When we do, put your heads down and close your eyes. If you're standing, squat and close them. My boss is coming to check on me. He'll be watching the cameras. Give me face."

A short time later, he came back with a handful of other officials and blew his whistle. We got up by row to get searched. Outside, we sat in rows on the floor. They found some contraband, picked two guys out, and escorted them away.

Monkei gave a pre-dinner speech. "We got a tip people were gambling. If I'm being honest, you can only gamble one hundred to three hundred NTD here. It's not worth it."

The factory responded with a collective shrug. We were criminals. If we'd cared about the law, we wouldn't have been there to begin with. I hoped he didn't think it really made a difference.

I spoke to Howard after things settled down. "You always single me out, yet I'm over here doing shit. You're always on my hip, micro-fucking-managing."

"Your work was unacceptable." Howard sneered.

I threw up my hands. "Because you didn't give anybody any instructions. You love to tell me how to do the little things, but when it matters, you're nowhere to be found."

"You do a lot of things wrong. Wrong is wrong."

"I'm not saying it was right." I stuck my finger in his face. "What I am saying is you're a shitty leader."

"I'm Heisenberg's right hand." He folded his arms. "You have to listen and respect me."

I rolled my eyes. "Wrong. Don't have to respect you. Don't even have to listen." I let it marinate, then roared, "Fuck it! This isn't getting us anywhere. I'm sorry. It won't happen again."

The mailman trustee and Prez Tsai's boyfriend noticed me gesturing and came over. The mailman started giving me a massage to calm me down when he saw how heated I was.

"Now I feel bad," Howard groaned. "Why you gotta act like this? It's no use talking to you."

After Howard left, the mailman whispered, "There's no use arguing. Nothing gets resolved, and nothing positive comes out of it. You're going home soon. Nod your head and say yes, or ignore him."

"You're applying for parole in a few months," Prez Tsai's boyfriend added. "You need to be on your best behavior. You can't even risk getting into an argument. It's not worth it. Leave as fast as you can, and don't look back."

CHAPTER 13

GROUNDHOG DAYS

Where a man can live, he can also live well.

—Marcus Aurelius

It was getting hot and sticky, but I slept in a good spot: in front of the water trough and the windows, near where the factory had put fans. The fans chapped my lips, and at night it was so chilly I used a blanket.

As we moved tables in the morning, a mouse scurried along the floor. It ran to the corner where we kept our mats stacked. Cockroaches skittered across the tables as we moved them. At least it was Friday. All morning, we heard squeaks from the corner. I'd never actually heard a mouse squeak before. It sounded cute. Its tail got caught under a box. A guy moved the box, and it ran under row 1.

I forgot about it until after dinner. While we cleaned, Mickey ran from row 1 to row 2, then from row 2 to row 3. It hid under table 1, then table 2, then table 3. Some of the young guys took off their slippers and tried to chase it down. It looked like a janky, real-life game of Whac-A-Mole. The chase went on for a few minutes. Finally, they cornered it under a table near the front of the factory. I half hoped it'd run outside, but it refused to come out. We moved the table, and it sprinted to the center. A guy caught it with his slipper, put his weight on it, and snapped its neck. The mouse died in the same place we ate and slept. No wonder we had skin problems. It was the smallest rodent I'd ever seen. The other ones looked like Bane versions of rodents: big, beefy, dirty, and mean. Chasing down and murdering the mouse gave me the feels. I wasn't sure why.

In the Taipei Retirement Castle, I thought about death a lot. I reflected on my life choices regarding my physical health and mortality. I needed to take better care of myself when I got out. It sounds morbid, but it wasn't. I never expected to be in the old people's factory in a Taiwanese forced-labor camp, watching geezers worked to death or waiting to die.

As the number of older people in Taiwanese penitentiaries increases, both proportionally and in absolute terms, the numbers of deaths will inevitably follow. The substantial increase of older people dying incarcerated means the Ministry of Justice has to grapple with risks and procedures they weren't forced to consider. Prisons are made for young people. Faced with an increase in the population of older inmates, and without a properly resourced and coordinated strategy for this group, institutions still face several challenges associated with aging populations.

* * *

A tweaker from row 3 would be released tomorrow, no parole. He'd done his full sentence. He passed a cigarette to everybody in his row and even gave me one too. I took it, lit it, and lit his.

"What're you gonna do when you get out?" I asked.

"My girlfriend is picking me up in front of the visitors' area." He took a few puffs. "I'm gonna send some food to my peoples here, then we're gonna go to a nearby motel to fuck and smoke some tweak."

"You're my hero." I smiled and took a puff. "Replace tweak with weed, and I'd do the same shit."

"I'm fifty-two. I've been in and out most of my adult life." He shrugged. "It's nothing. This stint was only eight months."

Taiwan is learning what America is learning: you can't arrest your way out of this drug problem.

* * *

In the afternoon, we took down all the windows and put them in storage.

"Every row has to send some kids to help. I'm sending you," Heisenberg told me. He looked around, then whispered, "Here's a tip. Stand in the back, and you won't need to do anything. They've got more than enough people."

"Thanks." I grinned. "I appreciate it."

"I wouldn't send you if I didn't have to. I hope you listened."

Nobody noticed I wasn't doing anything. Some guys broke a window putting it away. Another dude bumped his head on something and started bleeding.

Without glass, the "windows" were square holes with bars. I asked Heisenberg, "What happens when it rains or a typhoon hits?"

"We'll all get wet."

* * *

Sunshine came by for a chat on the morning of June 16. I'd missed the bastard. At least he'd let us watch movies and TV. I used to think he was an asshole, but now I realized he was okay. He'd worked us a lot, but he and the others were all de facto slave drivers. At least we'd had personal time. Monkei and his propaganda could go and fuck right off.

Later that day, I received a letter from the police department stating they agreed my three-month sentence for vandalism was too short. They also wanted to appeal. These bastards *would* give me this letter on a Friday. Didn't they have more productive things to do? Nothing the government did surprised me anymore. The absurdity of it all—thinking about it made my head hurt. If Taiwan wanted to waste more time and money they didn't have on me, it wasn't like I could do anything to stop them. But I cost them money twice—not only in transportation and everything, but also the loss of my factory production for the day. Joke's on them!

Court was like a craptacular elementary school field trip. I wondered if the snitch would dare to show up this time—and if I could bite my tongue when I saw him. Hoped so. I wished they'd leave me alone. Were these fools really trying to give me more time? Maybe because so many people were trying to leave a declining Taiwan, they resorted to forcing people to stay via the justice system.

Took some pills to ease some of the uncertainty and stress of Taiwan trying their damnedest to make an example of me.

* * *

Howard and Prez Tsai's boyfriend left last night. Big Face said it had been over a year since anybody had transferred. I thought it was annoying when people transferred from the dorms, but it was really a pain when people transferred from here. The entire factory was woken up. They turned on all the lights, and the tables and benches needed to be moved so they could get their stuff from storage.

"Why don't they let us know beforehand so we can do all this ahead of time?" I asked Big Face before breakfast as we rolled our mats.

"It's a secret. They don't want you telling people you're leaving. What if you got issues with somebody and decide to attack him?"

I nodded and scratched my head. "Makes sense, but why don't they do it like Kaohsiung? I was put in a separate cell the night before."

He shrugged. "Taiwan doesn't care about us. Who cares if we get woken up? We're inmates. We have no rights."

They transferred suspected gamblers. Ninety-Eight was a bookie, and Howard loved to gamble. I failed to see how moving gamblers to other dungeons stopped them from gambling. It just made them somebody else's problem. It turned out that a guy who'd recently been released from our factory had snitched them out. Officials needed to show they addressed the problem.

Imagine yourself in an elevator, and you press the button for your floor. A man walks in, presses a button for his floor. He waits, then presses it again, and then a third time. It doesn't make the elevator go any faster, but it sure looks like he's doing something, doesn't it? The man in the elevator is the Taiwanese government. Man, do they look like they're doing something!

In the morning, when I glanced at the head table, I smiled at Howard's empty seat. I was so happy. He was like a mosquito I could never quite smoosh—the only person I felt had it out for me. Our feud had been bubbling. At some point, it was going to boil. What would've happened then? Would I have been able to control myself? I'd love to tell you yes, but I'm not sure, and I was relieved it never escalated further.

* * *

In the middle of an afternoon movie, a trustee told me that AIT had come.

I met Nicky outside the factory, and we chatted all the way to the central desk. Guards searched us and took roll. Only six Americans, all short-timers—longest was Nicky with ten-plus years.

A CO wrote down our English names, inmate number, and factory, complaining about all the English he had to write. They met us in pairs. Nicky and I were first.

They searched me again before escorting me to a room. The AIT representative entered as I settled into a chair.

"What's your name?" asked the middle-aged lady.

"William Tsung."

She looked me over. "How come I've never seen you before? I know everybody. I come often."

I leaned back in my chair. "I'm a short-timer. Last AIT visitor was a middle-aged man."

She asked the usual questions.

I was annoyed about still being here past my original parole date and wanted to vent to somebody. I interrupted her and ranted. "How can they keep me here past my parole date? How can you people allow your citizens to be treated like this? Didn't seem to be about drugs at all. More like they want to lock people up and keep them locked up. Drug use is increasing, and the average age of a user is decreasing. Taiwan's war on drugs is unwinnable."

She put her hand up. "It's winnable." I opened my mouth to respond, but she cut me off. "We're getting off-topic. Do you have questions regarding your situation?"

"A couple. One, I entered Taiwan under my Taiwanese passport, but I only brought my American in. I have to leave a country with the same passport I used to enter, so what do I do? I was thinking of having an auntie mail my Taiwanese passport to me."

She wrote as I spoke. "I don't know. I'll have to ask my supervisors and get back to you."

"Two, when I'm released, immigration'll pick me up. How can I speed up the process? I don't want to be held in an immigration detention center.

Got money for a planet ticket and want to go from here to the airport. I'd like to leave the country ASAP. It's their job to make sure I leave, so I don't see the issue. I don't want to be here a second longer than necessary."

"The prison will hand you over to immigration upon your release, and it's their job to see to it you leave the country. The process takes one to two weeks."

I frowned. "Is there any way to speed the process along? To be taken directly to the airport?" I looked out the window at the garden. "I have the resources to be on the first flight available."

"I don't know. I'll ask and get back to you."

Lot she didn't know. Wonder what she *did* know. I thanked her for her time and implored her to reply ASAP.

Nicky and a white boy were in the waiting room when I left. Nicky said, "I asked your questions for you. According to my guy, you can walk out of here and stay, but why would you want to?"

"I'm over Taiwan," I growled. "I'm ready to get on with my life."

The white boy was called out, and Juan entered.

He nodded. "Sup, fool?"

I nodded back. "What up, G?"

"Why didn't your ass sign up for Christian Bible study?"

I blew my lips. "I ain't Christian."

"Who cares? Those dudes don't give a fuck. Come and kick it with your boy."

"It's not about religion," Nicky said. "I go to support the Christian missionaries. They do a lot for us in here; I want to show my gratitude. Also, it's an excuse to get out of the factory."

A CO entered. "It's time to go."

"Take care of yourself," I told Juan.

"Sign up for the Christian group." He grinned. "You need to reform your smuggling ass."

We bumped fists and parted. The CO gave me a bag of food to take to my factory. AIT's visit didn't address my concerns or accomplish anything except get me out of the factory. I was still concerned about my visa status, anxious about immigration and worried they'd try to keep me indefinitely. Pills kept me sane. I never heard from AIT again.

* * *

The row 1 chief left for camp. They promoted Fat Tiger to row chief.

"You excited about the job?" I asked when he, Justin, and I were smoking later.

He shook his head. "It's different here. These grandpas, a lot of them are weird. I can't be a dick because they're old. In a normal factory, I can be an asshole if they don't want to listen. I can slap them, but here I can't do anything." He sighed. "It's a lot of bullshit."

Sosa was still here, the last of the Mohicans. He applied for camp with the others, but he was denied even though he checked every box. I overheard him lamenting to Heisenberg. "I'm the most qualified, yet I've been here the longest. What's going on?"

"It's politics."

Later on, Heisenberg tapped me before dinner. "Join me at the head table."

"What for?"

"Since Howard left, there's an opening."

I straightened my posture. "Thanks."

"You get food, put it away, and wipe the table down," Sosa told me once I sat down. "Heisenberg likes you and wants to take care of you, but you're leaving in a few months, so it's unofficial. Your seat on the seating chart stays the same. He's too lazy to change it."

"Tell him I said thanks and that he's a cool dude. He doesn't have to look out for me, but I appreciate it."

Howard's transfer was the gift that kept on giving. Not only was it more peaceful, I got his job too!

It was great at the head table. A fan blew directly at us, and everybody in the row gave us a bowl of their food as a tribute whenever they had a visitor. Our row had twenty-three people, and I was third in command—crown prince of the slaves.

At night, I lay on my bed and thought about my promotion. I didn't ask for one. It fell in my lap. Not like I was unfit to lead or scared of responsibility. I was leaving soon and wanted to minimize my chances of conflict. I was concerned I'd get into an argument with somebody and get sent to the black room. Could easily see how it'd start too. Then again, I wouldn't be micromanaging a mofo, and I'd mostly let them do whatever they wanted as long as it didn't affect me.

* * *

Factory check. They happened every two months. In April, we'd placed second, and Monkei was pleased. It surprised me that second in a make-believe contest was enough for him. We didn't even get first in this sham inspection.

It was 200 NTD for factory-use commissary. Didn't matter I was broke—they'd collect it when somebody put money in my account.

Commissary sold a variety of seasonal fruits, and Sosa ordered a mango. I forgot they were in season. This was a place where time stood still. I helped him cut the mango, and he gave me a piece. Hadn't had one in over a year. Forgot how sweet it was. As I ate, all I thought about was how good a mango shaved ice would taste right now. While I wiped down the table afterward, Sosa said, "Besides food, you help with roll call, moving heavy things, making sure everybody does their job, and helping me whenever I need it."

* * *

Small Auntie visited. "I would've come sooner, but I got sick."

I smiled, "It's okay. I'm not going anywhere."

She chuckled. "It's getting hot. How are you sleeping?"

"As good as can be. I sleep near five fans."

She leaned back in her chair. "Sounds like you're doing well."

"I try. A young guy at the head table got transferred recently, and I took his place." A guard walked by and hovered a few moments.

"What do you do?"

"As little as possible." I chuckled. "I get food, wipe tables, move furniture —"

She leaned closer to the glass. "What do you get for this?"

"Nothing," I deadpanned. "It's just more responsibility and bullshit."

She nodded. "I bought pizza and beef jerky nearby, so it's still—"

The line disconnected.

* * *

Small Auntie found my passport and mailed it. I received it about a week later. It was close. I was worried for a while. I held my passport in my hand for a moment and felt the possibility of freedom.

"The prison will hold on to it until your release," Monkei said.

Hold on to my passport?! I wouldn't trust those bastards to take me to the movies. I gave him the side-eye, hesitated, and handed it to him.

* * *

"You're up for parole!" the mailman said gleefully during the after-lunch smoke.

"How do you know?"

He pointed at his desk. "I get a list of people who are eligible this month or next. You're up next month."

Fantastic news! First Howard left, then parole. I was on a roll.

* * *

One kid said he wasn't feeling well and was sent to the doctor. The doctor said he had a fever and quarantined him. Trustees took everybody's temperature in the morning, leading to seven more inmates being quarantined. Half the factory walked around with face masks. We worked, slept, and showered shoulder to shoulder. It was a coffin. What was a face mask going to do? It was a small wonder we didn't get sick more often. The Pimp, who did Sosa's laundry, came and tried to give Sosa a face mask, but he refused. Later, he came back and insisted. Sosa took it and put it on.

Before dinner, the teacher summoned me to his office. My ass had barely touched the seat when he asked, "Do you have Taiwanese citizenship?"

The question caught me off guard. "Uh . . . no."

He held up my passport. "Then how come you have this?"

"My parents are Taiwanese. They grandfathered it in."

He nodded. "Do you wish to stay in Taiwan after your release?"

189

"No, but I have another charge: vandalism. If it ends, I'll pay the fine and go home. But if not, I'm not sure I can leave. I have no choice but stay until it's resolved. If parole is denied, none of this matters."

"If you think there's a chance you'll be staying in Taiwan"—he opened a drawer and grabbed a folder—"I'll need some paperwork from you."

I looked at the floor and shook my head in disbelief.

He either ignored me or didn't care. "I'll need a relative to send me a photocopy of their ID card and a letter stating you can stay with them until your situation is resolved. If I don't get this paperwork by August 1, they will deny your parole."

I glared at him.

He looked me over. "Well, you can apply, but it'll be denied because those who don't have a place to live or somebody they can stay with can't be paroled." Apparently, the homeless and isolated are penalized.

I got up and left soon as he finished talking. I wasn't trying to hear anymore.

August 1 was seventeen days away. Should be enough time to get what I needed. I wished he would've told me sooner, but why would they do anything that made my life easier? Taiwan harassed me for shits and giggles. I was glad Small Auntie had mailed my Taiwanese passport, or else we'd have been having this talk after they denied my parole. I didn't know why the teacher waited so long to have this conversation. They knew I had an outstanding charge. I'd been in custody over a calendar year and in the justice system for almost two. Felt like they withheld this info purposely as a setup to fail and keep me longer.

* * *

Five more inmates caught fevers. Monkei said the sick bay was full and they were waiting for people to leave. Until then, those with fevers stayed. Face masks became mandatory. Trustees bleached the floor while we worked. Big Face told me the flu went around every year, but only three had caught it last year.

Some IT guys (inmates) came during work to lay cables. They put ladders on our tables, drilled overhead and rained dust while we slaved.

Nobody held the ladders. I didn't care if they fell. I just didn't want anybody to fall on me.

After the guys left, during a break, I was complaining about prison safety to Erik.

"One time, I stepped out of my cell, and there was water all over the floor," he said. "I slipped, hit my head, and tweaked my wrist. Even though it wasn't my fault, I had to pay for an X-ray, doctor's visit, and treatment."

"It's fucked up how Taiwan has arguably the world's best health care, but we're forced to pay for subpar medical treatment." I looked at my rashes.

"Tell me about it. In August 2016, eight days after arriving at the factory, I had a stomachache and was in a lot of pain. First, they took me to the prison doctor. He did a quick exam. 'You need to go to an outside hospital for surgery,' he said, then gave me a painkiller. They took me to Taoyuan hospital, where I spoke to a doctor for a couple minutes—"

"How'd you talk to the doctor if you can't speak Chinese?"

He threw his hands up. "That's what I'm trying to say! I don't think he understood me. I was in the main reception room, shackled and cuffed, surrounded by people. Never saw another doctor, nurse, or had another exam. I just sat there all day."

"Even if you saw a doctor, it's not like you can communicate with them," I joked.

He exclaimed, "I know, and they won't give me a translator. In the afternoon, I got an X-ray, a CT scan, and a bed. A nurse entered and felt me all over. 'Oh, you still hurt?' A few hours later, the nurse discharged me. 'Your stomach pain is because you had your appendix out when you were seven.'"

I grinned and shook my head. Over the half the stuff they put us through would have been comedy if it weren't life or death serious.

"Over a year later, it still hurts." He sighed. "Every time I eat, I get the shits. The best part? They charged me 11,058 NTD. I wanted to know why they charged so much, so my embassy and I complained."

"Did anything happen?"

"Nothing," he moaned. "They just took it from my account! Nobody ever showed me a bill. I had to tell my embassy to put money in."

"It happened to me too."

"After three months, they finally gave me a bill for 11,058 NTD, legitimizing what they had already took. I continued to complain. I was told I could go back to the same hospital again."

"Did you go back?"

"Hell no! When the regular CO heard what happened, he laughed. He thought it was so hilarious I went to the hospital and didn't get the medical attention I needed."

"It grinds my gears. It's all a joke to them." I offered Erik a cigarette. "Like they think we get sick on purpose. We're getting sick under their watch. They're responsible for this." I lit his cigarette, then mine. "Fucking condescending, patronizing dicks."

I thought because I was young and healthy, I'd be okay. But I'd be lying if I said this outbreak didn't weigh on me. Pills took the edge off.

* * *

They finally fixed the TV antenna. Before, I only got certain channels if I held it a certain way. Now all thirty-three channels were watchable. It'd been three weeks, and I'd forgotten how TV made time fly.

Heisenberg summoned me while I was chatting with an old man in our row. "Stay away from him," he warned.

I looked at the old man. "Why?"

"He doesn't have any friends here."

It was the first time we'd spoken. He didn't seem weird. "How come?"

"He raped his son's wife at knifepoint."

"Wow, what a piece of shit." I stared at the old man. "How long he get?"

"Twelve years."

Some people deserve to be in prison. Shit, some people deserve to be *under* the prison. I shook my head. "Not long enough."

Heisenberg nodded.

* * *

On July 24, I had court. Last time, I'd left after breakfast. This time, I wasn't so lucky: the CO came early. On my way out, Justin and Lion fist-bumped me and wished good luck. It felt strange to walk around the gulag so early; I heard the yells of roll call and the sounds of the people stirring from outside the cells instead of inside.

In the waiting room, the guard tried to take an old man's wheelchair, but he couldn't walk or sit without it. They haggled for a minute, and the guard eventually let him keep it.

An official called us individually to fingerprint a form, then waited outside. They shackled me! Why? They didn't shackle me last time. It was my understanding that only those with ten years or more needed to be shackled. I was annoyed. At least they were the shackles with keys instead of the medieval kind from last time.

They shackled us in groups of four, and we trudged to the administration building for another roll call. They herded us through the metal detector, and the handcuffs and shackles set off the detector as we passed. Guards ignored it every time. I suddenly understood how someone could to kill himself in a courtroom.

In June 2016, Tyrsel Martin Marhanka had slashed his throat with a pair of scissors in a Changhua courtroom after being convicted for marijuana possession. Upon hearing his sentence through an interpreter, Marhanka appeared incredulous and repeated, "Four years?" Suddenly, he pulled out a disassembled pair of scissors and shouted, "I don't want to live anymore!" and stabbed himself in the neck. He was pronounced dead shortly after.

In February 2015, inmates in Kaohsiung had used scissors from a workshop to take guards hostage. Among their complaints: low wages that forced them to rely on family support, which put relatives in financial difficulty. They broke into the armory and seized firearms, which six inmates used to commit suicide.

Their deaths should raise questions about security in Taiwan's judicial facilities. For example: What's really going on, and who is supervising? If they're not reforming us, what are they doing?

I'd thought all penitentiary transports were the same, more or less resembling armored school buses with rows that faced the front, but this one had rows that faced each other. As we boarded, we realized each row only sat two people. We sat two by two, across from each other, but because we were cuffed together, the dudes in the middle had to hold their arms out the whole trip. I was one of the unlucky ones. By the end of the ride, my arms had gone numb.

The judge was female; the prosecutor was male. Two young ladies were seated in the back of the courtroom before I arrived. I wondered why they were there.

"Are you the owners of the car?" the judge asked.

Why'd she ask that? I thought the snitch owned the car. *If they're not here with me, and they're not here with you, who are they here for?*

"No," replied a young lady.

I wondered if the snitch was too scared to appear in person and had sent two girls to watch. I was paranoid, but it didn't mean someone wasn't out to get me.

"May I have a translator?" I asked.

She looked at my dossier. "It says here you speak Chinese, and you didn't have one last time."

"The prosecutor said I didn't need one last time," I protested. "I want one. My Chinese is terrible."

"We're going to proceed. If there's anything you don't understand, say so, and we'll explain."

"All right." I told the same story.

"When are you eligible for parole?"

I tried to hide a smile. "Next month."

"If you're paroled, where will you be?"

"Kaohsiung."

"Is there anything you'd like to add?"

"Yes." I cleared my throat. "I'd like this to be wrapped up ASAP so I can go back to California. Also, do I have another court date after this?"

"You'll have one more court date with three judges."

I thought they reserved using three judges for serious or ten-years-and-up cases. My smuggling case had had three judges. Seemed strange they needed three judges for this nothing of a case.

I got back to the factory a few moments before Monkei clocked out. I checked in with the wing chief first. One of his trustees asked, "How'd it go?"

I shrugged. "Good, I think."

"Great. Now we wait for your aunt to mail your paperwork so you're all set."

I entered the factory as a conquering hero. All I was missing were heralds trumpeting my arrival. My people gave me fist bumps and welcomed me back. A trustee handed me my cigarettes and another my newspaper.

"You're on your own for dinner," Heisenberg said. "I didn't know what time you were coming back. I didn't save you anything."

I nodded.

"Oh, and two guys in our row got sick."

The fever had people dropping like flies.

A cool part of court was getting to shower after hours. I was the only one there—what a luxury! I had instant noodles and a pill for dinner.

At least I didn't have to make paper bags, I thought.

Big Face told me they had no work today.

Well, ain't that just about a son of a bitch.

* * *

Small Auntie filled out the paperwork and mailed it back. She came through in the clutch. During work, the teacher summoned me. "Where's your auntie's household registration?"

I gestured at the factory. "It's inside with the rest of my paperwork."

He ordered a trustee to retrieve it.

"It was from when I wanted to receive books."

He glanced at it. "I told you, you needed a household registration."

"I have it, it's right there." I pointed at it.

He held it up and showed me. "It's eight months old. How do we know she hasn't moved in the past eight months?"

I threw my hands in the air. "You can't be serious! She owns her house!"

"Well, how do we know for sure?" He eyed me suspiciously. "We need a recent one, up to six months. We'll need it by August third. Your paperwork needs to be correct and up to date, or they'll deny you."

I rolled my eyes. "You didn't tell me about it being recent. Isn't eight months close enough? I received it back in March. I showed you. You've had this the whole time."

"Showing it to your trustee friend isn't the same as showing me. I'm telling you now. Don't blame me if you don't have all the proper paperwork. Do you understand?"

I bit my lower lip and balled my fist. "Yeah."

"That's it. Write a letter to your auntie and hopefully you'll get it in time. August 3rd."

While escorting me back, a trustee offered some advice. "Write a report. Tell Monkei you need to mail a letter tomorrow and it's an emergency. You need paperwork for parole. Have Heisenberg write it."

Carmelo wrote my letter, and Heisenberg filled out the report. It was rushed because it needed to be submitted by 4:00 p.m. if I wanted it to be mailed the next day. We finished at 3:55 p.m.

Heisenberg brought me in front of Monkei, explained my situation, and showed him the report and letter. Mercifully, Monkei said, "Okay."

Back at my seat, Heisenberg gave me a tongue-lashing. "I remember telling you, you needed a household registration. You're a short sentence. They'll let you out on parole. But everything needs to be correct. You can't give them a reason to reject you."

I opened my mouth but decided to stay silent. When in doubt, shut the fuck up.

"They'll look for any minor reason to dick you. It's how Taiwan works. If your parole gets denied because of your carelessness, you'll have to wait another four months to reapply."

After he left, I hung my head. He was right. I hoped my arrogance and recklessness hadn't cost me my chance at early release. And it wouldn't be the first time those two traits got me in trouble either.

Carmelo came by. "Wanna smoke?"

"Yes, yes I do."

He didn't help my mood when he said, "I overheard Heisenberg lecture you." He took a puff. "It's how it is here, man. They purposely don't tell you stuff or tell you late or after the fact. Happens all the time. They try to keep us here as long as possible, and nothing is transparent. Rules change all the time without notice."

* * *

I moved back to my original seat. I didn't get a reason. Heisenberg told me to, and I did it. It had only been a month and a half, but it was fun while it lasted. I had nothing to be sad or angry about. He helped me out all the time—didn't owe me anything. And I'd gained weight from all the food at Heisenberg's table.

I received my receipt for the express mail, which meant Small Auntie had gotten the letter. I should have her new household registration by the following week, just in time for my application.

Monkei had the trustees bleach the floor in the morning. Fat lot of good it did. Three more caught fevers. It was getting serious. Three factories didn't work. The COs quarantined the cells instead of sending the sick to the doctor. I failed to see how that'd address the situation. Not everybody was sick, and those who weren't probably would be after spending all day in a cell with somebody who was. Three factories was about six hundred people. That'd be a lot of lost money for the state.

I cried crocodile tears.

Somebody from Bei Shuo was sick when he was transferred to Taipei. Instead of being isolated when he arrived, they put him in the freshmen dorms. He infected his cellies. Then the infection spread among the factories. One went to Factory 16, which was above mine, and came in contact with someone from my factory during visitation.

No thought was given to our living conditions or sanitation. We were denied timely access to doctor's visits, medicine and treatment. Small issues that could easily be cured or controlled if dealt with early were put off until they became uncontainable. We were forced to work no matter what, never alone, in constant contact with sizable groups of people in cramped, dank spaces.

The doctor couldn't see all the infected, and the sick bay been full for weeks. Their solution? Face masks. Amazingly, infected inmates were still allowed to be in contact with others at class, visitation, Bible study, and so on. This was the third week, and there were no signs of slowing.

Crowded living conditions, weakened immune systems, and limited access to health care. The hygiene situation was horrendous. Even someone who believed they were protected from these infections, like me, wasn't. These were all preventable diseases. It's unconscionable. It felt like the officials were giving extra punishment for your crime, when, most likely, they were the primary cause of the sickness and didn't have the resources or morals to help.

Whether in prison or not, I doubt anybody gets sick on purpose. But being sick incarcerated was another level of annoyance and frustration. That's without even talking about all the rules, which seemed designed to punish us for being irresponsible enough to get sick and having the audacity to seek treatment. Committing a crime doesn't give the government, or anybody, the right to treat us as subhuman—unworthy of proper medical attention. Like animals, they had us wallow in our own filth and be exposed to diseases and infections that had been eradicated in most developed countries.

I remembered a conversation with Erik, when I told him about my reoccurring scabies.

"At Bei Shuo," he said, "I caught it because I shared a cell with an infected guy. Had it for six months even though I saw a doctor and received medicine. He wouldn't prescribe what I requested."

"The medicine inside seems ineffective."

Because the difference in medical care was so drastic, I got to thinking: *Are they doing this on purpose?* Is there an unholy alliance between the prison, penitentiary doctors, and pharmaceutical companies? Were institutions purposely getting us sick and giving us ineffective medicine?

Most of the common health hazards arose because of poor sanitation, or worse yet, bad personal hygiene. I didn't even know what scabies was until Taiwan. In America, only the homeless catch scabies. In Taiwan, the homeless don't even get scabies; the inmates do. Every time I complained to a CO, he told me to see a doctor like it's a fact of life, or he chided me for not being "clean" enough. *What about the environment you let flourish under your watch, where healthy people are infected upon arrival?*

The simplest reason is money. The health care system is going broke. It relies on young, healthy people to subsidize the older ones with conditions. As Taiwanese people live longer, it puts more strain on the system. Coupled with a low birth rate, it's a double whammy. I'm not even including people who didn't pay their monthly health fees, like Prince. He hadn't paid insurance fees in ten years and owed 100,870 NTD. It's an exorbitant amount. I don't even know how he racked up so much debt. The monthly was only 500 NTD.

Maybe there's a more insidious answer. Perhaps doctors willingly prescribe drugs they know will do nothing. Health care is subsidized.

Pharmaceutical companies win, doctors win. The person who gets stuck with the bill is the government. Well, them and the patients who receive substandard care.

Take the Kaohsiung Armed Forces General Hospital, for example. Doctors and medical staff received kickbacks from pharmaceutical companies at the hospital. The hospital is managed by the Ministry of National Defense's Medical Affairs Bureau and is the largest military hospital in southern Taiwan. It mostly serves active-duty military personnel and their families. Allegedly, salesmen received a percentage of their sales, while the pharmaceutical companies gave doctors monthly kickbacks based on the volume and price of drugs prescribed. If it happens on the outside, why do you think it wouldn't happen here?

I took pills because Americans take prescription drug abuse to a level the rest of the world has yet to experience—and I hope it never does.

After hours, the old man Heisenberg told me to stay away from had an episode. He suddenly froze, dropped to the floor, and turned pale as a ghost. People carried him out. Heisenberg was furious. It wasn't the reaction I expected.

I found him smoking and asked, "Why're you so pissed?"

He took a deep breath. "This asshole stopped taking his medication these past few days. Hasn't been eating; his health is deteriorating rapidly. He refused to see a doctor and barely did any work. Because of his crime, he's ostracized. Mofo is sixty-eight years old with a twelve-year sentence. A few people, myself included, think it was an attempted suicide." He put out his cigarette and grumbled, "I was planning to relax tonight. Now I have to write a statement because I carried him out."

The next day, Heisenberg found me after work.

"The dude from last night died, but they resuscitated him. He's on life support in an outside hospital."

CHAPTER 14

THE MAN WHO LEAPT THROUGH TIME

Isn't it funny how day by day nothing changes, but
when you look back everything is different.

—C. S. Lewis

Small Auntie's paperwork arrived. She came through with a few days to spare. I hoped for a visitor soon. It'd been a while, and I only had 32 NTD in my account.

My first and only pair of prison sneakers arrived. They were only available once a year. We signed up to purchase them in June, filled out the order form in July, and they finally came. Until that point, I'd worn flip-flops. For all court appearances, they'd issued me shoes and socks.

The Jump 851s cost 750 NTD, were size twenty-seven, and were garbage. They weren't even exercise shoes. There were two Velcro straps instead of laces, and the shoes came in one design; gray upper, white sole, baby-blue inside. No cushion. It felt like I was wearing Chucks, but not in a good way. These shoes were so fugly, if I were free, I wouldn't wear them even if the company paid me. Even with this shoe's many, many flaws, at least it was a pair that fit. And they were mine.

It seemed strange to buy shoes after I'd applied for parole, but parole wasn't guaranteed. I'd likely get it, but anything could happen. I was tired of secondhand shoes. Most of the time, they were too small; I'd tried to squeeze my clown feet into size nines. When I left, I'd leave my pair to Carmelo or Lion.

* * *

Monkei put a new guy in our row, a sixty-eight-year-old thief. Short, small and so skinny he looked malnourished, he didn't seem all there. Some thought it was his age, but I disagreed. He'd been in and out his whole life, yet he still didn't understand what was going on. He entered with nothing; everything was donated to him. Maybe he was one of those who chose to be incarcerated—it was a place to sleep and provided three meals. (I'd write "three hots and a cot," but we didn't even get that.)

A guy came over and yelled at Thief in Taiwanese. "You took my cigarette holder!"

I was sitting to the left of him and jumped when the guy shouted. At first, I thought it was a mistake. Who'd steal something on their first day? We'd just given him a bunch of stuff.

Heisenberg rummaged through Thief's belongings and found it. He gave it back to the guy and took Thief to Monkei, who lectured him for a while, then chalked it up to a misunderstanding.

A little later, during a work break, Thief squeezed close to me.

"Back up a little," I barked.

"Do you want to play Chinese Chess? I'm pretty good." He was wide-eyed.

This dude had weird vibes. I didn't want to play with him, didn't want to hang out with him, and wouldn't have sat next to him if I didn't have to. "I'm not good, but Heisenberg is. He got second in the gulag chess tournament."

Heisenberg overheard and shot me a dirty look.

* * *

The first week of August, we made Din Tai Fung to-go bags by attaching plastic buttons with a pin on one side, like a thumbtack, to cloth bags. The pins weren't sharp. I didn't push, I stabbed them through. Another row's job was to press the other side so they'd clasp shut. We double-checked if they closed after. If not, we did it again.

Heisenberg taught Thief how to do it before we began. When the bags came, he sat there and looked around.

I turned to him. "Whatchu doing? Get to work."

"I don't know how to do this," he mumbled. "I want to collect the bags."

I showed him how again. He just sat there, annoying me.

After a few moments, he walked toward Heisenberg. "I don't want to do this. I want to collect the bags."

I'd never seen Heisenberg so mad. "You think I'm fucking playing? You do what I say. Sit down and make the bags," he roared as he jabbed buttons.

He went back to his seat and pretended to work. Heisenberg noticed and put the final three bags in front of him.

Thief sat and stared.

The work chiefs got mad and brought him back to Monkei.

"I don't want to make the bags, I want to collect them," Thief said.

"It's not up to you. You do what we tell you to do. You're old and work slower—fine. But work, or go to the black room," Monkei calmly replied.

Somebody from row one came up to Thief and shouted in Taiwanese during a lull in work. Thief had stolen the dude's glasses and tried to trade them for a bag of coffee. Wow. Just wow. At the rate he was going, he'd be lucky to last a week. They caused a scene, and the trustees brought them to Monkei for another lecture, another report.

Afterward, back at his seat, Heisenberg walked up to Thief, grabbed his ear, twisted it like he was a kid, and bellowed, "Stop fucking around!"

* * *

Justin and I saw Thief in the restroom while we smoked after dinner the next night; he'd shat himself and blamed the guy who slept next to him. Heisenberg made him pull down his pants to prove he'd lied. Shortly after, Thief got into a fight with another old guy. After lights out, Thief went to the front to get the attention of the guard on duty. The guard waved him away.

"I fear for my life here, and I want to be taken to the central desk," Thief said while waving his arms.

The guard shouted at him loud enough to wake up the factory, then escorted him away.

"Can you do that?" I asked Big Face.

"No. He's the only person I've seen ask. Especially at night. It's a hassle, and guards are lazy. It better be important."

He'd only been there two days! Never seen anybody wear out a welcome so quick. I thought I brought it out in people. This guy incited anger and hate like it was his superpower. Next to him, I was an angel.

* * *

"You have a visitor."

I looked at the trustee, then went back to work. "No, I had one on Friday. Must be a mistake."

He checked his clipboard of names again. "It's you."

"Can I see the visitor log?"

He showed it to me. It was Gonzo! I strutted to visitation. The last time I'd seen him was in May.

"Dude," he said as soon as I'd picked up the receiver, "I would've gotten here earlier, but I went to the wrong place. This is Taipei prison in Taoyuan, but there's also a Taoyuan prison. I went there. It's fucking confusing."

"At least you made it," I said. "It's the last visit of the day too." A CO walked by and hovered.

"I know. I wanted to buy Big Macs, but I didn't have time. Fried chicken is all I got."

I updated him on the pending case and parole.

He pulled a pen out of his pocket. "Let's get commissary out of the way first, yeah?"

I hadn't expected another visitor so soon. I didn't prepare a list. I rattled things off the top of my head. "Milk tea, Super Supau, instant noodles—"

"Do you still have herpes?" he quipped.

I grinned. "No, dick. But the medicine they gave me turned my balls black. The cure is worse than the disease. I appreciate you coming."

"No sweat. It's been a while, and I'm flying back to LA tomorrow."

I filled him in on my sleeping situation and promotion, then the line disconnected.

* * *

We received a new guy in our row. He sat on my right.

I nodded at him in greeting. "What's up, man. I'm William."

"Kevin." He gave a knowing glance. "You're not from here, are you? You have an accent."

"Yeah, I'm an ABC."

"I can speak English too. I was born in Singapore and moved to Taiwan when I was ten," he replied in English.

I smiled. "How old are you now?"

"Thirty."

Jackpot! A young kid who spoke English.

We spoke in a mix of English and Chinese (Chinglish). He had nothing, so we laced him up. Heisenberg gave him a box; Sosa gifted soap, shampoo and detergent; I donated toothpaste and snacks. I remembered what it was like to arrive unprepared, and it sucked. Once upon a time, people had taken care of me. Paying it forward was the least I could do.

Heisenberg pulled me aside. "Take care of him."

"I was going to do it even if you didn't tell me."

This week, our row was on chore duty. Heisenberg had Kevin shadow me so he could take my spot when I left.

Kevin was a cool guy. Tall, athletic build, good-looking teeth. Finally, somebody normal sitting next to me. Friday was when the kids would hang out. I showed him around and introduced him to everybody. He was good at chess. After I introduced Kevin to Carmelo, Carmelo pulled me aside and said, "You gotta take care of him. He sits right next to you."

Big Face said something similar when he was introduced. "He sits next to you, and he's young. It's your responsibility to look out for him."

I scrunched my face. "Why's everybody telling me that?"

"Because these kids look up to you."

"Exceptional leader, terrible role model."

* * *

Factory 11 let us do our laundry on any weekday. At Factory 15, it had been once a week when Sunshine was in charge. With Monkei, it was once every two weeks. Cleanliness and hygiene obviously weren't high on his priority list.

Junior started banging his head against the floor until it bled. Guards escorted him out of the factory after. Officially, he went to the black room. Unofficially, they took him into protective custody.

"What happened?" I asked Heisenberg.

"He's up for parole soon, his third try," he said, shaking his head. "But he knows he'll probably get denied again."

"How come?" I glanced at Junior's empty seat.

"People told him it's easier to get paroled if you have a serious medical condition. That, and it's hard for murderers and bananas to get early release."

Junior was in fantastic shape for a person his age; he ran whenever we exercised and could do most things without help.

"What do you mean, harder?"

"For you, a first-time offender and foreigner, you'll get out on your first try. Guys like Junior need at least four or five."

Heisenberg made it sound as if he'd tried self-harm in an attempt to get out earlier. I'd just thought he couldn't take it anymore. Seemed like a cry for help. Maybe the joint broke him.

Junior fascinated me. He was a murderous piece of shit who should be locked up for forever and a day, yet I felt complex emotions I hadn't ever expected to deal with. His physique astounded me, made me envious. When I'm eighty-eight, I hope I can move like him. I needed to exercise more. I felt sorry for him because he was old, but everybody there was old, and *they* didn't act out. He seemed to think he should get special treatment.

The fuck was I doing, caring about some old guy I wasn't related to? I was born and raised in America. Seniority doesn't mean shit there; they put their old people in homes. Out of sight, out of mind.

* * *

On August 16, I'd been in prison for one calendar year. Time flew.

Okay, that's a lie. Each day seemed endless, like the minute hand was ticking backward, but the weeks flew. I had a routine. I woke up and looked forward to breakfast. My eye was on the clock throughout work, and I couldn't wait until lunch. After lunch, I counted down the minutes until dinner. I drank as much water as I could so I'd have to take more piss breaks. Didn't plan or think about the future. I tried to make it through the day without getting scolded or fighting.

Everybody counted their time differently. Some counted days, others counted months, and a few counted years. I counted weeks. I'd never worked a corporate job, but I imagined my life was similar to what a person in a cubicle felt like. Throughout the week, I looked forward to the weekends.

I'd happily applied for parole and hoped I'd be out sometime soon. But fuck, I hadn't expected to be there so long.

Pills and codeine to cope.

* * *

When I submitted some forms to a trustee, he said, "Congrats."

"Why has everybody been telling me that today?" I looked around, then added in a low voice, "What happened?"

"Ours are the only two parole applications to make it out of the prison and to the parole board." He smiled. "Everybody else's got denied."

"For real?" I gave him a fist bump. "Wait, I don't get it. I thought an application means it goes to the parole board."

"Maybe in your country, but not in Taiwan. Let's say I'm eligible for parole. I submit my application, then they vote. It goes to the board if I get enough votes. If it doesn't, parole is denied. It never even gets to the board. If your application made it to them, it's not a guarantee it'll be approved, but chances are high. Let me give you an example: Let's say you applied for parole three times, but your application never made it out of the prison. You probably would've been approved on your second try, but the prison wouldn't allow your application out. Now, you'll probably be paroled on your fourth application."

I rubbed my forehead. "That's fucked up. And such a specific example."

"Because it's me. This is my fourth try. First three didn't even make it out."

People heard my application made it to the board and congratulated me the rest of the day. They seemed confident I'd be released on my first attempt. I didn't know what to think. The government had lied to me since day one. I didn't want to get my hopes up only to have them crushed. There's nothing worse than false hope.

* * *

August 22 was my last day in court, and tropical storm Hato hit. These fools *would* make me go to court during a typhoon. If an act of God wasn't a sign that my case was nonsense, what was?

They took me to the central desk to check in, then bent me over and did their thing. People trickled in. Thirty-three people had court, so it was packed as always. Once everybody arrived, we took roll. When the CO called out our number, we responded with our name, Taiwanese ID, and date of birth. Then, we were herded to the waiting room.

An officer came to take roll, again. Strange they took roll twice in such a short time. Must've been a slow day. Once my inmate number was called, they led me outside to be cuffed and shackled. The shackles hurt, but at least they were the kind with keys again. I didn't ever want to see the medieval kind that needed to be hammered. They cuffed me to Young'un (gun charge and bodily harm). He and his boy had court together but needed to be kept separate because they were accomplices. The CO put us in isolation in the back of the bus.

Guards shepherded us to the holding cells at the far end of the court-house's basement. There were five cells: three large and two small. I was in a large one. A clock hung above the guard's desk. Court was at 2:20 p.m. I thought I was last, but a dude had court at 4:20 and another had it at 4:30. We waited until everybody was done before we could leave. There were seven of us in all: five from Taipei and two from Hsinchu.

A hole about the size of a doggie door connected the cells. I didn't know what it was for. Shortly before lunch, Young'un got down on his hands and knees and talked to the person in the next cell, who turned out to be a woman—dope dealer. A CO overheard their conversation and moved the lady to another cell. The inmates from Taipei had a craptastic bento box of yesterday's leftovers. The two guys from Hsinchu had two pieces of bread from a bakery. I traded my bento box for one guy's bread.

Time passed slowly in the holding cell. The clock seemed to go one tick forward, two ticks back. I took three naps and still had plenty of time to kill.

A woman (my interpreter) was seated at my table when I arrived in the courtroom. We went through the evidence. I plead guilty. The judges displayed photographs of damages to the car and an estimated cost of repairs.

"Do you want to settle at one million?" the judge asked.

I stayed stone-faced. "No, I'm not paying. This's extortion."

"One million is the starting point." The judge straightened her glasses. "It can and will be negotiated down."

"I don't have any money."

"Your sentence is three months. How do you feel about it?"

"It's a fair sentence." I smirked. "If it could be lighter, I'd appreciate it. I already applied for parole. I wanna resolve this quickly so I can go back to LA"

"Your sentence will be handed down on August 31. Do you want to come back, or do you want us to mail it?"

"Mail it."

"Okay. Is there anything else?"

"Is this sentence final, or will there be another appeal?" I tapped my foot.

"The sentence is final, and the case will be closed."

Amazing that they put me through this without a lawyer.

Back in the cell, waiting for others to finish. The guards' restroom was near our cell. As one of them was going in, Young'un took his craptastic lunch and threw it at him.

The guard came out of the stall with rice over him, cleaned himself off, and yelled, "Which one of you threw it? Confess now and there won't be a problem. Confess now! Who did it?"

Everybody kept their mouths shut. The guard became more and more upset and moved us to the smaller cell. It wasn't big enough for seven people; two of us had to stand.

The guard put his hands on his hips. "If nobody confesses soon, I'll check the video, then you'll really be in trouble."

At 4:30 p.m., the bus was supposed to arrive, but it never came. The two guys whose hearing was scheduled for after four o'clock still hadn't been called up. I cussed at the CO in English.

"Where's the bus? This's bullshit. It's past dinnertime." I gestured. "Where's our food? I want to talk to my consulate."

"We were in the big room; now we're in the small room," Young'un complained. "There's no place to sit. I want to sit down."

"I want to smoke a cigarette," another dude added.

"Why're we being punished because you guys don't have your shit straight?" shouted another. "I don't want to be stuck here overnight."

Shit, I didn't think that was a possibility. "I want to go home."

"Boooo!" another dude yelled.

The guard ran his hands through his hair as he paced back and forth. He paused here and there to yell. We caused such commotion, a younger guard came for backup.

"Hey, why's your boss so weird?" Young'un pestered the younger one. "He's a weirdo, huh? What's it like working with a weirdo?"

The bus arrived twenty minutes later. I stuck my hand out to be cuffed to Young'un. I started walking away, but the CO barked, "Come back. We haven't put the shackles on yet."

I sucked my teeth and trudged back to be demonized.

"Why can't we ride in the front?" Young'un asked when the guard put us in isolation. "We already had court. It doesn't matter anymore,"

He had a point. I stopped and watched the guard expectantly.

He paused, looked back and forth between us, then snapped, "Get in the back."

It was stuffy in the transport. I kicked the door. "Turn on the AC! It's hot back here."

"It's on!" the guard screamed. "Stop banging!"

The ride back was a tease. People had recently gotten off work. We looked at all the girls on the street, on scooters, and in cars. I wiped a little drool off my mouth as we passed the restaurants.

"If we both kick hard, we can bust open this gate," Young'un said as he looked out the window. "The lock's flimsy. The doors and windows all have emergency releases. We can make a break for it."

I looked out the window, then at our feet. "What about our shackles?"

"They'd be a problem." He took a deep breath and shook his head. "I'm just dreaming out loud. I'm not like you. It's at least seven or eight years until I'm home."

I got back to the factory after hours. People greeted me and asked how court went. Kevin had my cigarettes because the trustee had gotten paroled. I took a long shower. Afterward, I sat with Heisenberg and told him about my day.

When I got to the part about trading lunches, Kung Fu Guy joked, "Did he thank you?"

I chuckled and shook my head. "He didn't say shit."

"I wonder if he thought he came up."

Between mouthfuls, Heisenberg warned, "You're lucky you didn't get written up."

Well . . . better lucky than good.

* * *

A smelly dude—serving seven years for rape—transferred from Justin's row to mine. Heisenberg called him Xiao Tian Tian ("sweetie") and treated him like a child. He slept next to Kevin. On the first night, Kevin moved him one spot over because he smelled so bad.

I talked to the row 5 chief and Justin the next day. "Why'd you guys give us the smelly dude?"

Justin opened his arms. "We took Junior. You owe us one."

Dude had a point. All we did was swap weirdos.

One Wednesday a month we ended early because the gulag threw a birthday party for the officers. I hoped they choked on their cake.

* * *

A sixth guy joined my table. At some point in the conversation, he said, "I've used heroin for thirty years."

I glanced at his arms. "How come I don't see any track marks?"

"I shoot up between my thighs and balls." He lifted his shorts. "No visible marks. Don't do drugs. Heroin destroyed my body."

No kidding. He was in his midfifties but looked ninety. He was anorexic, with sunken skeleton eyes, and constantly sniffled and coughed. I felt uneasy, like I was sitting across a Dementor—a wraith-like dark creature from *Harry Potter* that feeds on human happiness and makes any person close to them feel depression and despair.

* * *

I woke up in the middle of the night to discover Big Face and I had switched blankets. This'd never happened before. The blankets weren't even used—they were still folded. I needed to cut back on the pills.

It is believed that ghosts of our ancestors haunt Taiwan for the entire seventh lunar month. Activities include preparing food offerings for the visiting spirits, burning incense, and making joss paper, a papier-mâché made of clothes, gold and other goods. We ordered special commissary as offerings for Ghost Month: snacks, cookies, biscuits. An announcement at noon instructed everybody who had an offering to package or wrap it with tape, write their factory and name on it, then set it aside. We moved tables outside as an altar. They laid the food from Factories 15 and 16 at the foot of it. The trustees and row chiefs went first. Row by row, they handed everyone an incense stick. It wasn't mandatory. A lot of incense was burned, and there was so much smoke it was hard to breathe.

I hadn't realized Taiwan was so spiritual. Felt like there was a holiday every month. I didn't participate, but I was all for anything that postponed work, even for a little while. We brought in the food after the ceremony. I regretted not buying snacks.

At 2:30 p.m., a group of monks escorted by a guard entered our factory, blessed it, and left. It took less than a minute. A drive-by blessing.

I received the vandalism case sentence. The judge had thrown out the snitch's appeal. The original sentence stood: three months, and I could pay 1,000 NTD per day instead of time.

If I can throw money at a problem and it goes away, it's not a real problem.

Pills to celebrate.

* * *

The teacher saw me outside the factory as I was waiting for an escort to visitation and called me in.

"Congratulations!" he said before I even sat down. "Your parole has been granted." He shook my hand.

I looked at the calendar displayed on a wall. "Today is September eleventh. How much longer will I be here?"

He looked at the calendar as well. "I can't say because we're waiting on paperwork."

I fidgeted.

"Could be a week or two, or it could be as fast as the end of this week."

A guard came to the office and shouted, "Three-four-four-three!"

I raised my hand. "Yo!"

"You have a visitor."

I paraded to visitation like I'd just killed the Wicked Witch of the West.

Small Auntie looked concerned, but I was grinning like the Cheshire Cat when I sat down. She was probably worried because I'd told her not to come anymore the last time she'd visited, about a month ago. I'd said I would write when I heard from the parole board. I hadn't written yet because I hadn't heard yet.

"How come I haven't heard from you?" she scolded. "We were—"

"My parole got granted!" I blurted.

She smiled from ear to ear. "What? When?"

"Right now." I pointed in the teacher's direction. "They just told me."

"So now what?" She pushed her glasses farther up her nose. "How long until you're out?"

"Could be as fast as the end of this week or as long as two. I'm low on necessities because I didn't expect to be here this long. What should I do?" I leaned closer to the glass.

"Buy what you need and leave whatever's left for your friends. I brought you fried and popcorn chicken."

I grinned. "You're the best. Have I told you lately how much I appreciate you?"

When I returned to the factory, they'd already moved the tables and chairs. I grabbed a mop; it was my row's turn to clean. People congratulated me as I mopped. When Justin got back, we combined our food and had a feast with our friends.

I counted down the days. The board had taken their sweet-ass time with my judgment—six weeks! In the end, it was granted. I couldn't complain. Even so, I couldn't help but feel Taiwan wanted to keep people in for as long as possible, even first-time, nonviolent offenders.

That night, I took so many pills, you'd have needed a space shuttle to reach me.

* * *

"Pay the 92K NTD fine, or you'll still be here," Heisenberg reminded me two days later, during a smoke break.

Between puffs, I endorsed the air. "Check's in the mail."

Later, during work, a trustee summoned me to his desk and pointed at my name in a book. The number 904 was next to it. "Sign and fingerprint," he said.

I put my John Hancock. "What's this?"

"Work paycheck."

"This month?" I fingerprinted.

He laughed. "No, total."

I didn't find it funny. That 904 NTD was less than $30. I spent more on monthly factory supplies—and wouldn't even be enough for a high-speed rail ticket back to Kaohsiung. I'd have to take the bus. I needed some context.

"It's Kevin's first month. How much did he make?" I asked.

He flipped through the pages until he found Kevin. "Thirty-two NTD."

I shook my head. Less than a bowl of instant noodles.

Heisenberg helped me fill out my paperwork. I couldn't risk anything going wrong. Another trustee summoned me to go over what I had to take with me: TV, radio, nail clippers, electric razor, video game, fan, and sneakers.

"But I wanted to give Carmelo my sneakers," I objected.

"You have to leave with a pair." He looked around, then whispered, "Just swap your new ones with his old ones."

I signed a bunch more paperwork.

The trustee shook my hand. "If it's quick, they'll release you tomorrow, most likely sometime next week."

*　*　*

Three guys transferred to prison camp: two guys from row one, and Sosa. Good for him. Sosa—a seventy-two-year-old white-collar criminal and first-time nonviolent offender—shouldn't have been in a place like this with drug-dealers, rapists, and murderers.

I patted him on his shoulder. "Congratulations."

He flinched. "For what?"

I motioned to our surroundings. "You're transferring to a nicer place."

"A nicer prison is still a prison." He sighed and slumped. "I'm still an inmate. You're going home. It's not the same." He gave me a look over his shoulder as he packed. "Settle down. Get a wife and a house. Stay out of trouble. Tell your dad you love him. He cares. He might not say it because he can't find the words."

I shuddered. He'd hit a nerve

"It's strange." He took a deep breath. "I'm the same with my son. It's hard for me to tell him how I feel."

I grunted softly.

"You lost weight. You should quit drugs. This time has been good for you. I've seen you change from how you were when you first arrived. Your parents would be happy and proud."

I smiled. Hope he was right.

"What's the first thing you're gonna do when you get out?" he asked, mercifully changing the subject.

"Go see my grandma, then call my parents."

His eyes lit up. "I'm surprised you didn't say 'get a girl.'"

"I thought about it, but family first. My grandma tells me all the time, 'If you don't have family, you don't have anything.' Imma go see the queen." I bowed exaggeratedly. "I feel like a piece of shit for all the trouble I put them through."

"Yes." He smiled. "That's why I'm proud of you. I believe in you, and I want you to know you can do so much better. You don't even know how big a mistake you made. For Asians, smuggling is the worst crime you can do, short of murder. Some of our neighbors still execute smugglers." Sosa lowered his voice and leaned in. "You're too talented to get caught for drugs again. It's not worth it."

"If you're ever in LA, look me up." I gave my number. "I'll take you to dinner."

He chuckled. "Thanks, but that's not how it works." He gave me his. "I'll take *you* out."

He had a visitor before he transferred and left his food for us.

Kevin took Sosa's spot at table one. Heisenberg saw us smoking in the restroom and came up to me. "You're leaving soon. That's why I moved Kevin and not you."

"No worries, boss." I shrugged. "I sat there before, and could do without it. Don't get me wrong—I enjoyed the head table, but it's a lot of bullshit too."

The look on his face made me feel like I was the first person to complain about the job. "It's not that bad, is it? It has its benefits."

"It does." I took a puff and passed him the cigarette. "But there's a lot of things to pay attention to. I suspect that's why you're a row chief and not a trustee. You could be one if you wanted to."

He nodded and took a puff. "A trustee isn't as great of a job as it looks."

"I don't think it's a great job at all."

"If it were up to me, I wouldn't even be row chief." He took another draw, then passed the cigarette back.

I took it between my fingers. "Being a peon ain't bad, yo. Nothing's ever my fault. Anything happens, I tell them to talk to you."

He chuckled. "It's not what you say." He impersonated my ABC accent. "I don't speak Chinese."

We both laughed. "Thanks for the heads up. You didn't have to explain."

"You know what the difference is between a mobster and a street-corner gangbanger?"

I couldn't tell if it was a joke or a rhetorical question. He looked at me as if expecting an answer. "Uh, money?"

"Class."

I nodded. He was right, but I'd never heard anybody say it like that. "I wanna be like you when I grow up," I joked.

He leaned in and whispered, "Stay out of trouble, and you can do better than me. A lot better."

I jerked my head back. Didn't expect him to say that. Coming from somebody like him, it meant a lot. I chuckled awkwardly and flicked the cigarette butt into the squatter.

I was happy for Sosa. If I was worried and scared to be locked up with murderers and sexual predators, imagine how he felt. Maybe that was why Heisenberg had been put in charge of him. Sunshine knew he had the clout, and having him as our boss had absolutely made life easier.

Pills because I missed Sosa.

* * *

During work, the trustee #1 summoned me, looked around, and whispered, "Don't tell anybody, but you're going home tomorrow."

I cocked my head. "For real?"

He nodded and smiled. "I told you as soon as I could."

I wanted to jump for joy but played it cool. It didn't feel real.

"Congratulations, man." He shook my hand, then watched me run to tell my peoples.

At night, I cooked everything I had: ten bags of instant noodles and twenty cans of peanut milk soup. Somebody had leftover dumplings from visitation. We celebrated! I went around and asked if anybody needed me to do anything outside.

"Two of my kids have birthdays in October," Lion said. "Can you buy and mail some stuffed animals to them, from me?"

"I gotchu." We bumped fists.

Lion was my age, with four kids from three baby mammas. Married three times, divorced three times. Say what you will about Taiwan's declining birth rate, but Lion did his part to make Taiwan young again. His second ex-wife was the mother of two of his children. She visited often, and was hot.

"When you get out," I told him, "marry the second one again, and be married four times to three different women. You'd win if you marry her."

He tilted his head. "What would I win?"

"You'd win at life," I joked.

I couldn't wait for the day to end. Tomorrow, I'd finally go home. Parole was the first step, but I still needed to get out of Taiwan. Still, I didn't feel as happy as I should have. I tried to figure out why I wasn't more excited. My mind raced with all the ways they could still dick me.

I'd been told it would be hard to sleep the night before release. Not for me. I was tired from a long day of slaving—and still full from the feast. I passed out quick.

* * *

I was so excited to be released, I was packed before breakfast. I donated everything to Kevin and Carmelo. Whatever they didn't want was Heisenberg's for the newcomers. I got my stuff from storage, and the trustees collected my electronics and ID. I handed out fifty cigarettes that I'd squirreled away for a rainy day, said my goodbyes, and waited.

I only took my notebooks, mat, and books. I thought about leaving them, but only three people in the factory could read English, and they'd already read all my books. They'd just be thrown out. Plus, every book I'd received had been marked with my name, inmate number, and penitentiary stamp. They were souvenirs. I used my pillow and bedding to smuggle out my journals and paperwork.

After Monkei arrived, a trustee took me aside and said in a low voice, "Two inmates assaulted a guard in the waiting area as they prepared for court."

I fidgeted. "Will they push my release back?"

"I don't know."

Midmorning, a CO came to retrieve me. The head trustee arranged a cart for my belongings, so I didn't have to carry them far. Looked like I was getting the VIP service on my way out.

I arrived first at the central desk. A guard took me to the side, searched my stuff, then bent me over and did his thing. A cavity search when I'm about to be released? Harassment.

Another guard brought in the rest. Tofu passed by and saw me. "William! You're going home? Congrats, man! Remember to write."

The CO lectured him, wrote down Tofu's name and number, and threatened to send him to the black room. After he'd dismissed Tofu, he leaned toward me. "Don't worry. He's not going to the black room. I just wanted to scare him a little."

Ain't nobody scared. One of you got fucked up this morning. Bullshit like this is why.

Guards escorted us to the waiting room. About a half hour later, an official came and spoke in a friendly tone.

"I'm here to verify your identities. After, I'll take you to the office to get your clothes, let you change, then give you your belongings and the money in your account. It'll be quick—you'll be out by 10:00 a.m. The prison notified your family of your release. If somebody wants to pick you up, they know where and when."

Three guys were picked up by their moms, one by his wife, another by his brother.

The official looked at me. "You won't be leaving with us."

I scrunched my face. "What's that mean?"

"Kaohsiung Immigration is picking you up. Sit tight. It'll be a while."

Depending when they left, I could be there all day. Soon, I was the only one left. Dammit. What if they didn't let me leave?

Guys came and went. An official offered me lunch.

I looked at it, then looked the other way. "I don't want it."

"We have to hand them out," he grunted, and put it on the floor. "Whether or not you eat is up to you. Just take it."

I put it in the corner. A dude came back from court shortly after and gave my lunch a wistful look. I picked it up and handed it to him.

As he ate, I asked, "Were you here this morning?"

He nodded.

I moved closer to him. "What happened?"

He looked around and whispered, "Two dudes jumped a CO"

I could hardly contain my excitement. I practically squealed, "They stomp him bad?"

"Not that bad, but pretty bad. He deserved it, though. He's an asshole."

I nodded. "Most of them are."

"You're right. This guy yelled at everybody the whole time for nothing. But he was really picking on one dude. He thought the dude talked when he didn't. Told him to turn around and face the wall. Dude said, 'Why? I'm not the one talking.' They got into an argument, and the dude slugged him."

I smiled. "Yeeee."

He chuckled. "Another guy jumped in. It popped off after. I minded my business, but I saw the whole thing."

Immigration arrived during lunch. There were three people: a man, a lady, and a teenybopper with a face full of acne. I changed clothes in the restroom. It took a long time to get dressed. I paused every time I put on a piece. Everything felt surreal. Finally—clothes that weren't washed in dirty water or worn by God-only-knows-who. I looked in the mirror and brushed my shoulders.

I looked forward to an actual shower. I'd probably need two of them to wash this place off me. Two might not even be enough. I wanted to go to a spa for a deep pore cleanse and body scrub.

I lost track of time admiring myself in the mirror. The CO entered and barked, "Hurry!"

The walk to the transport felt strange without cuffs or shackles. First time I'd left the gulag without them. I was happy this part was over, but I knew there was more. I expected somebody to pop out and take me back on some bullshit. But nobody did.

I watched the dungeon's metal gates slam shut behind the transport—and breathed a sigh of relief.

CHAPTER 15
PAROLE

The reports of my death are greatly exaggerated.

—Samuel Clemens

September 19, 2017

"I'll just taxi to my house from Kaohsiung Immigration," I said from the van's backseat, watching the passing scenery. There was a hook on the floor where handcuffs could be attached, and a bar on the window.

"It's better if a family member comes to get you," the lady replied curtly.

Somebody needed to sign for me like I was a piece of property. "Call Small Auntie to let her know."

"Your uncle is coming."

"I thought I'd take the HSR down." I stared out the window. "It's easier and faster."

She sighed. "We wish you could take the HSR too, but we had to come."

They stopped by a Cantonese barbecue place before we got on the freeway. I inhaled my lunch. The food was so good. I'd forgotten what warm food tasted like. The pit-stop restroom looked like a palace. I had prison goggles. Every girl I saw was gorgeous. And all the space! I'd never appreciated how big outside was and frenetic life was. Even though I was on the sidewalk, I jumped back when a car whizzed past. It was all so overwhelming. I felt like a deep-sea diver. My head would explode if I came up too quickly; I needed to take it slow.

It was dark when we arrived at immigration, and Big Uncle was already there. Officials sat in the office, thumbing through rules and regulations to find a code or section that would've allowed me to stay. I had a Taiwanese passport and therefore was a Taiwanese citizen, but I had entered on a ninety-day visa that expired on April 28, 2016. I couldn't legally stay, but they couldn't deport one of their own. My visa had expired so long ago they couldn't just issue a new one. I'd apply for a ten-day visa, then leave. I felt like one of those immigrants Trump always bitched about.

I filled out paperwork for a while. They settled on a ten-day visa for now, but they needed to talk it over with their supervisors. They'd call me soon with further instructions. I thought I was supposed to check in with a probation officer (PO) within twenty-four hours of release, but immigration said I didn't have to. On the way home, I stopped by the Zuoying police station to inform them of my release and where I'd be staying.

The drive from immigration to the station to my apartment was a blur. Uncle said nothing. He probably didn't know what to say. He didn't even play music. Local news was on the radio. Didn't matter to me, I was so excited to see my grandma and go home. Everything else was background noise.

I arrived home at nighttime. I was bouncing up and down as I waited for the elevator. Inside, I pressed the floor's button once, but I wanted to press it eighty-eight times.

I got to the door first and reached in my pocket, only to realize I didn't have the key. It'd been a while since I'd been home. I leaned against a wall and waited for Uncle to unlock it. My grandma was preparing for bed when I walked in.

She did a double take, then came up to me with the biggest smile. She felt my face with her hands.

I opened my arms. "Do you still remember me?"

She clapped. "Of course I do. You're my baby."

We hugged.

She grabbed a handful of my stomach. "How much weight did you lose?"

"Seven keys."

"Seven kilos!" she exclaimed. "I could eat for over a month!"

I chuckled. "Why you always gotta compare me to a piece of meat?"

She giggled, then pointed a stern finger at me. "If you're gonna stay out late drinking, you need to let me know."

I pulled away. "Okay, but why?"

She frowned solemnly. "If you don't come home, I'll think you're in jail. If you're not where you say you are, maybe you've been arrested. I worry about you."

I hugged her again. "Don't worry, Grandma. I'll check in." I'd missed my grandma. She fell asleep while I was hanging out with her.

The first shower was amazing. It'd been over thirteen months. The water pressure made me jump. I stared at the dirty water as it circled the drain. *That could've been my life.*

I wasn't as excited as I thought I'd be when I sat on a throne. The squatters took getting used to, but now I preferred it. They felt quicker and more natural. I thought about installing one in my restroom, then realized how stupid it sounded.

I used to be a shy shitter. Not anymore. I could go anywhere now. But I still don't like it when people talk to me when I'm in the restroom. It's weird.

My mattress was too soft. I didn't know if I was getting older or if it was because of all those months I slept on the floor, but I'd swap it for a firmer one.

* * *

Immigration called and told me to come in to apply for the ten-day visa. When I arrived, nobody knew what to do.

"Your situation is unique, and I need to ask my supervisor," the lady at the counter said.

Her supervisor wasn't much help. "This is the first time I've encountered this." She photocopied my paperwork. "I'll call with further instructions."

I received a phone call two days later. They'd consulted the Ministry of Justice, and the official stance was that I had to stay in Taiwan until I completed parole on May 2, 2018. However, I could ask my PO for permission to leave. If he approved, I could. They assigned me a PO and told to check in on October 18.

There was a second issue with immigration: I had another charge pending: the vandalism from July 2016. Court for the case wasn't until March 2017. My uncle thought I scared the dude, and he'd waited so long to press charges because he wouldn't get insurance money any other way.

Hindsight is twenty-twenty. I probably shouldn't have done it, but I controlled myself. It was an insignificant case—petty vandalism. Paperwork was supposed to come two weeks after my last court date, but it'd been over a month. I didn't know why it took so long.

I couldn't leave the country until they sorted this case out. Couldn't stay because I didn't have a visa. Couldn't leave because I didn't have a visa. I needed two ministries' approval, Immigration and Justice, just to leave. Worst case, I was stuck there until May 2, 2018. Best case, I'd be home by Thanksgiving.

Most countries know how to incarcerate people, but they don't know what to do with them after. My life was in a holding pattern. This country. This fucking country. Her justice system is fucked up beyond all reason, and her parole system is worrisome; it's a danger to the public. It would've been in the best interest of all parties involved to get me out of the country soon as possible, instead of whatever the hell this was. I went from a prisoner of war in the war on drugs to a refugee. I was a drug-war fugee.

* * *

In prison, everything is tomorrow. Tomorrow my commissary will come. Tomorrow I'll get to exercise. Tomorrow I'll get a visitor. Tomorrow I'll get a letter. Tomorrow I'll get a phone call. Tomorrow parole will be granted. Tomorrow I'll get to go home. Well, tomorrow had finally arrived.

My first full day out with no plans, and I didn't know what to do with myself. So many choices! When would I eat? What would I eat? Where would I eat? And that was just food choices. There was so much more. What time would I get up? What would I do? When should I sleep? I was like the dog that caught the car: I wasn't sure what to do with it.

I saw a doctor because I wanted proper treatment for whatever I had. Went to the one who'd vaccinated me before my surrender. I told him I recently got out of prison and wanted a full physical.

He looked me over. "It's scabies. It's known as the prison disease here."

I rubbed my hands on my thighs. "How do I make it go away?"

"Wash all your clothes and everything you touched using hot water." He handed me two bottles of lotion. "After you shower, rub this over your body. You need to be thorough, or else they'll keep returning. Don't worry, you're out now. They'll go away after two or three weeks. Inside is so dirty, the government doesn't care, some people are unhygienic, and this is an extremely contagious skin disease. All inmates get it eventually."

The diseases might've been gone, but I still had scars all over my body. The longer it took a scar to heal, the more I wondered if it ever would. Even so, it was the scars I didn't see that troubled me.

* * *

My birthday was six days after parole was granted. Freedom was the best present I'd ever gotten. I had lunch with my grandma, then spent the night and the next day in Taipei. Biggie said it better than I ever will: "Birthdays were the worst days, now we sip champagne when we're thirs-tay."

During a nice dinner with Mrs. Juice, Houston, Big Bro, and his fiancé (in town for engagement pictures), I mentioned I'd met Justin Lee.

Houston gasped. "Whoa, I didn't expect you to say that."

"Me either." I sipped my beer and leaned back in the chair.

"Do you know what he did?" Big Bro said in between mouthfuls.

"I heard, but I hadn't seen the videos."

"Don't watch them, they're bad," Houston said in a hushed tone. "In one, the girl is crying the whole time. In another, she's saying 'no, no, no' in English and Chinese."

"What he did is fucked up," said Big Bro.

Houston put down his utensils. "You're not from here, so you may not know, but some of his victims were celebrities. Models, actresses, artists, things like that. He ruined careers. Some of them lost endorsements and contracts. Others were mob wives. People are looking for this dude. He's radioactive."

I slumped in my chair. "I didn't even know he was famous."

"All this happened before your time," Big Bro added.

"When Mr. Juice and I first started dating," Mrs. Juice said, "we once sat at Justin's table, and he handed me a drink. Mr. Juice came from across the table, slapped it out of my hand, and said, 'Don't take anything from him.'"

My mouth hung open. "Shit. So people knew, huh? Yo, this ain't funny, but it kinda is: if it wasn't for Mr. Juice, you might've been in one of those videos."

"Shut the fuck up."

The waiter cleared the table.

"I didn't know you had so many visitors, homie," Houston said. "You're popular, huh?"

I titled my head. "What do you mean?"

"I had work Monday to Friday, but I knew I could visit on Sundays. Whenever I had a free Sunday, I'd call Taipei and ask if I could visit, and they'd always say no. I thought somebody came before me. I know you only get so many every couple of days."

I shook my head. "Man, when I got to Taipei, I'd have like one, maybe two a month if I was lucky."

His head snapped back. "What the . . . That's—"

"Wait," I interrupted. "Did you get the letters I sent?"

"I was about to ask. I got yours, but every time I sent one to you, it'd get returned."

"They say why?"

Houston shook his head. "It comes back stamped Return to Sender."

A few more of my friends told me the same.

"How about the money?"

I stared. "What money?"

"When they said I couldn't visit, I mailed a few racks your way. You didn't get that either?"

I shook my head and pounded the table with my palm. "I didn't get anything."

Taking money out of inmate's mail. Damn. I didn't know Taiwan needed money that badly. I'd paid my debt to society. Taiwan could keep the change.

* * *

My first check-in was October 18. The office was on the third floor of a building in the middle of nowhere, a twenty-minute moped ride right north of my grandma's. It resembled a DMV. A person behind glass checked me in, then there was a big waiting room with rows of seats and TVs listing the queue numbers about to be called. The place was packed; I waited almost two hours.

My PO had six fingers on his right hand—two thumbs. I'd never met a mutant before. I wondered if he knew Jean Grey.

"I don't need to drug test you, do I?" he asked.

"Of course not. I don't do drugs." I smirked. "How often do I have to meet you?"

He looked me over. "You don't seem like a troublemaker. Once a month, how's that?"

I nodded. "Seems fair."

"Check in on November 16. Come anytime between nine thirty and one or between two thirty and four thirty."

"Thanks, man. You're an all-right dude." I shook his hand. "See you next month."

He gave me a form to fill out and bring back.

"Do you want to go back in for three months?" Small Auntie asked in the car on the way home. "I mean, you have to be in Taiwan, anyway. Save 92K NTD."

"To hell with that," I snapped. "Nobody goes to prison unless they have to. I'm not going back in. I got the cash. I'll pay the fine."

* * *

I went to Taoyuan to pay the fine. Afterward, I visited Carmelo at Taipei to drop off food. He told me Big Face and the Pimp had gone home. Lion thanked me for the stuffed animals I'd mailed his kids. Visits used to make my day. I hoped it made theirs too.

It was weird being on the other side of the glass, and also made me feel a little guilty. Guilty for what I'd put my family and friends through. Guilty because I'd had it better than some Taiwanese guys. I felt the way an animal must feel when it escapes a trap, only to discover it has left a piece of itself behind. Don't know if I'll ever get over it, but I can get past it.

I don't think I'm a victim, and neither should you.

*   *   *

Since being out, I noticed I couldn't be in a room for longer than two hours without getting antsy. Like the walls were closing in. I wasn't freaking out or anything, but I wanted to be outside doing something, not in a room all day. It was so strange. I'd never felt like this before. It wasn't PTSD, right? After all that time in a cage, I wanted to be out and about as much as possible.

Every time I saw a bag with a shoestring handle, I couldn't help but wonder if an inmate had made it. I boycotted every company that made me make bags. I hoped those bastards would all go bankrupt or see their stock value fall off a cliff. They got enough of my labor. They weren't getting my money.

I stopped eating instant noodles or any of the snacks I ate inside. The food was so bad, most of the time I filled up on junk food. I don't eat congee anymore because I'd had it every other morning. I started eating a lot healthier. Used to be a picky eater, but now I was just happy to have food—and I even differentiated between quality food and junk food. I tried not to eat junk anymore.

If marijuana counted as a drug, then I went in with a regular drug problem and left with a prescription and alcohol problem. Ain't shit got changed—it got worse. No weed to smoke to help me cope when I was released, but there was plenty of alcohol. I was so happy to be out. I over-indulged. I'd drink until I blacked out. That never used to happen before. I was loud, belligerent, unleashed, and wild. I'd forget where I was and how to act. In social settings, I'd sometimes forget how to act. I wasn't incarcerated anymore and needed to readjust to society. It was difficult. Often, I'd take things the wrong way and overreact.

I'm not trying to justify or condone my behavior. I want people to understand where I'm coming from and why I act the way I act. It's a work in progress.

*   *   *

I went to Taipei to get a suit fitted for a wedding. As I walked around Ximending, a policeman saw me from across the street and jogged over.

"What's in your backpack?" he asked. "I want to look inside."

I stared at him and pretended not to understand Chinese.

He repeated, "Let me look inside your backpack," then reached for it.

I stepped back. He gasped air.

"I want to see your ID," he said sternly.

I gave him a puzzled look. I didn't know why I was being profiled.

"I want to see your ID now." Some moments passed. Finally, he said, "Are you Taiwanese?"

I took out my California driver's license.

He had a sheepish look. "Sorry for the trouble."

What just happened? Did I get profiled? Were stop-and-frisks legal here? I called my people who grew up in Taiwan and asked them if this was normal.

"It's definitely not," one told me. "Normally, if you tell them you're American, they'll leave you alone."

"Even if you spoke Chinese, I don't think they've the right to do that," said another homie.

My favorite response was, "I'd have told him to fuck off."

Maybe I'd overreacted. I wondered if being an ex-con made me look suspicious, or if the guy was just a dick.

* * *

"Hey, wake up," a man's voice said as someone shook me.

I woke up and looked around. I was lying on a couch. "Where am I? Who are you?"

"You're in the lobby of the High Rise. I am the security guard."

"How come I'm missing a shoe?" I asked hazily.

"Dunno. You came in like this."

I rubbed my temples. "How about a cell phone? Did you find a cell?"

"No. You didn't have that either. You said you know somebody here by the name of Houston? Well, we can't get ahold of him, and it's 6:00 a.m. You can't stay here any longer. You're disturbing our residents."

"I'm sorry." I sighed. "May I borrow your computer to look up the name of my hotel? Then I'll be on my way. I have no other way to find the address. I'm so sorry."

In the taxi on the way back to my hotel, I tried to piece together my night. After barhopping, I'd gone to a club with the groomsmen. After I blacked out, I lost my phone. I'd had both shoes on when I left . . . I think. My best guess was that my shoe got caught when I'd left the taxi. I'm pretty sure I didn't leave the club with one shoe.

It was 9:00 a.m. when I got back to my hotel. Check-out was at noon, but I slept in until 2:30 p.m. The front desk didn't wake me. I only had this hotel for one night. I'd booked one that was close to the wedding venue.

After checking out, I went to a shoe store. The employees gave me the side-eye. Couldn't blame them; I probably looked homeless. I hoped to buy the same shoes I'd lost, but they were sold out, so I picked a pair of Jordans. I had a new pair of socks in my pocket, and I put them on and told the worker, "Lace me up. I'm gonna wear these out."

In my new kicks, I checked into my new hotel and rested for the wedding the following day.

Houston was a groomsman. When I saw him at the afternoon ceremony, he shook his head at me. "Damn, you're on another level, homie. I've lived there for ten years. You can't be doing this kind of shit. It was six in the morning! People are going to work and walking through the lobby, and there you are—drunk, snoring, missing a shoe, no cell phone. I had four different concierges call me at work. There's nothing I could do."

I face-palmed. "I am so sorry, man."

He shoved his hands into his pockets. "I'm not going to lecture you, but you're thirty-three. You know you're too old to be acting like this."

I looked at the floor.

"What's going on?" He fixed his tie. "You never used to do this before. This is new and, to be honest, reckless, homie."

"Don't know what to tell you." I avoided eye contact and fumbled with my jacket. "Did a bunch of pills to help me get through the day. I don't need them anymore now, but it became a habit. It's not like I tried to lose a shoe and my cell phone." I made eye contact and opened my arms. "You gotta understand, I can't legally work, leave, or stay. I'm so bored. I'm drinking every day."

"It's all good." He put his hand on my shoulder. "I get it. You've been through a lot. If you need help, we're here for you, but you're persona non grata for two months. Wait for this to blow over, then come back."

We slapped hands, then embraced. "Thank you, but I probably ain't coming back. Ever. I'm ashamed to show my face. Imagine what it was like for the workers, dealing with my drunk, belligerent ass for two hours."

He shook his head. "I avoided walking through my lobby this morning."

"It felt good to let loose." I chuckled. "It's been awhile."

He sucked his teeth. "You're fucking wild. You need to calm your ass down."

* * *

"You're here early," my PO said when I walked in. He glanced at the clock. "It's nine thirty. You're the first one."

"I'm so happy today is finally here and excited to put this behind me. This is our last meeting. The sooner I do this, the sooner I'm done."

"Congratulations." He smiled and shook my hand. "You're all done."

"That's it? It's all over?"

"Yes, it's all over."

I stood up and pumped my fist. "Hell yeah! I leave on May second?"

"Not so fast."

My heart sank. I needed to sit down.

"First, you need to buy your plane ticket, then you'll show immigration and apply for a visa to leave on that date."

How much longer did they plan on holding me hostage? "How long is the process?"

"Hard to say," he shrugged. "Anywhere from one to two weeks."

I practically jumped out of my chair. "Another two weeks?!"

"You already made it this far. What's another couple weeks?"

I thought about what I was going to do for another two weeks on the moped ride back: say goodbye to my friends, drink, smoke, party, and try to stay out of trouble. Same shit, different day.

When I got home, I called my mom to fill her in, and she cheered.

"Did you hear your sister had a kid?" Mom asked.

"Yeah, I got the letter. It's a boy."

"You're an uncle now. Have you thought about what you're going to do when you get back?"

"Well, weed's legal."

"Yes, and you can stay with us until you get on your feet."

"I appreciate that. Sorry for all the trouble, but sometimes you gotta make the wrong choices to get to the right ones."

"You'll be okay. We just need to get you on American soil. Anything can happen when you're still over there."

Mother knows best.

I didn't realize the family dynamics had changed so much in a short amount of time. I needed a moment to process it all. Pops had retired. In a handful of years, my mom would too. Sister had a kid. Grandpa died. A cousin was in college. There was a lot to catch up on, not including whatever feelings they had toward me.

People talk a lot about resilience. I had a built-in resilience. I could bounce back when I got knocked down, but I wouldn't be bouncing back to what I was before. I wasn't the same person. If I thought I was, I'd encounter problems. I'd had an experience that changed me. Society and others' perceptions of me had changed too.

A lot of my friends had gotten married. A handful were divorced, and few were on their second marriage. Some had had their first kid; others were on their second. A few had come out. I was happy for all my friends. Happy to be free and able to attend their life events. But I couldn't shake the feeling I was behind in life—and I still can't. It made me wonder, *Do I want that? What do I want?* My friends talked about weddings, pregnancies, and mortgages. *Damn, I'm not even close.* I was just trying to put the pieces of my life back together.

If I were from Taiwan, this book wouldn't exist. I'd still be in prison—another casualty of the war on drugs. No different from Carmelo, James, Kevin, or One. When they get out, where's their support?

Prisons are repositories for some of the most disadvantaged groups in society. They're monuments to failed education, social, health care, and welfare policies. Systemic failures. Most of the people I met inside only had an elementary school education. Most of the people locked up simply should not be there. Having been chewed up and spat out by a system the outside world knows little about, I realized most people don't care about what happens inside prisons. As long as it locks away criminals, people believe the government is safeguarding society.

But what about how often prisons fail those in its care? I'm not arguing against prisons. They are an integral part of society. A locked-up burglar can't rob your house. But prisons have diminishing returns. A ten-year sentence costs ten times as much as a one-year sentence, but it's not ten times the deterrent. After society has locked up all the dangerous, violent criminals, then each criminal after would be less and less dangerous.

Taiwan has an alarmingly high rate of recidivism. Four out of five prisoners in the country's prisons are repeat offenders. I'm one of them. This leads to questions about whether they're serving any corrective or educational purpose. Inmates are a class of marginalized, desperate, idle people, many of whom turn to drugs and crime. Some may be threats to the safety and security of the rest of the population. Most, though, probably aren't. The government's response? Build more prisons.

Building more gulags doesn't reduce crime. If it did, America would be the safest country in the world. If the only solution to crime is more prisons and more prison time, it's an endless cycle of crime and punishment.

* * *

My Taiwanese passport expires a few years from the time of writing. I'm not sure if I'll renew. There's no real benefit. Taiwan has fewer and fewer diplomatic allies. The writing's on the wall: Taiwan has, maybe, a generation before she's done. There's a real risk of being a nation of leftovers. Anybody with any skills, talents, degrees, capital, or connections is already gone. It's why my parents left. Taiwan has fundamental, existential problems she either refuses or doesn't know how to address. Even more troubling, she doesn't seem to care. There might not be a Taiwan for my kids to visit. It'll be called Chinese Hawaii.

Taiwan's economy is stagnant, with no real long-term growth in sight. The birth rate is dwindling, but the population is rapidly aging. Entitlements are killing her. Pension funds are running out of money. She's short on water, power, and skilled labor—and it'll only get worse. Wages aren't competitive. Schools are failing. To put another way, Taiwan is getting poorer and dumber. At least they're tough on crime. Maybe if the education system were better, they wouldn't need to be so tough on crime. Perhaps if Taiwan's economy weren't so stagnant, there wouldn't be a need for "law and order."

* * *

I went to Taipei one last time to say goodbye to my friends. When I came back, I discovered my grandma had gotten sick. It was bad. She was bed-ridden. I stopped by the hospital every day. I'd thought my grandma would be the same as when I left. She was old, yeah, but she'd been old for as long as I'd known her. When people get older, their health deteriorates slowly, but it can also fall off a cliff. Everything happened so fast.

A few days later, my aunties told Pops to come home. It wasn't look-ing good.

Another aspect of men coddled by Eastern culture. As they age and become grandparents, if the men die first, the women are fine. They live another decade or longer. However, if the women die first, the men often seem lost. I use my family as an example. My maternal grandma passed when I was eighteen. I moved in with my grandpa to keep him company, but it wasn't enough. He moved back to China and remarried. I don't think his new wife loved him. Met her a few times, and it seemed like she only married him for the green card. I wondered why he even wanted to remarry. He had a whole new family. What about us? When my paternal grandfather passed, my grandma lived another thirty years.

She and I had spoken about this before. "Was I lonely after your grandpa died? Of course. But I wasn't alone. I have my family—my kids and grandkids."

* * *

"Your grandma passed during the night," my Big Auntie said solemnly on May 11.

"Wait, what?" I'd just woken up. It took me a moment to process. I didn't know what to do. I stood there. Wasn't even sure I responded. I might've walked away.

I was in a daze on the way to the airport to pick up Pops. When I saw him, I took his luggage and said, "Grandma passed last night."

He looked at me, then looked at the ground. "Shit."

I'm sure he wanted to be there, to say his goodbyes, but I hope he took solace in the fact she was weak and in no capacity to respond. Neither of us said anything on the way home.

Back at the apartment, my aunties filled in Pops while I stared at the floor.

"Her conditions worsened last night, and she has a DNR. It was time to let her go."

"What's a DNR?" I asked.

"Do not resuscitate," Pops said. "You know, your maternal grandpa didn't have one. When something happened, your mom was the one who pulled the plug. It was tough on her and the family."

It made me want to have a DNR.

After everybody went to sleep. I was alone, and drinking. After the first glass, my lip quivered, and I cried. It was uncontrollable. I hadn't cried when my grandpa died. I was inside and didn't want to look weak and vulnerable. Not anymore. It was like two years of emotions had finally caught up to me.

I didn't realize it at the time, but keeping a journal is most likely what kept me sane. That and the pills. It was therapeutic, but it also left me feeling exposed. If my grandma had passed before all this happened and you asked how I felt, I'd have said, "Sad." If she passed while I was inside, I'd still have said, "Sad." But I'd want to give you more, so I'd say something like, "I feel how Simba felt when Mufasa died." Now, I'm trying to reconcile the person who seems to need drugs or alcohol to show emotion with the person who has no problem telling you, "I know how Spider-Man felt when Uncle Ben died." I don't know what's wrong with me. I felt like such a punk for crying. Probably looked like how Howard thought he looked. I was glad nobody saw me. Is toxic masculinity why Howard was mad at me for no reason? I bet my grandma could take Howard. I chuckled, then drank until I blacked out.

* * *

An auntie came over a few days after to get the clothes grandma wanted to be buried in. As I let her in, I asked, "Do you need time to pick out outfits?"

"No, your grandma already picked out what she wanted to be buried in."

"For real? Like an outfit or two?"

"She has a whole drawer full." I followed her, confused. I saw the drawer. It had at least four outfits, a few pairs of shoes, and a couple of purses. I'd heard about being ready to die, but not about a wardrobe packed. There was not a thuggish bone in the little old lady's eighty-pound body, but that was some gangster shit people only see in Scorsese movies.

It was the coolest damn thing I'd ever seen.

* * *

I went to immigration to see if they'd allow me to postpone my flight so I could attend my grandma's funeral. "You have already applied, and you have to leave on that date."

And that was Taiwan's final fuck-you.

EPILOGUE

You can't go home again.

—Thomas Wolfe

I moved in with my parents in Monterey Park, California.
The snitch moved back to Kaohsiung when he got word I'd left for good.
He sued me in civil court for damages to his car. As if I was going back to court. To this day, there's a warrant out for my arrest in Taiwan. While I can go back, I won't. If the tragic deaths of Malcolm X and Nipsey Hussle taught me anything, it's that motherfuckers be hating. People want to see you do well, but not better than them. Naysayers and nonbelievers can watch me do whatever I can to help from the summit.

They want me so badly? Extradite me.

A month after my homecoming in July 2018, I got a job. I'm a Southern California regional account manager for a lab that does, among other things, marijuana compliance. One country's smuggler is another country's white-collar worker.

It all kind of worked out for me, but what about those who aren't so lucky? For every one of me, there are tens of thousands rotting.

Drugs won the war on drugs. End this forever war. Invest in education, community outreach, social welfare, and community services. Free all nonviolent offenders in for drug-related offenses. Free the trappers.